Academic Leadership in Higher Education

Academic Leadership in Higher Education

*From the Top Down
and the Bottom Up*

Edited by Robert J. Sternberg, Elizabeth Davis,
April C. Mason, Robert V. Smith,
Jeffrey S. Vitter, and Michele Wheatly

ROWMAN & LITTLEFIELD
Lanham • Boulder • New York • London

Published by Rowman & Littlefield
A wholly owned subsidiary of The Rowman & Littlefield Publishing Group, Inc.
4501 Forbes Boulevard, Suite 200, Lanham, Maryland 20706
www.rowman.com

Unit A, Whitacre Mews, 26-34 Stannary Street, London SE11 4AB

British Library Cataloguing in Publication Information Available

Library of Congress Cataloging-in-Publication Data Available

ISBN 978-1-4758-0803-2 (cloth : alk. paper)
ISBN 978-1-4758-0804-9 (pbk. : alk. paper)
ISBN 978-1-4758-0805-6 (electronic)

∞™ The paper used in this publication meets the minimum requirements of American National Standard for Information Sciences Permanence of Paper for Printed Library Materials, ANSI/NISO Z39.48-1992.

Printed in the United States of America

Contents

Contents

Preface

"Now what should I do?" This is a question academic leaders ask themselves with great regularity. As ironic as it may seem, very few academic leaders have had any formal training in academic administration, or in any kind of administration at all. For the most part, academic administrators learn on the job. They also seek advice wherever they can get it. The purpose of this book is to offer such advice.

ABOUT OUR BOOK

In May of 2013, when Bob Sternberg was provost and senior vice president of Oklahoma State University, he wrote to all of the provosts of the Big XII universities asking them whether they would be interested in collaborating in editing a brief book providing advice to academic leaders at all levels, from department chairs, up through deans, provosts, and presidents. The idea proffered was to seek out academic administrators at various levels and types of institutions and ask them to write brief chapters providing advice, especially but not exclusively to those newly starting out in their positions.

All of the Big XII provosts, as of May 2013, agreed to take part as coeditors of the book. But, life has a way of intervening, and in the meantime some of the provosts left for other positions and other provosts left administration altogether. Some other provosts just got busy with alternative endeavors. In the end, six (past and present) Big XII provosts stayed with the book. Thus, the book has continued on, and you are reading it now. The book is written both for academic administrators at all levels and for those who aspire to academic administration.

We have divided the book into six parts.

Part I comprises an introductory chapter by Elizabeth Hoffman, formerly provost at one of the Big XII universities, Iowa State. (Hoffman also is a past president of the University of Colorado.) She provides a panoramic overview of the chapters in the book.

Part II provides advice from (present and past) presidents and chancellors, that is, chief executive officers of universities. These individuals have a telescopic or wide-ranging view of all of the functions of a university.

Part III furnishes advice from present and former provosts, that is, chief academic officers. These individuals probably have a more encompassing view of the academic side of their institution than does any other single person in the institution.

Part IV contains advice from present and former deans. Deans are chief executives for schools or colleges within universities and, in some institutions, are almost like presidents of portions of the institution. They differ from presidents, however, in the more limited scope of the problems they are likely to confront.

Part V offers advice from present and former department chairs and heads, the ones who, from some points of view, have the most difficult jobs in the university. They have to deal with administrative problems on the ground, and they frequently encounter those problems in their original, unfiltered, and raw forms.

Finally, part VI contains two concluding chapters: one by Jeffrey L. Buller and one by Robert J. Sternberg, one of the coeditors. These chapters summarize major points of the book.

Each of the six parts is grouped by the highest level an individual has achieved (e.g., some presidents or chancellors have been provosts, but if an individual has been or is a president or chancellor, his or her chapter is grouped with the other ones of individuals at that level). Within the provost and dean categories are included chapters by associate provosts and deans as well as full provosts and deans.

Enjoy the book! We hope you will learn as much from reading each of the chapters as we have as we prepared the book.

We are grateful to Patty Moore of Oklahoma State University for her tireless work in helping with the preparation of the book.

Robert J. Sternberg
Elizabeth Davis
April C. Mason
Robert V. Smith
Jeffrey S. Vitter
Michele Wheatly

I

Introduction

Chapter One

What Have We Learned about Academic Leadership?

Elizabeth Hoffman

When Bob Sternberg embarked on this project in May of 2013, I was nearing the end of a year's administrative leave after stepping down from my fifth major administrative position, an administrative career spanning twenty-three years. My latest position was a five-year term as executive vice president and provost at Iowa State University. I had been one of the Big XII provosts who formed the original set of contributors to this important book.

Now, a little more than a year later, only two of the original Big XII provosts who wrote for this volume are still in those positions. Some have retired, others have returned to faculty positions, and still others have moved on to other administrative positions. Yet, we have remained close friends and colleagues and Bob has wisely expanded the range of perspectives represented in these essays to include leaders representing other institutions and administrative positions ranging from department chairs and faculty members to campus presidents and chancellors.

This change makes this a much richer narrative of academic leadership, while also highlighting the similarities among the challenges we all face. So, while it is clearly true that "where you stand is where you sit," as articulated by Bob Smith, it is also true that we face many similar challenges, independent of position. In this introductory chapter, I will attempt to bring together themes that permeate many, if not all, of the chapters, regardless of academic leadership position.

STRATEGIC PLANNING

Strategic planning (or just planning) is probably the most pervasive theme in the book. Strategic planning may be discussed directly, as exemplified by the chapters from both the University of Kansas and Kansas State University. University of Kansas Provost Jeff Vitter writes about the importance of the process of strategic planning as a way of bringing the different constituents of the university together to define the university's future during difficult economic times. Kansas State University Provost April Mason outlines a similar process and its importance. Both emphasize the value of having a plan whether you have the good fortune to distribute additional resources or have to respond to a budget shortfall. They agree that a plan guides resource allocation to make sure the strongest and most important areas of the university are strengthened in good times and protected, to the extent possible, in lean times.

Continuing the theme of strategic planning, vice provost for administration and finance at the University of Kansas Diane Goddard describes how the university went about transforming its business and organizational structures to be more efficient and effective in order to free up resources to implement important goals of the new strategic plan. John Floros, dean of the College of Agriculture at Kansas State University, describes how a large and central college at a land-grant university developed its own strategic plan to mesh with the new university strategic plan, while maintaining its own key strategies.

Ann Brill, dean of the School of Journalism and Mass Communication at the University of Kansas, describes how long-range planning in advance of the long-run decline in newspaper circulation allowed the college to prepare for the digital age in advance of most of its peers.

Lise Youngblade, head of the Department of Human Development and Family Studies at Colorado State University, used to work for April Mason when April was dean of the College of Applied Human Sciences at Colorado State University. Lise writes in her chapter about the importance of a strategic plan for a large, complex, multidisciplinary, and growing department. Her department not only has traditional academic programs but also an early childhood lab school, a family therapy program, and an extension program. She outlines how strategic planning sets the vision for the department, helps the department understand the context within which it operates, allows the department to take advantage of new opportunities, helps stakeholders with buy-in and commitment to the department's mission, serves as a structure for a business plan, and provides a framework for marketing the department's work.

Other chapters also focus on strategic planning. Marc Johnson, president of the University of Nevada, Reno, titles his chapter "Strategic Planning through Thick and Thin." The state of Nevada was one of the states hit hardest by the Great Recession. While the University of Kansas and Kansas State University sustained budget cuts along with much of higher education, budget cuts in Nevada were bordering on catastrophic. Whole colleges and departments were eliminated. Faculty lost tenure. Marc describes how the university's strategic plan made it possible to decide what to eliminate in order to preserve the university's ability to rebound strongly when better times came: "Under conditions of catastrophic resource reductions, the strategic plan guides decision makers toward institutional preservation."

David Hodge and Bobby Gempesaw of Miami University of Ohio, in their chapter "Effective Academic Leadership," also focus on strategic planning. They use three examples of changes at Miami that were informed by the university's strategic plan: redefining the role of an interdisciplinary school; upgrading the university's two-year branch campuses to four-year degree-granting campuses; and responding to the budget challenges resulting from the Great Recession. They also describe how the new strategic plan (Miami 2020) was developed after the Great Recession. They concur with the leaders at the University of Kansas and Kansas State University that involving the entire campus in developing a strategic plan is crucial to achieving widespread buy-in for the plan and support for major changes that result from decisions based on a strategic plan.

Mary Ellen Mazey, president of Bowling Green University, and Anne Balazs, head of the Marketing Department at Eastern Michigan, use a chapter about effective shared governance to discuss strategic planning in a unionized environment. They make the important point that unionized faculty put more emphasis on increasing the numbers and salaries of faculty than on the financial health of the university. "What becomes the most difficult task in such a unionized setting is building consensus on that budget, even if the strategic plan represents a shared agenda. The process becomes a 'teachable moment' guiding faculty, staff, and administrators to fully understand and agree on the assumptions and data needed to make good financial decisions." Bowling Green used a consulting firm to help them frame the issues, which then led to a successful campus-wide discussion of the key issues facing the campus following the Great Recession.

Alan Mathios, dean of the College of Human Ecology at Cornell University, uses the language of strategic planning without directly describing the writing or implementation of a strategic plan. He begins by talking about the importance of a mission statement for a multidisciplinary college in conveying the college's values and strengths to multiple audiences. He goes on to outline the importance of "creating a culture of community," among a faculty inclined to "think otherwise." Again, while not using strategic planning terminology, he talks about how a culture of community allowed the college to take advantage of faculty turnover to renew the college in ways that made it more relevant to the demands of twenty-first-century students and research areas of importance. He continues by emphasizing the importance of guiding principles. He recommends using data to drive decision making. And he describes how he partnered with other strong programs in the university to help build a neuroscience MRI facility and a population program. He then outlines how he built a multidisciplinary team of department chairs and dean's office staff to implement the implicit college plan.

COMMUNICATION, ACTIVE LISTENING, ETHICAL THINKING, AND CLARITY

Another theme that runs through many of the chapters is the importance of communication, active listening, not compromising one's ethics, and being clear about what you will and will not support. Ed Ray, who has held every leadership position from department chair to campus president, is very emphatic about the importance of clarity and ethics. He describes how, as a young department chair, he had to tell a colleague old enough to be his father that his research and teaching were weak and he would not get much of a raise. He was honest and direct, but kind. The faculty member thanked him for his directness. Apparently, previous department chairs had blamed his low raises on the dean not giving the department enough raise money. Later, he talks about "taking one for the team" when tough, but unpopular, decisions have to be made.

Kenneth Ruscio, president of Washington and Lee University, uses a series of books he has read and cherished through his life to illustrate the importance of ethics in leadership: *Red Badge of Courage*, *All the King's Men*, and *Billy Budd*. In each book, an individual or individuals face an impossible ethical dilemma. He compares the ethical dilemma faced by Henry Fleming, who was forced to kill during the Civil War in *Red Badge of Courage*, to the challenges faced by young college students who were forced to go to war in Vietnam. *All the King's Men* reminds him of Watergate. *Billy Budd* reminds him that college and university administrators often have to choose between a just process and a just outcome. Kenneth contends that it is not always possible to have both. While he does not give any specific examples, one we encounter every year comes to my mind. Do you tenure someone you believe has promise, but whose record does not yet meet the university's written standards? My strategy has been to offer the faculty member a two-year tenure clock extension with specific expectations, signed and agreed to by all parties. About half the time the faculty member fulfills the expectations and earns tenure.

Ana Mari Cauce, provost and executive vice president at the University of Washington, describes how she used her communication and listening skills when she was asked to serve as an outside chair of the American Ethnic Studies program when it was in such disarray that no internal or external chair in the field could be found. Her leadership was protested from day one. Department members posted "wanted" pictures of her or targets on the walls. She visited every class to talk with students and faculty members about their concerns. At the end of the year the students awarded her a "Rookie of the Year" certificate, the department was able to make its first consensus hires in a decade, and the department was able to agree on a set of goals and priorities. At the end of her three-year term, the department gave her a positive review and commended her leadership. She has used the skills she learned from that experience in each administrative position she has held.

Elizabeth Davis titles her chapter "The Art of "No." Her message is that clarity is more effective than equivocation. And, if you can't say yes or no right away, tell the person when you will be able to give an answer and stick to your commitment. She also contributes to the theme of planning. She recounts how she spent most of her career at Baylor University, where religious commitment is an important component of the educational process. As provost she had to say no to proposals for excellent hires of faculty without a spiritual commitment, as well as to strongly religious individuals without a reputation for scholarship and a commitment to education. It was important to the mission and vision of the university to have a community of excellent scholars who were also individuals of faith. She also talks about procedural clarity, whether in the university's tenure policy or in a course syllabus that outlines what does and does not count toward a student's grade. She offers some advice about how to say yes or no as clearly and kindly as possible: "be timely . . . be transparent . . . be self-reflective . . . be consistent/fair/reasonable . . . be willing to own a bad decision . . . be compassionate." The result will be trust, even by those who disagree with you.

Richard McCarty, provost and vice chancellor for academic affairs at Vanderbilt University, talks about the importance of a rigorous and clearly understood tenure and promotion system and of the provost setting aside enough time every year to evaluate each faculty case carefully and fairly. He describes the time it took to bring all sides together to effect a new undergraduate curriculum when he was dean of the College of Arts and Sciences. As provost, he tries to answer e-mail questions as quickly as possible and to be as transparent as possible in all communications. He describes how he and the dean of students worked together to resolve a tricky conflict between the university's nondiscrimination policy and religious freedom. They are currently working with the general counsel and with law enforcement to respond to a gang rape allegation, both compassionately and in keeping with both the law regarding sexual assault allegations and with new federal Title IX guidelines. Both issues required carefully listening to all sides, while remaining in compliance with the law and with university regulations.

Sally Reis, vice provost for academic affairs at the University of Connecticut, emphasizes the importance of active listening, asking the right questions, collecting the right data, being honest and respectful, and projecting optimism and good humor. She enjoys solving problems, but recognizes that she cannot effectively solve problems if she does not follow the simple rules outlined above. She also emphasizes the importance of teamwork: "I try to rally a group of creative people, put incentives in place, and establish opportunities for them to work with me to create something new and innovative."

Jane Halonen, dean of the College of Arts and Sciences at the University of West Florida, offers "Ten Strategies for Enhancing the Academic Leader's Communication Effectiveness." Her excellent recommendations include remembering that every faculty group you work with includes "the smartest kids in the room," each of whom wants you to listen carefully to his or her concerns. You are going to have to deliver bad news. Do it as humanely as possible. Recognize that you are dealing with very busy people. Don't waste their time with meaningless meetings. Realize that some people are uncomfortable coming to your office. Hold office hours at Starbucks! "Publish a monthly newsletter." This is one of Bob Smith's recommendations, as well. "Make no promises you can't keep." And, don't be afraid to subject yourself to rigorous evaluation.

Diane Halpern, dean of social science at the Minerva Colleges of the Keck Graduate Institute, focuses on shared governance, which fits well with the theme of communication and transparency. She writes about how working with faculty on difficult decisions makes it possible to effect seemingly impossible changes. She uses the example of a hypothetical German department that no longer has enough students to maintain minimum enrollments, but the faculty members are tenured. Resolving a problem such as how to close the German department and find positions for faculty in other areas of the university requires involving as many stakeholders in the university as possible.

Michele Wheatly and Jennifer Bott, associate provost at Ball State University, recount Jennifer's experience as an ACE Fellow, learning about academic administration from Michele when Michele was provost and chief academic officer at West Virginia University. Effective mentoring is an important communication skill. While Michele and Jennifer touch on many topics, one important theme is women serving as mentors for other women because only another woman can truly understand and communicate the life trade-offs that women academics face. When should a woman have children? How can a woman successfully balance work life and family life? What is the future of women's leadership in higher education?

Larry Lyon, vice provost and dean of the graduate school at Baylor University, writes about how to lead "without portfolio." His point is that as dean of the graduate school he has no real power, controls few resources, and has a small staff. How is he to make a difference? Communication, data collection, developing a shared understanding of which data have relevance to shared goals, and not trying to be perfect all the time are some of his recommendations for how to accomplish real change in a role "without portfolio."

David Perlmutter, dean of the College of Media and Communication at Texas Tech, emphasizes the importance of keeping a written record of all decisions and "mutual expectations." He recommends sending an e-mail to himself after every meeting that involves a promise to do something. He offers the same recommendation to faculty members. After a meeting with the chair, if you believe you have been promised something, send an e-mail to the chair confirming the commitment. This serves as a record and gives the chair a chance to confirm or disconfirm that your memory is the same as the chair's. He adds some important advice to chairs and faculty for how to maintain cordial and productive relationships: pick your battles carefully, don't whine, appreciate that your chair is busy and may be stressed, appreciate that your concern may not be the most important issue the chair is dealing with on any one day, offer to help when you have special expertise of value to the chair, and recognize that chairs change either because they rotate out, they get other jobs, or they are asked to step down by the dean.

Jean Sander, dean of the Center for Veterinary Health Services at Oklahoma State University, describes herself as having a "direct to the point" style. She had to learn that many people she found herself working with as dean either did everything possible to avoid confrontation or felt the need to talk about every other subject possible before getting down to the business of discussing what was really on their minds. "I've had to work at controlling my inherent style to allow those who come to me to discuss something the chance to get to the point on their own terms." She describes a particular interaction with another administrator. She knew immediately what he wanted and kept trying to get to the point. But he was not going to stop telling his story first. "So I leaned back and listened, and listened, and listened until we were able to finally address the problem. Had I continued to try to move it along, we might still be in that office trying to get through the conversation!"

Henry Roediger, chair of the Department of Psychology at Washington University in St. Louis, recommends never making a decision about one faculty member's concerns without making sure you have heard all the other sides. Listen to the faculty member coming to complain and then say that you will get back to him or her. Do your homework and then come back as quickly as possible with an answer. Often the answer will be "no," so learn how to say no as nicely as possible. And, since you will be saying no a lot, you have to listen and repair any hard feelings as soon as the faculty member has stopped being mad. Finally, he recommends always portraying kindness and optimism, even when you are truly tired of a particular faculty member's constant requests. "Ten percent of the faculty take up 80 percent of your time."

Heidi Bostic, chair of the French Department at Baylor University, titles her chapter "Chairing Stories." The central theme of her chapter is that the stories chairs are able to tell and bring out of their faculty are important ways to bring people together. Her first example is learning to identify Alfred Hitchcock's MacGuffins, "an apparently unimportant object that forms the goal of someone's quest." A question about a piece of equipment was really about space restructuring. A chair has to be able to "see all sides" and help faculty see beyond their own, sometimes narrow worldviews. A chair also needs to celebrate her faculty achievements and weave narratives that link the achievements of multiple faculty and staff members to one another and to the success of the department. Sometimes a story about linkage, combined with good data, can yield new resources for the department. Finally, a chair must at all times display empathy, humility, and integrity.

Frank Keil, professor and chair of Psychology at Yale University, perceptively points out that most academic administrative decisions involve difficult trade-offs. Do we make ideologically pure or pragmatic decisions about such thorny issues as admission of legacy students, including investments in fossil fuels in university portfolios or setting policies on speech that violate the principle of free speech? Are committees empowered to make real recommendations or simply to lend validity to decisions already made? Do we hire the most prestigious faculty members, regardless of how disruptive they may be, or have departments full of nice people who may not push the boundaries of their disciplines? Do we hire groups of faculty working on important problems and risk creating silos or hire one faculty member in each subfield and end up with intellectual mush? Each time we make a decision we must weigh these trade-offs and try to balance ideals and reality.

MAINTAINING A CONNECTION TO YOUR ACADEMIC DISCIPLINE

Almost all of the contributors who have faculty positions either explicitly or implicitly make the point that staying close to your academic discipline is important for an academic administrator. Ed Ray thinks and writes like an economist. Thomas George, chancellor of the University of Missouri, St. Louis, titles his chapter "Maintaining a Personal Program of Research and Scholarship while Serving as President/Chancellor." He talks about the importance of setting the tone of expectations of all faculty members if the chancellor is still an active scholar. Bob Sternberg maintains an active research agenda and has taught at least one class every year. Ana Mari Cauce also has taught every year and works to maintain a funded research agenda.

Donald Foss, professor of psychology and formerly provost at the University of Houston, has written about leadership throughout his administrative career. Bob Smith wrote and taught throughout his administrative career. Richard McCarty recommends teaching as a way of staying connected to students.

Not surprisingly, the chairs are more consistent about the importance of continuing to teach or to maintain a research agenda. Henry Roediger recommends continuing to teach. C. J. Brainerd, chair of the Department of Human Development at Cornell University, titles his chapter "The Science Chair as Scientific Leader." While the rest of the chapters in this book focus on administrative advice, he focuses on the role of the chair as an educational and scientific leader. He describes studying at the University of Iowa under the leadership of Kenneth Spence, "a world renowned experimental psychologist and chair of psychology." Spence led a department focused on theory-driven research, combined with a strong connection between theory and experimental design. He would make sure the graduate students took the train to Chicago every year to go to the Midwest Psychological Association meetings. While at the meetings they would decide which theories had the most promise for testing over the next year. They would go back the next year to present their research. By maintaining a consistent strategy of faculty and graduate student recruitment and mentoring, he built a department that sent its graduates to the best faculty positions in the country and maintained a national reputation for excellence. Brainerd contends that is the main role of a department chair.

CONCLUSION

This is an important and valuable collection of chapters on academic leadership. Unlike most books on leadership, it represents the different perspectives of people whose leadership experiences range from campus president/chancellor to faculty leader. The book allows the reader to "see" leadership from many different perspectives. Yet, as summarized above, common and important themes emerge. I have not covered every important theme. Fundraising, for example, is mentioned by some. And shared governance is only addressed directly in one essay, although all of the essays on strategic planning implicitly show the importance of shared governance in developing and implementing an effective strategic plan.

I will end by referring to another theme that is alluded to by some and addressed directly by others. As academic administrators, we serve at the pleasure of both our supervisors and those we serve. It is not about us; it is about the institution, and sometimes we have to move on to allow the institution to move on. Frank Keil puts it succinctly. "Know when it's time to say 'time's up' for being a chair." For those of us who have been presidents or chancellors, provosts, and deans, there may come a time when we have to step down or move on. Most of us who started as Big XII provosts when this project started are no longer in our posts. It may happen because a new leader is hired who wants his or her own team. It may come as retirement. Or, it may be a conscious decision not to make an ethically challenged decision demanded by a board or a supervisor. I have faced both the new supervisor and the demand to make an ethically challenged decision. In both cases I returned to a faculty position and to the classroom.

These experiences have taught me the importance of having an exit strategy negotiated in advance. First, if you are a faculty member taking a position at another university, don't sign a contract that does not include a position of tenured full professor in your discipline, or a related discipline if your new institution does not have your department. Second, negotiate what your salary will be, adjusted for future inflation, when you step down. In addition, try to negotiate an administrative leave if you serve for a certain amount of time. Use a reputable academic labor lawyer to negotiate for you if you run into difficulty getting what you want in writing. Remember that you won't get what you want when you are leaving. You are most likely to get it when you are being recruited. If you have a signed contract and a good lawyer, you can step down and never have to compromise yourself. Finally, if you have maintained a scholarly agenda and done some teaching, the transition will be relatively painless, and you will not have to compromise your principles to keep a job.

I don't want to end on a negative note. Serving as an academic administrator is a calling as strong as being a world-class scholar, a social worker, or a minister. There are amazing days when you land a great scholar or close a large gift. The time you spend with the "smartest people in the room"— faculty, staff, students, alumni, donors, and community members—is one of the great joys of the job. Unlike the life of a scholar that requires considerable delayed gratification waiting for publication, as an academic administrator you can solve problems and go home feeling you have accomplished something important that day. I wouldn't have given up those experiences for anything.

II

Presidents or Chancellors and Past-Academic Executive Officers

Chapter Two

Thoughts on Leadership

Edward J. Ray

Throughout my career, I have held a number of leadership roles. Thanks to luck, timing or fortunate twists of fate, these opportunities have provided me with invaluable lessons and experiences that shaped my views on leadership. My beliefs about leadership are described and illustrated below with some key examples.

I believe that effective leadership must be ethical leadership. Unless grounded firmly on a sound ethical foundation, leadership will not be successful. Lacking an ethical base, sooner or later, things will and do go badly. Yet a sound moral compass is not enough. While ethical leadership is admirable, it is not enough to be successful.

Leadership is about getting things done. In today's 24/7 world where we are all connected all the time, leadership needs to be dynamic, just in time, and authentic. There is no time for posturing and nowhere to hide. Leaders are doers, not just delegators. We drive, we push, and we follow up to ensure progress is being made on whatever initiative or matter of concern has our attention. Getting things done almost always takes a team effort. Good leaders recognize the contributions of others, celebrate their accomplishments, and recognize that we are all imperfect instruments.

Finally, I have a "no whining" rule. One cannot lead by whining, grousing, complaining, and being stuck in a negative place. When challenging situations arise—and they always do—true leaders, quite simply, carry on and direct the discussions, decisions, and actions required by circumstances.

Let me share some leadership lessons I have learned and explain how they came into play during my academic career and my service with the NCAA and elsewhere.

I became the chairperson of the economics department at Ohio State University at the age of thirty-one and was the youngest department chair in the history of the university at that time. I had no good role model for being a department chair. So I decided to apply the Golden Rule. I aimed to be the kind of leader I myself would be proud to support and that I would model the behavior that I expected to see in others. As department chair with new administrative obligations, I continued to teach, publish research in leading economics journals, and serve on university committees.

I believe that the mantle and honor of leadership carries a responsibility to serve. As a leader, you speak and act for others. People count on you to empower them by looking out for their interests and aspirations. Given this responsibility, which often can change the trajectory of one's career—and even possibly one's life—I believe that leaders should always deal directly with individuals whom they supervise and always take ownership for their decisions. Deliver the good news—and the bad—yourself. People have the right to expect that you will be honest with them and respect them. Early in my career, I told a colleague old enough to be my father that his teaching and research were weak, and I could not give him much of a raise. He turned before he left my office and thanked me for respecting him enough to be honest with him. He said previous chairs blamed the dean for low raises. He knew they were lying and that they assumed he could not figure that out.

On a daily basis, leaders are privy to information that must be processed, contemplated, and often acted upon. When appropriate, leaders should share information as quickly and fully as possible. This will reduce the distractions of rumors, rife in today's world of social media and twenty-four-hour news cycles. There cannot be an inner circle if everyone is up to speed on important issues. Similarly, make all decisions openly and transparently. If all decisions are subject to the light of day, you will be more objective, thoughtful, and disciplined.

Positions of leadership require great teamwork and the ability to chart a course with well-trusted teammates. As a leader, understand, articulate, and advance the team's mission. Promote teamwork, focus, and accountability. Give colleagues responsibility and hold them accountable for results. Team dynamics are interesting to manage and change from team to team and project to project. As a leader, it is always important to avoid favoritism. Good leaders focus on collecting success, not friends. Study problems together, but do not dither. Most importantly, leaders must take responsibility for team success—and failure. If you cannot lead like this, quite simply move out of the way and do not stymie progress.

Just as teamwork is inherent in leadership, so are mistakes.

Leaders make mistakes. No one is perfect, and no one has a perfect day. When these inevitable mistakes occur, quick action is required. It's important to recognize and acknowledge mistakes, apologize when necessary, and move on. I apologized to a colleague once, and when I told my wife that it went very well, she said she was not surprised because I had a lot of practice apologizing in my life. Mistakes invariably teach us valuable lessons. Pay attention to these learnings, but don't be too hard on yourself when you make mistakes. Do take time to make amends, but move on quickly.

As leaders, we must work to surround ourselves with trusted allies—people who align with our organizational goals and vision but who also have the temerity to push back, raise questions, and even tell us "no" on occasion without worrying about it limiting their careers. It's vital to make the chain of command work for you. Understand that most information should flow upward and unfiltered. When you have identified key staff willing to tell you when you are wrong, make sure to thank them for having the character and respect for you to speak candidly and tell you what you needed to hear.

As you assemble your teams, it's essential that you have the ability to identify leadership potential in others. Make sure you have regular, reserved, and dedicated time to give guidance, share direction, and foster feedback. I ask my direct reports for three or four goals each year in two pages or less and evaluate them based on reported results, also in two pages or less, each summer. While regular communication is always advised, do not micromanage people—it distracts leaders from doing their own jobs, and it prevents others from getting better at theirs, from learning and from growing into their roles.

Just as it is important to work with your team, it is equally imperative to strategically and proactively manage up. In other words, keep your boss or bosses—and we all have them—up to speed and ask for their help and guidance when you need it. Heroic efforts to solve problems above your pay grade usually make matters worse. Additionally, be honest when you disagree with a decision your boss has made and be sure to keep it "in-house." Remember, everyone reports to a higher authority.

The toughest lesson I have learned was the realization that you cannot always find a safe exit when addressing a problem. Sometimes you have to "take one for the team" and simply do the right thing, as you understand it to be at that moment in time. With that said, it's not always easy to know what the right thing to do is. Like my Golden Rule strategy, this is where one's sense of right and wrong has to be relied upon.

As provost at Ohio State University, I approved extending the tenure-clock timeline for medical faculty from six to eleven years. This was a very controversial decision and one I could have left to others. Already in place in most top-fifty academic medical centers, 625 medical faculty members voted for the tenure timing change. Yet opponents of the new policy urged me to reject the request on a rules technicality, arguing it was an assault on the tenure system. However, I made the change and took the attacks; it was the right thing to do, and it cost me some friends and a lot of political capital.

The decision to have a new governance model at Oregon State University represents one recent example of a decision that I had to make. I took the time to consult with faculty, staff, students, alumni, and friends of the university before I made a decision. I wanted to hear what these very important stakeholders thought. After all, I represent them, and they should have a voice. I also needed to balance my sense of what is in the best interest for Oregon students as well as the people of Oregon, not just OSU. Early on in this discussion, I made the case against the creation of institutional boards for Oregon's public universities. In 2013, the Oregon legislature created institutional boards at two of the public universities and gave Oregon State University the option to create a board. After further broad consultation with stakeholders, I decided we would create our own board. Now I am working hard to help all of us make institutional boards and a new pre-K–20 educational governance structure work as well as possible for the people of Oregon. I believe that is the right thing to do.

Every day, I carry with me the lessons I have learned in every leadership role I assume. Here are a few more examples of how I have applied these lessons.

Here at Oregon State, like any Division I school, athletics compliance is a big responsibility. We make it pretty simple at OSU. Athletics is part of the university, and *all* students are here to fulfill their goals to complete their college educations. Our student athletes should be part of campus life, succeed academically, and be safe and healthy. They are students first. As president, my job is to put good people in charge. Bob DeCarolis, our athletic director, deserves a lot of credit for the coaches he hires, and the coaches deserve credit for their steadfast focus on doing things the right way. I learned something from our coaches that I took with me in my leadership role with the NCAA, the governing body for intercollegiate athletics. Honest coaches, who genuinely care for their student athletes, become frustrated when there is little accountability required of coaches or institutions that cheat and behave unethically. In turn, good, ethical coaches—who play by the rules—are made to feel like chumps for doing the right thing.

There are three membership divisions in the NCAA, and Division I consists of the largest schools, such as Oregon State University. Each division maintains its own rules on personnel, amateurism, recruiting, and eligibility, among other things. These rules must be consistent with overall NCAA governing principles. In 2007, I joined the NCAA on the Finance Committee and the Executive Committee and served for almost six years. I became chair of the Executive Committee in October 2009 following the death of Myles Brand, president of the NCAA. In this role, in 2010, I monitored negotiations for the NCAA's new media contract—which is worth $10.7 billion over fourteen years. I also chaired the search committee that hired Mark Emmert as the new president of the NCAA with the concurrence of the entire executive committee.

As previously mentioned, I have always believed participation and transparency are essential within all major organizational issues, debates, and decisions. When I joined the NCAA, board meetings did not include student voices, even though the NCAA is dedicated to student-athlete success and well-being. I helped to change that. Now, the three-division student-athlete advisory committee presidents meet with the executive committee to share their concerns. Additionally, the NCAA represents all three divisions—I, II, and III—but I learned that the presidential councils of the three divisions never met together. So I changed that, as well. Each executive committee meeting now has a breakfast that includes the presidential leaders from all three divisions.

While at the NCAA, I also helped initiate a conversation about rules enforcement. Approximately twenty-five major violation cases are filed each year; about 80 percent stem from Division I schools. Historically, the Committee on Infractions (COI) handled each case separately. Justice was not swift; repeat-violator coaches avoided accountability, and the public had more questions than answers and suffered a lot of frustration. The enforcement group that I chaired proposed changes to speed things up and improve the process. We expanded COI membership from ten to as many as twenty-four members, and panels of five to seven members now manage cases simultaneously. Additionally, a defined violation structure and specific penalty guidelines were established with mitigating and aggravating conditions defined. Violators now know the penalties, which are more severe than in the past, and penalties are more consistent from case to case. The enforcement staff at the NCAA is expanding, and case time is expected to decrease 50 percent while penalties become more predictable and consistent. All aspects of enforcement are now audited annually. These changes went into effect August 1, 2013.

The Penn State case involving former assistant football coach Jerry Sandusky was an unexpected, extraordinary challenge, and in July 2012, I found myself participating with NCAA President Mark Emmert in a national press conference after announcing serious sanctions against Penn State. I could have sidestepped that event, claiming my term was up in two weeks. I did what I thought was right and helped to explain the NCAA rulings.

Through all of my different leadership roles and challenges, I have had to draw upon a diverse set of skills. I am a firm believer in the foundation of an education that offers much experience and exposure to the liberal arts. I'm well aware that today's anxious parents often counsel their children to pursue STEM disciplines because job prospects are seemingly better in these areas. But in today's world of changing demographics and a global marketplace, the liberal arts are critical to success in every economic sector. There can be no doubt that they play an essential part in providing a foundation for learning in every professional field.

Clearly, all successful careers require critical thinking, teamwork, sensitivity to cultural, demographic, economic and societal differences, and political perspectives. A liberal arts education provides this grounding. Most people will have six to ten jobs during their careers, and liberal arts majors are the most adaptable to new circumstances. No one knows what the jobs of the future will be, but a liberal arts degree provides a great foundation for adjusting to new careers and further education. We do know that a third of all Fortune 500 CEOs have liberal arts degrees. For example, Leslie Moonves, who leads CBS, has a degree in Spanish from Bucknell University, and Starbucks' CEO, Howard Schultz, majored in communications at Northern Michigan.

The Association of American Colleges and Universities recently launched the LEAP Employer-Educator Compact to make the quality of college learning a national priority as employers seek college graduates with a broader set of skills and knowledge. LEAP—Liberal Education and America's Promise—is a national advocacy, campus action, and research initiative that champions the importance of a twenty-first century liberal education for individuals and for a nation dependent on economic creativity and democratic vitality.

I was among one hundred college presidents, all members of the LEAP Presidents' Trust, who developed the compact in concert with employers who are advisors to this initiative. These education leaders and visionary employers were the initial signers of the compact. More than 350 colleges, community colleges, and universities, and eight state systems of higher education are working through LEAP to ensure that all their students achieve this essential learning.

Increasingly, the information we receive from many sources—including 140-character Twitter feeds, videos, and other social media—is tailored to our presumed interests. Search engines and social networks track our online habits to influence our preferences. The ability to quickly assimilate information, analyze what's needed, and aggregate content for personal or professional use are skills that stem—no pun intended—from liberal arts training and are critical in all aspects of life today. Leaders put these skills to good use through their various trials and tribulations. I am so passionate about advancing liberal arts education because I know it fosters skills critical for effective leadership.

People often ask me about leadership. And I always urge them to explore what motivates their own style of leadership. I genuinely like people. I like helping others solve problems and being part of causes more important than me. I always felt that if I had children—and my wife and I have three—I would want them to be able to be proud of me. My wife Beth and I celebrated our forty-fourth anniversary in 2013, and, for most of my life, I have been trying to impress my girlfriend.

So in closing, I ask: What motivates you?

NOTE

Acknowledgment: To my partner and best friend Beth.

Chapter Three

Maintaining a Personal Program of Research and Scholarship While Serving as President/Chancellor

Thomas F. George

PATHWAYS TO BECOMING PRESIDENT/CHANCELLOR

There is no unique pathway to becoming a president or chancellor. While the most common pathway entails progressing through the academic faculty and administrative ranks, successful presidents and chancellors have come from outside academe, such as from the corporate world, government, and private foundations. Generally, a president who moved through the academic faculty ranks has at one time had a successful program of personal research and scholarship, and my chapter here will apply largely to such a person. However, my comments also can apply to those taking other pathways, depending on the individual. Let me also indicate up front that my faculty appointments have always been in chemistry and physics so, while I understand and appreciate the entire array of disciplines represented by the faculty of a comprehensive university, I will frequently draw on my own experiences and the practices of a scientist in the research arena. When I use the words "research" and "scholarship," the reader can interpret them according to the particular discipline, like exhibitions for artists and performances for musicians, among others.

STILL A FACULTY MEMBER?

I was appointed dean of natural sciences and mathematics at the State University of New York, Buffalo, at age thirty-eight, never having served as a department chair, although at the University of Rochester I had been on numerous committees, both departmental and university-wide, and for five years I was the sole lecturer and person in charge of general chemistry, a course of 750 students, which required administrative as well as teaching skills. A question that I was asked when I arrived at SUNY, Buffalo, was: "When will you shut down your personal research program?" I "naively" said that I had no intention of doing so, and during my six years as dean, I maintained three major grants from the Air Force, Navy, and National Science Foundation, which supported a team of postdocs and graduate students.

This was possible because I came in with a robust, funded research program—such a program could not have been started from scratch in a decanal position—and I had a supportive provost and president at the university. Upon moving to the position of provost at Washington State University with a wider range of responsibilities, the size of my research group and level of external funding were reduced. However, I started capitalizing on the power of the Internet and collaborators around the world that I had met at various international conferences—the world became my research group.

Moving on to my two chancellorships (in Wisconsin and now Missouri), my research group was reduced to the size of one (i.e., just me), but the Internet collaborations became my main *modus operandi* in the research arena. I have opportunistically sought external funding, and during my past decade at the University of Missouri, St. Louis (UMSL), I have served as principal investigator on research and teaching grants from the Office of Army Research, National Science Foundation, North Atlantic Treaty Organization, and St. Louis Institute of Nanomedicine. Analyzing my list of publications, you would find that 150 of my 750 papers (journal articles and book chapters), two of my five authored and five of my eighteen edited books have been written since I became chancellor at UMSL in 2003, and I periodically present invited research lectures at universities and conferences, albeit not with the same frequency as in my earlier years when I was a faculty member or dean. It is probably safe to say that in regard to research and scholarship, I have indeed maintained my role as a faculty member.

Furthermore, I have insisted at the beginning of each of my administrative appointments that my faculty appointment as a tenured professor go through the rigorous process applied to other faculty at the university. I should add that I am a theoretician, such that my research takes place with computers and "pencil and paper" (but, I do interact with experimentalists in different fields), so I do not have the burden and expense of running a laboratory.

DEFINING AND SUCCEEDING AT A
PROGRAM OF RESEARCH/SCHOLARSHIP

To be successful in maintaining research and scholarship without compromising the position of president/chancellor, one must define well the type of research and its place within the administrative portfolio, both with respect to content and to the devotion of time and energy. It helps to personally be savvy in the use of computers and the necessary software relevant to one's discipline.

While you can lean to a certain extent on secretarial assistance, you must realize that your primary position is president/chancellor—the program of research and scholarship takes a back seat and should never interfere with your administrative responsibilities. You will have to compromise on how much "free time" you might have, since your research often will take place in the wee hours of the morning or on weekend mornings (if they happen to be free). It is important to get into a rhythm with respect to both research and administration. If one is absent too long from one's discipline, especially in the sciences, it can be very arduous and time-consuming to get back to speed without taking a sabbatical.

COLLABORATIONS, TEAMWORK, AND SIMILARITIES
BETWEEN RESEARCH AND ADMINISTRATION

The extent one would work in teams varies across the disciplines; in much of the sciences and engineering, research is carried out in a team setting. The skills developed there can translate directly to the team approach, which is so prevalent in administration. One learns to capitalize on the strengths of others, recognizing that one person alone will probably not accomplish a given task. The varied backgrounds of team members help broaden the perspective and expand the arsenal of tools that can be brought to bear on a given problem/challenge.

In addition, since research/scholarship is not necessarily expected of a chancellor/president, and hence not used to evaluate his or her performance, one can "loosen up" and more easily explore new directions. In fact, here at UMSL, while my particular expertise is in laser-induced processes in chemical and materials physics, with special emphasis on nanoscience and nanomedicine, I have coauthored eight different papers with faculty collaborators across six academic departments: finance, management, music, chemistry and biochemistry, physics and astronomy, and mathematics and computer science. What a joy it is to work with these outstanding faculty members and to learn from their wealth of knowledge! It has also helped me gain a better appreciation at the ground level for the way publishing is done in different disciplines, including the unique challenges for each discipline.

In some cases, as one gets more entrenched in administration and becomes more removed from the cutting edge of his/her original discipline, research and scholarship can take different forms, such as focusing on how the academy functions and evolves its role in society. In this case, the president/chancellor draws on his or her administrative expertise and how this can be used to address important issues in higher education, leading to authored papers in appropriate journals and to authored/edited books.

BENEFITS/REWARDS AND DRAWBACKS OF A PERSONAL RESEARCH PROGRAM

Let me start with the benefits and rewards. One's visible engagement in research and scholarship helps set a tone for the institution. We expect full-time tenured/tenure-track faculty to maintain a program of research and scholarship, and leading by example can help in this regard. Creating or discovering something new and then presenting it to the outside world, such as through peer-reviewed publications, exhibitions, performances, and so forth, keeps an administrator attuned to the practices of faculty. Fighting the journal referee battles and proposal reviews is an ongoing challenge, and doing it yourself imparts a special appreciation for the successes and challenges of faculty. Besides interacting with peer colleagues in the disciplines, an active research program enables one to make substantive presentations to various lay and student groups, as I will do, for example, to high school students. And then there is the overall sense of self-worth and the added dimensions to one's life made possible through research and scholarship.

Assuming one's research does not lessen one's ability to serve as a president or chancellor, it is difficult to find a drawback to having a research/scholarship program. A president or chancellor must of course realize that their performance will be assessed on how they succeed as an administrator, not as a researcher or scholar. While it can be fun and entertaining to talk about one's research at a reception/dinner, which I will do especially in regard to my work in nanomedicine and laser-cancer therapy (there is that instance when someone asks what I do, and I reply "quantum physicist"—now there is a conversation stopper!), most of the time I am wearing my "chancellor's hat" in my conversations both on and off campus.

TEACHING

While this chapter has focused on research and scholarship, I tip my hat to those presidents and chancellors who continue to teach, either in a classroom or online. Teaching is another way of keeping engaged with the responsibilities of faculty and, of course, having substantive interactions with students. Teaching and research are not necessarily mutually exclusive endeavors—they often reinforce each other and even merge in some cases, especially in regard to working with graduate students. One can engage in the "scholarship of teaching," leading to publications in pedagogical journals. Introducing undergraduate and even high school students to research is encouraged at many universities. As an example, a physics colleague and I worked with high school students on the topic of how birds learned to fly, where we applied Newtonian mechanics to describe the motion of wild geese on our campus; this ultimately led to a jointly authored paper in the journal *The Physics Teacher*.

MUSICAL HOBBY

I would be remiss if I did not mention the value of a constructive, passionate hobby. A president/chancellor could call research/scholarship a hobby and intellectual pursuit, since it is a kind of outlet and release for different kinds of creativity, but frequently one encounters presidents and chancellors who are adept at something outside their official office. In my case, it is music. While I have studied jazz piano with some prominent musicians, such as at the Eastman School of Music in Rochester and the Berklee College of Music in Boston, I do not have an academic degree or certificate in music. In K–20 I was a student of classical piano and pipe organ, and I eventually switched to jazz in my early twenties. I started performing in clubs, restaurants, churches, schools, and other venues, often "gigging" several times a week in Rochester, which is how I "developed my jazz chops."

Since coming to St. Louis, I have been fortunate to perform in major concert halls and other settings with some of the very best musicians in St. Louis, often in connection with fundraising events for UMSL and other community organizations. I often play with faculty and students, which is most rewarding. I have taken my playing overseas, such as on recent trips to Bosnia, China, Croatia, Hungary, Kuwait, and Romania in connection with trips on behalf of the university.

In a trip in 2012 to develop academic partnerships between UMSL and the University of Sarajevo (Bosnia) and the University of Dubrovnik (Croatia), I also gave jazz concerts at both universities as well as a research seminar at the former location. While I would not label my musical activities as research or scholarship, I get the same sort of "rush" from these as from basic scientific research and having a paper accepted in a leading journal or a grant funded by an outside agency.

MUTUAL REINFORCEMENT OF ADMINISTRATION AND RESEARCH/SCHOLARSHIP

While I have commented above that one's research/scholarship should not interfere with the responsibilities of the administrative post, let me be as bold to say that, crafted appropriately, research/scholarship can actually enhance one's ability to function as an administrator, and vice versa. Granted, there are a number of superb administrators who do not have a personal program of research and scholarship, but in the case of myself and various others I know, I feel that wearing multiple hats besides the "chancellor's hat" has made me a better (or at least a more interesting) chancellor. At the same time, I have leaned on my chancellorial skills to address problems and issues in working with my research collaborators.

The distinction of my multiple hats was recently emphasized by my receiving two honorary doctorates. The first was from the University of Szeged in Hungary for my research as a physicist, which went through a rigorous review by the faculty, including an examination of citations, before it was granted. The second was from Phranakohn Rajabhat University in Thailand for my role as chancellor in economic development in the St. Louis region. It was fun being purely a faculty member during my trip to Hungary, where I presented the Doctor *Honoris Causa* Lecture on laser-induced electronic and vibrational excitation of nanoparticles, and being exclusively a chancellor in Thailand, where I made a presentation on the role of higher education in economic, cultural, and social development. As an aside, while in Bangkok in 2013, I had a chance to ride an elephant—one of the perks of being a chancellor, I suppose.

Wearing just one hat at a given time can have its amusing moments. I recall being invited to present a seminar on my research on optical intersubband transitions in semiconductor heterostructure quantum wells to the Department of Physics at the University of Jyväskylä (170 miles north of Helsinki in Finland) when I was provost at Washington State University. Besides my seminar, I spent a lot of time with the faculty discussing science and their university overall, and I recall their complaining about the upper administration to me as a colleague physicist, since they were not receiving sufficient resources and faculty positions for their department—I of course commiserated with them.

CONCLUSION

To conclude, let me mention that a colleague of mine is fond of Chinese scroll paintings, especially those that depict mountains with many different paths to the top. Certainly, there are many different approaches to blending research and scholarship with a top administrative, or for that matter, any administrative post. I hope the personal story and examples portrayed herein will be useful to our readers.

Chapter Four

Effective Academic Leadership

David Hodge and Bobby Gempesaw

In his book, *Managing in Turbulent Times*, Peter Drucker noted that "the greatest danger in times of turbulence is not the turbulence—it is to act with yesterday's logic." Despite the fact that faculty are aware of the importance of new ways of thinking in their research and pedagogy, higher education institutions ironically tend to be resistant to change, and creating change is often a slow and arduous process. This presents a challenge to academic leaders as colleges and universities across the nation deal with shifting student demographics, reduced public funding, increased public demand for accountability, heightened competition, rising tuition cost and student debt, rapid technological advances, and other factors that call for significant change. Responding to these challenges will inevitably require changing long-held ideas and practices. In this chapter, we share three examples of recent major initiatives at Miami University that demonstrate how academic leadership can effectively bring about change in a university: changing the structure of an academic unit, changing budget priorities, and changing the approach to strategic planning and accountability.

Miami University is a public university located in Oxford, Ohio. With a student body of 16,000 undergraduate and 2,500 graduate students on its main campus, and another 5,000 students on its regional campuses, Miami is recognized as one of the most outstanding undergraduate-focused institutions in the United States. In the 2014 edition of *America's Best Colleges, U.S. News and World Report*, Miami was ranked third among the nation's top universities for its exceptionally strong commitment to undergraduate teaching and as the second most efficient university for producing high-quality results.

CHANGING AN ACADEMIC UNIT

Although the educational mission of a university may not change drastically over time, it is now clear that universities must evolve to remain relevant and successful in fulfilling their missions. The ever-changing patterns of expectations, resources, and demand for higher education place significant stress on universities—especially within their academic units. Thus, university leaders increasingly must make difficult decisions regarding such controversial options as downsizing or closing academic programs, merging academic units, limiting faculty hires and increasing teaching loads, reducing professional development support, and imposing higher standards for personnel evaluation. Implementing these kinds of changes presents a great challenge for academic leaders. Robert Diamond, president of the National Academy for Academic Leadership, states that "in higher education, particularly at larger institutions, individuals are more committed to their unit or in the case of faculty to their discipline or department, than they are to the institution. Any shift of resources away from their own area is viewed as a loss to be avoided at all costs."[1] Thus, proposed changes are invariably met with strong opposition.

Successfully implementing major change requires the careful balancing of engaging and pushing. On the one hand, it is important to solicit the input of those who will be most affected by the proposed change. Solutions should come from the collective efforts of the administration, faculty, staff, students, and alumni who must work together to achieve the desired outcome. With the board of trustees often demanding immediate solutions, it is tempting for academic leaders to simply dictate what needs to be done, but such an approach will most likely result in low faculty morale and implementation stalemates. Because change generates anxiety and uncertainty for those who will be affected by it, academic leaders will find it productive to listen to their concerns and engage them constructively in finding a solution. On the other hand, it is also critical that academic leaders resist the urge to delay the development of a path forward because of the loud opposition from those who refuse to recognize the need for change. Academic leaders must have the courage to do what is right, while earnestly following the appropriate procedural guidelines to enact change.

In 2006 Miami University, after three years of turmoil and resistance, downsized and reorganized an interdisciplinary school from "school" status to a program located within another college. The school had been experiencing a decline in student demand for several years, had received two less than favorable program reviews, and had a very low student to faculty ratio. Nonetheless, the decision to remove the school status was met with considerable opposition, which, fairly or unfairly, criticized the process as much as the rationale. As a result, the university senate, with the concurrence of the administration, passed a resolution in 2008 that required a substantially rigorous process for making administrative decisions that involve eliminating, partitioning, or merging academic units.

The university senate resolution influenced the way the university managed a similar scenario in 2011, when evaluating the viability of reorganizing our regional campuses. Created in 1966 to provide two-year degrees to residents of the regions and to prepare students to relocate to the main campus to complete baccalaureate degrees, the structural relationship of the regional campuses to the main campus had remained largely unchanged. It was especially noteworthy that faculty appointments and curricular matters at the regional campuses all reported up through departments on the main campus. However, over time, the number of students transferring to the main campus declined significantly to less than 6 percent of students enrolled on the regional campuses.

In 2008, the Ohio Board of Regents emphasized the importance of distinguishing the mission of the regional campuses throughout the university system of Ohio and to build them into institutional entities that more purposefully serve the people of the state of Ohio, specifically the Ohioans who live near the regional campuses and have the most direct access to them. Over many years, we had been evaluating the mission and role of the regional campuses. In 2010, the matter was addressed in the university's strategic priorities task force. Prior to that in 2009, a regional campus committee was convened to examine the issue. The main recommendation of each of these groups was virtually identical: (1) the university needed to re-envision the regional campuses as locations where we can increase the availability of affordable four-year degree opportunities, and (2) students must be able to be fully complete those four-year degree opportunities on the regional campuses.

Clearly the mission of the regional campuses had changed while the organizational and academic structure had not. All of the committees who had studied the regional campuses had recommended some form of unit reorganization and other changes. However, many recommendations were not implemented primarily due to the vocal opposition from the faculty on both the regional campuses and the main campus as well as from members of the community.

By 2011, with the growing emphasis on four-year degrees and the reluctance of the departments at the Oxford main campus to approve new degree programs—like criminal justice—on the regional campuses, the tension between mission and structure had reached a critical point. Instead of imposing change through a top-down approach, we followed the procedural guidelines and intent of the university senate resolution and engaged those affected fully. We described in detail the challenges and opportunities faced by the regional campuses in fulfilling their mission and the serious consequences of maintaining the status quo. Of equal importance, we engaged in authentic discussions with faculty, staff, and students that yielded valuable insights that shaped the final recommendations.

Working with various faculty committees and in coordination with the university senate and the full support of the board of trustees, the university was able to complete the creation of the new division, with curricular autonomy and the responsibility to appoint tenure-track faculty, in two years. This outcome has provided the new academic division with the flexibility to offer new programs and degrees to meet the educational needs of the region and to hire faculty that align with those programs.

In less than two years, the new division has developed five new four-year degrees that were readily endorsed by state government and are experiencing early signs of success and better signs of financial stability. Do all of the faculty members and staff support these changes? No. Even with this approach to change, there was strong opposition to the reorganization and many difficult moments. But the process worked, and effective change was achieved. Academic leaders must have the courage to lead and make difficult decisions about academic structure in order to avoid what could be even more difficult decisions down the road.

CHANGING BUDGET PRIORITIES

Like many higher education institutions, Miami University faced extraordinary fiscal constraints brought about by the recession of 2009. Typically, in this scenario, the central administration would decide where to make cuts, how to reallocate, or what specific budgetary changes to make to resolve the shortfall faced by the institution at that time (which in our case was $40 million). Instead, the president formed a task force of faculty, staff, and students representing all divisions and levels of the university. The task force was very carefully chosen to include forward-looking and respected individuals. Few decisions are as important as who is chosen for this challenge.

The task force was charged to construct a forward-looking framework to guide decision making over the next five years (and beyond) in order to advance Miami as a premier national university. The task force's specific charge was to prioritize and align the university's strategic goals with the new economic reality and competitive context of higher education by creating a sustainable baseline budget that would yield an even more successful and highly regarded university.

Our role as leaders included defining and contextualizing the problem, asking important questions, and providing accurate data to help shape the recommendations. The task force was asked to distinguish enduring values from those traditional practices that were no longer serving us effectively in order to develop creative and entrepreneurial recommendations. Task force members were explicitly encouraged to use their area expertise but to take a university-wide perspective while working independently of outside influences. It took a bit of time for the task force to fully grasp what this meant, but their success in doing so was vital to the quality of their recommendations. They took their work seriously and exceeded our high expectations. The group examined all areas of the budget and produced an ambitious set of thirty-five recommendations regarding the academic and administrative organizational structure, graduate education and research, student life, intercollegiate athletics, administrative support services, physical facilities, and, most importantly, new sources of revenue, budgetary cutbacks, and a new performance-based budgetary framework.

The task force performed its work as the university faced the perfect storm affecting higher education. Guided by the task force recommendations, we selectively reduced our workforce (mostly through attrition), froze hiring, and chose not to award salary increases for two years. At the same time, we embraced new structures and measures of accountability. It was a difficult time, but four years later the university is flourishing. We are aggressively (but selectively!) hiring faculty and staff, enjoying record numbers of applications, recruiting the most academically accomplished first-year classes in our history, and providing annual salary increases. Do we believe that all the employees agreed with the task force recommendations when they were made? No. But because the task force represented all parts of the university and not just the administration, these recommendations were widely embraced. The task force proved that an institution that is able to plan with focused goals, anticipate challenges with an inspiring vision, and is disciplined enough to implement much-needed changes will be a better institution for everyone in the community—and particularly our students.

CHANGING THE STRATEGIC PLANNING PROCESS

In the fall of 2007, in what was a favorable economic environment, the university launched a process to determine its strategic goals for the next five years. The process was led by senior administrators and then vetted with university stakeholders. The goals were not controversial, and, as was common at the time, included only a handful of university-level goals.

In the summer of 2012, in a much more uncertain and challenging context, the university initiated the development of a new strategic plan (the Miami 2020 Plan) to achieve its vision to offer "the best undergraduate experience in the nation, enhanced by superior, select graduate programs." Unlike the previous strategic plan, we recognized that this effort would require a more inclusive strategic-planning effort to secure shared ownership since this strategic plan would require specific metrics and accountability at the unit level as well as at the university level. The stakes were high, given the headwinds confronting higher education and the general resistance to change that is found in academia. Fortunately, we completed the process on time and with a strategic plan that is forward looking, emphasizes metrics and accountability down to the unit level, and is widely embraced by the university community. We achieved this outcome by adhering to several leadership principles.

Build an Effective Team

In *The Wisdom of Teams*,[2] Katzenbach and Smith advise that, more important than selecting team members with charismatic personalities, it is best to select members who possess the complementary technical, functional, problem-solving, and interpersonal skills to address the problem at hand. When forming the fiscal-priorities task force team in 2010, the faculty who were selected to co-chair the task force came from different academic divisions but had keen knowledge of faculty governance, budget, and finance principles. The rest of the team was comprised of members from all levels and areas of the university, who brought with them diverse, complementary skill sets. In developing the Miami 2020 Plan, we followed this same logic by appointing the faculty chair of the university senate and the dean of Arts and Science to co-chair a coordinating team of twenty faculty and staff members who shared those attributes that made the fiscal priorities task force such a success.

The coordinating committee initially settled on five broad goals and set up a subcommittee for each goal. In consultation with academic deans and vice presidents, we then appointed another thirty members of the campus community to be part of five target goal teams. The deliberations in each of the target goal teams were shared/discussed/debated with the full coordinating committee, and the coordination committee co-chairs reported directly and regularly to the president and provost. Thus, we had both an outstanding core coordinating committee and an extended group of faculty and staff focused on the initial set of five broad goals.

Establish Urgency as well as Clear, Meaningful, and High Expectations

It is important that team members understand the urgent and worthwhile purpose of solving the problems at hand. The more that urgent and significant problems are understood, the more likely it is that a high-performing and functional team will emerge. To highlight the urgency and importance of the Miami 2020 Plan, the president focused his State of the University address on the challenges faced by the university, the urgency of meeting the timetable in developing the plan, and the expectation that all units in the university should participate and contribute to the university's strategic plan. He highlighted the evolving challenges facing higher education by emphasizing that we could either "anticipate and lead" or "react and follow." He concluded the address by stating: "The Miami 2020 Plan will provide the vision of where we want to be, the measureable objectives that will both inspire us and hold us accountable, and action plans that integrate our individual and collective efforts. Together, we, the extended Miami community, will determine all of these elements, and we will own our future." In order to deepen the understanding of the challenges to higher education and the need for urgency, the university also invited several national leaders to educate the community. These independent voices engaged the coordinating committee and the broader community most effectively.

Empower the Team

To ensure that the team stays on task and makes effective progress, leaders should encourage frequent interaction among team members. Team members' time together should ideally be both formal and informal. Indeed, creative insights as well as personal bonding require casual interactions just as much as analyzing spreadsheets, poring over the professional literature, and interviewing stakeholders. As senior leaders of the institution, the president and provost met regularly with the coordinating and target goal team leaders to review their progress, provide guidance, and answer questions. We invited members of the board of trustees to participate in the discussion and sought their opinion on the general direction of the plan. We also invited alumni and other external experts to help the team understand the critical task on hand. During all of these interactions, though, we emphasized that the coordinating committee had the responsibility for driving this forward. Effective leaders guide their teams to uncover their shared aspirations for success, analyze their assumptions, and identify breakthrough possibilities. As progress is made, they applaud and celebrate those accomplishments.

As Heifetz and Linsky suggest in *Leadership on the Line*, leaders need to "give the work back" to members of their organization to promote a shared ownership of the need to solve the problem. The Miami 2020 team leaders held numerous open sessions with faculty and the community to discuss their progress and seek broader consensus. These meetings were at times quite contentious, underscoring the value of having broad and respected leaders on the coordinating committee. The council of deans engaged their department chairs and program directors in defining their unit contributions and challenges in meeting the university goals. Regular updates were presented at the university senate, faculty assembly, and academic administrators meetings. Open faculty meetings were also held to solicit feedback from the campus community. The team leaders also worked closely with the communication and marketing staff to make sure timely updates were provided through the university's electronic newsletter and website.

Listen, Expect Conflict, and Take Risks

Effective leadership requires that leaders be willing to listen as well as push the process. One trademark of academia is the presence of free and open discourse. Academic leaders must be willing to share the podium with others and to listen for ideas where win-win situations can be achieved. Effective leaders also, though, use clear timelines to keep momentum going. Effective leaders understand that disagreements are unavoidable; however, disagreements can be managed more productively by carefully listening to all input before making the difficult decision. Effective leaders must also be willing to take risks during the process. At the start of developing the Miami 2020 Plan, we received numerous ideas and suggestions for possible goals and objectives. Some of the proposed goals and objectives were problematic because team members understandably brought their divisional or disciplinary priorities to the debate of ideas. After carefully listening to and working closely with the coordinating and target goal team leaders, we pushed the committee to focus the strategic ideas and took the risk of alienating team members whose ideas were not integrated into the 2020 plan. We explained that it was critical that we develop focused goals at the university level that will advance the whole university and not just one or two units. The divisions, departments, programs, and other units were then given the flexibility and support to be creative in crafting their specific contributions to the university goals.

The result of this process is a new strategic plan that is forward looking, provides metrics for all goals, identifies goals for units as well as the university, and is widely embraced by the university community. The Miami 2020 strategic plan is the shared pathway to our future.

CONCLUSION

Universities and colleges undertake many new initiatives every year, and every year the urgency of making change becomes more apparent. However, not all of these initiatives will be successful, usually because there is a lack of buy-in or support from constituents during the process. In our experience, for major and often controversial initiatives to be successful, academic leaders must provide a compelling vision, be honest about the challenges at hand (including admitting mistakes in dealing with these challenges), and follow appropriate procedures. The leadership must also be willing to take appropriate risks and spend political capital in making difficult decisions to achieve the objectives set forth.

The practice of effective academic leadership requires following shared governance principles, or what is known as *distributive leadership*. It is important for academic leaders not only to follow the governance planning process but to also distribute the responsibilities of achieving the institution's goals with deans, chairs, faculty, staff, students, alumni, and other constituents. Major initiatives can be sustained only if the campus constituents own the creation of the goals along with the responsibility for achieving those objectives. Effectiveness in academic leadership requires that we not only share in developing the strategic direction of the institution but also share the accountability for developing the pathway toward those goals. Finally, and most importantly, academic leaders must share the rewards and recognition with everyone who contributed in elevating the university toward greater excellence in ensuring the success of our students.

NOTES

1. Diamond, Robert M. (2006). "Why Colleges Are So Hard to Change." Trusteeship, November–December 2006 issue. Retrieved at www.thenationalacademy.org/readings/hardtochange.html.
2. Katzenbach, J. R. and Smith, D. K., (2003). *The Wisdom of Teams: Creating the High-Performance Organization*. New York: HarperCollins.

REFERENCES

Diamond, Robert M. (2006). "Why Colleges Are So Hard to Change." Trusteeship, November–December 2006 issue. Retrieved at www.thenationalacademy.org/readings/hardtochange.html.
Drucker, Peter F. (2009). *Managing in Turbulent Times*. New York: HarperCollins e-books.
Hodge, David (2012). *Annual Address 2012*. Retrieved at www.miamioh.edu/about-miami/leadership/president/reports-speeches/annual-address/2012/index.html.
Katzenbach, J. R. and Smith, D. K., (2003). *The Wisdom of Teams: Creating the High-Performance Organization*. New York: HarperCollins.
U.S. News and World Report (2013). "Best Undergraduate Teaching: National Universities." Retrieved at colleges.usnews.rankingsandreviews.com/best-colleges/rankings/national-universities/undergraduate-teaching.

Chapter Five

Strategic Planning Through Thick and Thin

Marc A. Johnson

Strategic plans guide preservation, inertia, and growth of an institution. The subject of a strategic plan is the institution. The strategic actions guided by the plan carry the institution from its current condition to a desired condition through the unknown sequence of future, exogenous forces that reality provides. Each institutional strategic plan is different; each institution starts with a unique current condition, represented by parameters that are mostly unchangeable, like tenured personnel, policies, contracts, and facilities. The desired, realistic, future condition is affected by institutional mission, economic realities, governance structures and personalities, and the consensus vision of the actors within the institution.

The example used in this chapter is the University of Nevada, Reno. The university was founded in 1874 and remained the only institution of higher education in the state of Nevada for the state's first seventy-five years of existence. As such, it has developed as a broad liberal arts and sciences university: the land-grant university, the agriculture school, the mining school, and the medical school. When the university developed its last strategic plan, covering 2009 to 2015, it was classified by the Carnegie Foundation for the Advancement of Teaching as a "Comprehensive Doctoral, Arts and Sciences/Professions—Balanced, High Research University" and ranked by the *U.S. News & World Report* Best Colleges edition as a Tier I institution.

THE INSTITUTIONAL STRATEGIC PLAN

The Institutional Strategic Plan, 2009–2015, www.unr.edu/president/strategic-and-master-planning/strategic-plan, was initiated in the summer of

2008 after the first announcement of a likely major budget reduction for fiscal year 2010 but before the magnitude of the reduction was known. The plan was ready for approval by June 2009 but was not actually approved by the board of regents until December 2009. The plan was developed through processes that included much information synthesis; numerous faculty, staff, and student meetings; and subsequent drafts and reviews. The transmission letter from the president to the board of regents describes the "current condition" of the university, the priority to preserve the ability to fulfill core missions, and the imperatives of service to address critical issues facing the state:

> The University of Nevada has served the State of Nevada for 135 years, first from Elko and then from Reno. The University of Nevada, Reno has evolved through time to become a comprehensive institution of higher education for learning, discovery, and community engagement across the full range of academic disciplines. The University has developed special emphases to reflect the important industries and social conditions of the State, e.g., adoption of the Land Grant University principles, development of the Mackay School of Mines, and growth in agriculture, medicine, health care, engineering, business, education, and journalism. Today, the challenges of Nevada include: young people's success in school, economic and environmental opportunities with renewable energy, health care for citizens, environmental quality, and diversification of the State's economy, in addition to support for Nevada's traditional industries. The University continues to evolve to address these challenges with professional workforce development, new knowledge and technology, and direct community involvement, relevant for citizens of Nevada, the Nation, and the world.

> While planning for the period 2009–2015, the University's community recognizes the difficult economic realities of this period. Beginning at a time of deep economic recession with an uncertain path to recovery, the most important values and capabilities of the University will be protected so the University can emerge in a strong position to continue as cultural and economic pillars of Nevada's progress. In the next six years, the University of Nevada, Reno will diminish a number of the programs which developed in good economic times, to assure capacities in the fundamental teaching, research, and outreach functions of a comprehensive research university. Primary values include the ability of students to obtain a quality education, the ability to discover and apply new knowledge, and the ability to share this knowledge with citizens of Nevada and the world. The University will emerge from this recession and resume growth at a rate and in directions largely determined by the entrepreneurship of its faculty in response to opportunities in the State and the Nation.

> This institutional strategic plan is a requirement of the Nevada System of Higher Education. The plan has been developed in accordance with a procedure developed by the Executive Board of the Faculty Senate. After collecting large amounts of information from across the university, central administration

developed a first draft. The draft was presented to all university faculty, student leadership, and administration for review. A second draft incorporating comments was reviewed by a large committee composed of students, faculty, and administrators to suggest additional changes. The third draft was shared with college advisory committees for additional input. The final draft was then submitted to the President for approval and presentation to the Board of Regents.

The transmission letter summarizes several messages: (1) the current condition of the institution, (2) the priority to preserve momentum in the core capacities of mission fulfillment while sacrificing some programs, and (3) the path of emergence dependent on entrepreneurship of faculty rather than reliance merely on state funds. The entire plan is best summarized in the one-page statement of institutional vision, mission, and goals.

Institutional Vision, Mission, and Goals

Preamble: The University of Nevada, Reno was constitutionally established in 1874 as Nevada's land grant university. In that historical role, the University has emerged as a nationally and internationally recognized, comprehensive, doctoral-granting research institution of higher education.

Vision: The University of Nevada, Reno is an internationally-respected, high quality, accessible, arts and sciences university, fully engaged with Nevada's citizens, communities, and governments to improve economic and social progress.

Mission: The University of Nevada, Reno: (a) prepares graduates to compete in a global environment through teaching and learning in high-quality undergraduate, graduate, and professional degrees in the liberal arts, sciences, and selected professions in agriculture, medicine, engineering, health care, education, journalism, and business, (b) creates new knowledge through basic and applied research, scholarship, and artistry, in strategically selected fields relevant to Nevada and the wider world, (c) improves economic and social development by engaging Nevada's citizens, communities, and governments, and (d) respects and seeks to reflect the gender, ethnic, cultural, and ability/disability diversity of the citizens of Nevada in its academic and support programs, and in the composition of its faculty, administration, staff, and student body.

Goals of the University of Nevada, Reno:

Goal 1: Serve as an accessible, comprehensive, doctoral-granting, research university with characteristics of a high-quality liberal arts university and Nevada's land grant university, combining undergraduate and graduate education, fundamental and applied research, and engagement with Nevada's citizens, industry, and governments.

Goal 2: Serve Nevada's traditional mining, agricultural, gaming, manufacturing, news, and logistics industries, and the emerging renewable energy resource industries, with professional workforce preparation, modernizing research, and involvement in innovation.

Goal 3: Prepare Nevada and Nevadans for the diversified knowledge economy.

Goal 4: Cooperate to prepare Nevada youth to participate in the world economy through education.

Goal 5: Improve the physical and mental health of Nevadans.

Goal 6: Enhance sustainable environmental quality in Nevada.

Goal 7: Participate in Intercollegiate Athletics with success in sports competition and success in graduation and character-building of student athletes.

Goal 8: Build the University's infrastructure to provide facilities, operations, and policies which enhance the productivity of students and personnel in fulfillment of the University's missions.

USING THE PLAN THROUGH REDUCED BUDGETS

During fiscal years (FYs) 2009 through 2014, the University of Nevada, Reno, sustained four major budget reductions, which amounted to more than a third of state fund revenues ($76 million less in state funds in FY 2014 than in FY 2009). (After increasing student registrations fees significantly and attracting robust growth in enrollment, the net result still is nearly $50 million less revenue in FY 2014 than in FY 2009.) In the first round of reductions, many special academic centers were stripped of most of their state funds (most survived), vacant positions were closed permanently, and administrative and student services were curtailed with layoffs. Two vice president positions were put on hiatus for five years and one was closed. Active faculty positions were preserved in hopes of maintaining all academic and research programs.

Nine months into the fiscal year 2010, the state legislature was called into special session to address significant revenue shortfalls; a second round of budget reduction was required in midyear. In the second round of reductions, closures of academic and research programs were required, with associated layoffs, in addition to further reductions and layoffs in administrative and student services. Reliance on the strategic plan and data were essential to carry the university forward through severe resource reductions in an effective way. When approaching academic program closures, reorganizations, and downsizing, procedures in the Nevada System of Higher Education Code and faculty contracts guided the process of decision making. Policies require following a process of curricular review before reducing or closing a program or unit. The preamble to the curricular review proposal of March 1, 2010, states the principles followed:

> The University of Nevada, Reno will maintain strength in quality teaching, research and outreach capabilities with a two-part approach. First, the University will narrow its scope by closing some programs completely to protect the current size and quality of remaining programs. This will leave the University in a position to spring forward at the end of the recession with much of its current strength. Second, the University will make further reductions in state fund expenditures in other areas.

> The primary criteria for the review of programs include:

> 1. Degrees granted.
> 2. Enrollment in the major.
> 3. Student Full Time Equivalent production.
> 4. Scholarship productivity.
> 5. External scholarship grant award and expenditure performance.
> 6. "Connectedness" or importance to the fulfillment of other programs at the University.
> 7. Centrality to mission.
> 8. National and international uniqueness of the program.
> 9. Other considerations to preserve complementary elements of programs.

The strategic plan states clearly that protection of the core missions of learning, discovery, and community engagement are central and that sacrificing those programs with lesser mission fulfillment would be the cost of preserving "the size and quality" of remaining programs.

In the third round of reductions, curricular review processes were accomplished again with more academic program closures and significant reductions in budget and personnel in the university's larger public service units of the Nevada Bureau of Mines and Geology and the University of Nevada Cooperative Extension. During consideration of the third round of large budget reductions, a faculty budget advisory committee confirmed the desire to protect those academic and research programs that had built the highest volume of student enrollment and research revenues and the importance of maintaining a path of hiring tenure-track professors into vacancies, rather than being tempted to hire less expensive part-time faculty. The purpose of the latter is to maintain a balance of learning and discovery missions, consistent with the strategic plan.

The fourth round of budget reductions was less severe; student fee revenue increases exceeded the loss of state funds. No further program closures or layoffs were necessary. Continuous use of the principles of the strategic plan and continuous mention of elements of the plan throughout budget adjustment processes helped to maintain a focus throughout the university on maintaining the core programs at a high quality level. The third year accreditation review by the Northwest Commission on Colleges and Universities noted two commendations: (1) the strategic approach to absorbing massive budget reductions was done in a way to preserve the core missions of the university in a quality fashion and (2) recruiting materials for undergraduates are friendly and encouraging. By maintaining the size and quality of those academic units attracting most of the undergraduate and graduate students and performing most of the research, while preserving the core of outreach unit capacities and administrative and student services, the university has emerged in a strong position to move forward into the future. The results of these strategic actions include record enrollments, record numbers of graduates, record proportions of ethnically diverse students, record numbers of National Merit and Presidential Scholars, and record research expenditures. There has been strong progress in the five topical goals in service to Nevada.

The greatest challenge of adjustment came from an alternative view that protection of all existing faculty positions should take priority over protecting the "size and quality" of those programs contributing most to the institutional mission. The university continued to fill vacancies in units to be preserved, while layoffs continued in programs being closed. With small budget reductions, both objectives can be accomplished. Under conditions of catastrophic resource reductions, the strategic plan guides decision makers toward institutional preservation.

USING THE PLAN THROUGH RECOVERY

State revenues are growing again in Nevada. Along with strong increases in enrollment year after year, conditions look good for revenue increases for the next few years. The strategic plan serves as a useful guide to grow the impact of the university's core missions in the future. The university will not reinvest in programs that were closed during the times of budget collapse. Rather, the university will deepen its investment in the units and programs that were preserved. The university will seek to move toward a Carnegie classification of "Comprehensive Doctoral, Arts and Sciences/Professions—Balanced, Very High Research University," as well as a "Carnegie Engaged University." The university will continue to serve National Merit and Presidential Scholars while serving as an access university for first-generation and low-income students ready to succeed in college. Graduate education and research will encourage multidisciplinary approaches and drive more research results toward commercialization. The university will expand graduate teaching-assistant positions and faculty, almost exclusively tenure-track positions, to balance growth in both teaching and research missions and improve quality with a reduced student-to-faculty ratio. Staff and operating resources in academic, administrative, and student-service roles will complement faculty growth. The university will continue to focus teaching, research, and outreach resources on the key issues identified in the strategic plan (viz, seeking to add well-educated workforce and innovative research to diversify and grow the Nevada economy, to enhance healthcare in the region, and to preserve the Great Basin and Lake Tahoe).

CONCLUSION

Strategic plans are living documents that chart a path from the institution's condition at one point in time to a set of conditions at some point in the future. These are roadmaps that bind employees of an organization together in a common direction and purpose. Strategic plans are useful when guiding preservation and growth, through thick and thin.

Chapter Six

Strategies for Effective Shared Governance

Mary Ellen Mazey and Anne L. Balazs

Shared governance is a fundamental norm at most institutions of higher learning. It has, of late, been threatened by a rising concern for financial sustainability. In recent years, higher education has developed toward a model of corporate governance rather than shared governance. This shift has occurred because of the decline in state funding and a need to find new sources of revenue for the institutions. Before these changes, colleges and universities operated in a decentralized system, which fostered duplication, created silos, and led to inefficiencies in some of these organizations. The question then arises, how will colleges and universities need to change in order to still foster shared governance, but at the same time deal with the "new normal" of budget realities? This chapter will discuss the value and challenges of shared governance, the need to build a cooperative community, and the leadership requirements for developing productive campus relationships.

THE VALUE OF SHARED GOVERNANCE

Because of the nature of their work, colleges and universities have always prospered in a shared governance system. Academic freedom and the tenure system are essential in the academy. Such freedom produces a value added that is based first upon discovery and creation of knowledge from multiple disciplines and perspectives and then the dissemination of this knowledge. Diversity of thought is highly respected in the academy and is essential to producing knowledge, though in a practical sense, a multitude of opinions also can produce conflict. Faculty members are in charge of knowledge

49

production, while administrators are responsible for the effective leadership of the academic enterprise. Understanding these role definitions is critical. As a matter of fact, most senior university leaders have risen through the ranks of the faculty and are familiar with the day-to-day realities of the academic mission. However, not all faculty members are interested in administration, and some indeed refer to it as "the dark side."

Since faculty members play the major role in creating and delivering the curriculum, they often believe their knowledge base goes beyond their academic role and challenge the university administration about how best the university can be operated. Even though administrators focus on the environmental scanning and strategic planning to move the institution forward, the faculty takes a major interest in how the budget is administered because of the ownership of their disciplines and programs. For example, in a unionized environment there tends to be an emphasis by union leadership on increasing the number of faculty members and salaries rather than on the financial viability of the university. The strategic plan should drive the budget. What becomes the most difficult task in such a unionized setting is building consensus on that budget, even if the strategic plan represents a shared agenda. The process becomes a "teachable moment" guiding faculty, staff, and administrators to fully understand and agree on the assumptions and data needed to make good financial decisions.

Recently at Bowling Green State University, we hired a consulting firm, Accenture, to evaluate our overall efficiency and effectiveness as an institution of higher education. An outside perspective offered objectivity, but when the final report was released, the faculty, staff, and even some administrators were apprehensive. What were the opportunities we all failed to see? And worse, how would it affect our respective areas? Therefore, in the name of transparency, we allowed time for all employee groups to read the report and its recommendations and offer input. In addition, as we began the implementation of the Accenture recommendations, we formed advisory groups composed of faculty, staff, students, and administrators to allow them the opportunity to provide input. The goal was to focus the campus on achieving the goals of increasing institutional revenues and lowering our costs of operation and at the same time allow all governance groups to participate in the implementation phase. The goal was to move forward, together, as a stronger, more viable university.

This campus-wide effort promotes shared governance in a variety of ways. The future of the university was at stake, which affects everyone in the campus community. This feeling was palpable and could invoke fear. By creating the working groups, all constituents are represented and have a stake in the outcome. A diversity of opinion would foster creative solutions on how best to address the budget challenges. Ideally, ownership would beget determination and team building. Alternatively, a top-down authoritative leader could handle the budget cutting alone and face the consequences of excluding others from the process. If the university as a whole recognizes the seriousness of the situation and then acts in a coordinated fashion, this should lead to greater resolve and compliance with the solution.

This is not an isolated case. Budget cutting, restructuring, and balancing are annual exercises for most institutions, and rarely does a president experience the luxury of a budget surplus. Creative solutions are required each year to exhibit good stewardship of resources borne of the students, donors, taxpayers, and others. While some have resorted to extreme measures of deleting programs, other institutions have offered incentives for reengineering degree programs, collaborating with new partners both public and private, recruiting lifelong learners with new technology, and retaining current students with the personalized support they require. In a period of retrenchment, some of the extras, such as elaborate celebratory events, free parking, and sports ticket giveaways, are being replaced with extended computer refresh calendars, reduced travel budgets and early retirement incentives. If everyone can agree to the "belt tightening," it makes the experience much less painful.

THE CHALLENGES OF SHARED GOVERNANCE

Colleges and universities are organized as hierarchies but do not function as a hierarchy. This means we have levels of authority that ultimately report to a president, but because of the tenure system and shared governance system, presidents do not have the authority to terminate many of the individuals within their span of control. What we have are faculty and staff members who report to chairs and directors, and they in turn report to deans, who in turn report to vice presidents who report to a president. Despite a small span of control, there always seems to be a (mis)communication issue. The bureaucracy doesn't allow for information to flow directly, and the message gets lost in translation. Whether it is good news ("We have met our capital campaign goal!") or bad news ("We are facing a budget shortfall and must look for ways to economize."), there are always some who interpret the message contrary to its intent. ("See? There is money out there. We should have set a higher goal." Or, "The University can simply fund academic affairs with money from the athletic budget.") Administrators must be prepared for their communications to be interpreted in multiple ways and be prepared to address fallacious reasoning.

A number of presidents limit their communication with the faculty, which is the constituency group most interested in and in need of good information. Again, in a unionized environment, the perception of an adversarial relationship gets more attention and response from the membership than in a cooperative climate. Conflict seems to be inherent on many unionized campuses, and this hurts the entire organization. Bargaining often centers on workload, benefits, and salary increases. Shared governance would promote the valued input of the faculty on ways to innovate, economize, and thrive. Faculty members should be incentivized to creatively contribute to the discussions of institutional sustainability. If universities are to build a strong financial future, they will need to break the mold and adopt new avenues of discourse and problem solving to meet the demands of a world that is rapidly changing, while maintaining the valued relationship with their constituents.

BUILDING A COOPERATIVE COMMUNITY

In order to grow and prosper as a university, a climate of cooperation and collaboration must be built. So the question becomes, How can this take place? From our experience, creating a strategic plan with common values is the first step. In doing so, a process for the strategic plan must be developed that guarantees "buy-in" from all constituent groups—faculty, staff, students, alumni, and administrators. The process itself will take four to six months, but in the end it produces a blueprint that everyone feels they had an opportunity to create. The administrators should view themselves as facilitative leaders throughout the process of developing the strategic plan and as the implementation takes place. It is essential that the environmental scan be open, transparent, and with data that provides everyone an opportunity to reach the same conclusions about the future needs of the university. The vision statement should have ennobling language and target the place the university hopes to be, at some point in the future. The core values need to encompass the current uniqueness of the university and also be coordinated with the major goals of the plan.

Once the strategic plan is finalized, each unit in the university should develop its own strategic plan that further operationalizes and corresponds to the university's plan, fulfilling the goals that were delineated in the process. Chairs, directors, deans, and vice presidents, as facilitative leaders, should ensure that the strategic plans developed move the institution forward on a continual basis. Once the unit's strategic plan is approved, annual goals for all faculty and staff should align with the plan. Deans/directors should account for progress at least annually on their unit's accomplishments and the extent to which goals were achieved. Any adjustments or refinements to strategies or targets should be documented and shared. Collectively, the campus will address overarching goals together. Recruitment, retention, and graduation are critical issues on our campuses, and we must ensure that all members of the academy are working toward these common goals. Sharing the information at regular intervals is the first step. Creating a culture of continuous improvement is ongoing.

The key to successfully creating a cooperative community within the university setting of shared governance is bringing groups of faculty, staff, and students together in facilitated sessions to address key and critical issues for the institution. Universities tend to be in silos, and breaking out of these silos is important. For example, it has been determined that incoming freshmen should have a freshman seminar that promotes their potential for success in college. Such a seminar can be developed through a facilitative process to fit the institution's incoming students, and training can be given to graduate students, faculty, and staff to implement the seminar. This will bring individuals from across the university together who have never worked together as a community to collaborate and produce a freshman seminar that is key to the university's retention program. Again, collective action toward a common goal builds community.

LEADERSHIP REQUIREMENTS FOR DEVELOPING PRODUCTIVE CAMPUS RELATIONSHIPS

Leadership is the key to building a productive campus that embraces shared governance and has a sense of community. Facilitative leadership will be the key to building a strong shared governance system in a university. A facilitative leader has excellent listening skills, is able to study and absorb the university's culture and issues, and addresses these issues strategically to move the institution forward. Moreover, the facilitative leader focuses on others and understands that it not about what she or he accomplishes but about what the leader can get others to accomplish. That is the reason a consensus-built strategic plan is so important to a university's future, because all constituents must be moving in the same direction.

The facilitative leader always privately and publicly recognizes the accomplishments of others and only privately provides criticism of others. The focus must be on institutional success and collective success rather than individual accomplishments. The individual successes can accumulate into institutional success, especially in the case of nationally and internationally recognized faculty members. There are many facilitative leaders on any campus, and their ability to collaborate with each other will ensure that the institution is moving forward. Moreover there is a sense of shared accomplishment of "everybody pulling on the same rope" after a milestone is reached. There is always a need to problem solve in any university, and mediation skills for an administrator are a tremendous asset. Over the years we have engaged in open and active conflict resolution. When a problem arises, all parties are invited to discuss the problem and possible solutions and to agree on how to resolve the conflict. This takes place in round-table fashion, with all individuals present. In this setting, mediation skills are essential to the facilitative leader in resolving the issue.

At Bowling Green State University, we have recently begun to use forums for greater communication to all and selected constituent groups, such as the one to the unionized faculty on how we allocated raises or the one to all employee groups on the status of the budget. In addition, we continue to have meetings with chairs and directors to assist them as they transition from a nonunionized environment to a unionized environment (since 2012). It is important to communicate electronically and via one-on-one and collective personal interaction. In a decentralized administrative environment, there is no such thing as too much communication or over-communication. Transparency and consistency of the message are critical.

As administrators, we must communicate our message and direction for the future of the university as much as possible. That communication will create a sense of a common vision and direction in a time of uncertainty and fear for the future of higher education in general and at individual institutions. We must be willing to change and communicate how that change will occur. Even in this day of so much electronic communication, the personal touch is still needed in the academy. As administrators, we must be willing to attend university senate meetings, departmental meetings, and forums to assure our multiple internal constituencies that we can achieve that future by everyone working together. In a unionized environment, building trust through continual communication is even more important because a mutually agreed-upon agenda for the institution is extremely important and many times more difficult to achieve.

A PRACTICAL NOTE FOR ASPIRING
ACADEMIC LEADERS

For those who are considering a shift in ranks from faculty to administration, or union to management, a period of adjustment is required. Aside from the change in responsibilities and vantage point, the orientation to the role should reveal some shared and time-honored values. One certainty is the knowledge that no matter which position you hold, your commitment to the university's mission and well-being is transcendent. All members of the university have a vested interest in its success. Thus, the respect for shared governance that you held as a faculty member does not disappear. You are simply playing a different role in the process.

For recently appointed administrators, we strongly urge you first to understand the role of the new position. Furthermore, there must be an understanding of how your administrative role can be differentiated from other administrator, faculty, or staff roles. We have found that once there is a common understanding of administrative roles, the new administrator must work to build trust and transparency. It is with this trust and transparency that the shared governance system can prosper even in these difficult budget times.

Although a unionized faculty can generate conflict, there are ways to facilitate "buy-in" for the strategic agenda of the university. This can be accomplished by creating working groups across colleges and departments to foster collaboration on important issues such as online learning, recruitment, retention, and research. Even though faculty unions are often critical of the administration, it is important for all administrators in a unionized environment to problem solve and mediate conflicts that arise before these conflicts create an unworkable situation. In all university settings, but even more so in a unionized setting, continuous communication to the constituencies is very important to building trust and transparency.

CONCLUSION

In conclusion, the mark of a good, strong academic leader is in including the campus community in generating a strategic plan, providing updated information on its progress and other issues of concern to the faculty, and further sharing that information with as many constituencies as possible. Shared governance and your institution will prosper by your creating an environment where every faculty member, staff member, and student can feel empowered to propel the institution to its next level of national and international recognition, both on an individualized and collective basis, through a common vision and strategic plan. It is incumbent upon administrators to instill strategic thinking and planning across the campus to ensure the university embraces change and meets the challenges for its future development.

Chapter Seven

Literature and the Leadership Lesson of House Mountain

Kenneth P. Ruscio

In 1839 George Ruffner, the president of Washington College (now Washington and Lee University) wrote a novel entitled *Judith Bensadi*. It contains a passage about how groups of college students would go hiking and gaze down on the valley below from high atop a place called House Mountain, which is a landmark near the campus formed eons ago when the land around it collapsed, leaving a mound of limestone suspended prominently in its midst.

Here is how the students described their experience:

> The little homesteads that spotted the hills and valleys under the mountain, the large farms and country seats farther away, and the bright group of buildings in the village of Lexington relieved the mind from the painful sublimity of the distant prospect and prepared us, after hours of delightful contemplation, to descend from our aerial height and return with gratified feelings to our college and our studies again.

I have sometimes cited that passage to our students at Washington and Lee as a reminder that occasionally it pays to step back from our daily lives and our deep engagement with problems and view the world from a different perspective. It is a message those of us in positions of leadership need to be reminded of as well. It is too easy these days, given the pace of change and the advancements in communications and information technology, to become immersed in the minutia and the specific, to follow intensively the challenge of the day, to be overwhelmed by the complexity and to seek refuge in simplicity.

The case I want to make is that we have to be more intentional and deliberate in finding ways to see our worlds from a different perspective. One way—not the only way—is through literature.

Many of us can remember what I would call our first intellectual epiphany, that moment of youthful insight when we saw something in a different way. It might have been in fourth grade when a math equation with letters and symbols as well as numbers suddenly made perfect sense. Or maybe it was during a music lesson when notes came together in a sequence that struck us as beautiful. Or maybe it was watching the tide roll out along a shoreline and leave behind strange creatures that dug into the sand before we could grab one, and we marveled at their movement and the mystery of their destination.

My epiphany happened in seventh grade. I picked up a book called *The Red Badge of Courage* by Stephen Crane. I can't remember why I read it. A teacher hadn't assigned it. It was not my usual fare, which to that point in my life consisted of Superman comics and paperback biographies of Mickey Mantle, Yogi Berra, and Willie Mays.

I discovered at the moment, clear as day, the power of the written word. *The Red Badge of Courage* is the Civil War story of Henry Fleming, a soldier in the Union Army, anxious and fearful of his first battle, but eager to prove his mettle. I read passages over and over again—depictions of brutal fighting; expressions of a young man's conflicted emotions; and vivid portrayals of loss, of death, of command.

I was stunned by how a skillful writer could convey through his characters and narrative the moral complexity of pursuing a righteous cause by killing fellow human beings.

My discovery of Crane's novel coincided with the discovery of a wider world beyond our neighborhood. Some older kids down the street were being drafted into the military to fight a war in a place called Vietnam. Watching the evening news, which everyone did back in those days, and thinking of Henry Fleming, I sensed how those neighborhood kids must have felt. I could only imagine it, of course, but that was precisely the point. I could imagine it.

I began to understand as well the moral debates within our society. Those of us who lived during that time remember the personal losses; we remember also the uncertainty of knowing what we were fighting for, the divide within our nation, the heated arguments among neighbors over fences in the backyard and among family members around the dinner table.

I remember all that and I remember how a work of fiction depicting another time, another place helped me understand the world in which I lived.

A few years later, the country was facing another crisis. President Richard Nixon had been resoundingly reelected in 1972. There had been a few news stories during the election about a burglary in an office complex called Watergate. Nothing major, it seemed, until several months later the break-in was revealed as the tip of a massive iceberg of political corruption. There were congressional hearings and Supreme Court cases and presidential news conferences where Nixon proclaimed he was not a crook and would never lie and suggested that the accomplishments of his presidency should outweigh whatever means he used to pursue them.

By that time I was a college student majoring in political science and taking a course on the legislative process. We followed the news closely and even simulated the impeachment hearings, each of us playing our assigned roles, and each of us feeling deeply connected with the events of the day and fully aware of the high stakes our country faced.

On the side, I was reading a wonderful novel, mainly to escape from the arcane language of lawyers and constitutional scholars. I had heard about *All the King's Men*, written by Robert Penn Warren many years before. Here was the fictional political world of Louisiana, the story of a powerful populist governor named Willie Stark, of his admiring and conflicted aides, especially Jack Burton, and of political enemies and scores being settled.

In the hands of a skillful writer was yet another complex morality tale, this one about how the raw exercise of power was not the same as leadership.

Do the ends ever justify the means? You can't grow grass without dirt, Machiavelli might have said. Governor Stark put it this way:

> Dirt's a funny thing. . . . Come to think of it there ain't a thing but dirt on this green God's globe except what's under water, and that's dirt too. It's dirt makes the grass grow. A diamond ain't a thing in the world but a piece of dirt that gets awful hot. And God-a-Mighty picked up a handful of dirt and blew on it and made you and me and George Washington and mankind blessed in faculty and apprehension. It all depends on what you do with the dirt. That right?

I returned to my course with a much deeper appreciation of why power corrupts, and how our own constitutional order tries mightily to come to grips with a fundamental problem of human nature.

A work of literature again helped me see the world differently. And it is a lesson that sticks with me to this day. In positions of authority, we sometimes confront painfully and uneasily the cold reality of Machiavelli's political science (for he was, after all, the first political scientist who advised seeing the world as it is, not as we wish it should be.) The ends never justify the means, we know, but Machiavelli cautioned that the problem for leaders who want to lead a life of virtue amid those who are not virtuous translates into ineffectiveness and loss of authority. It's an ethical and political dilemma we have been sorting out ever since. Here's one more example.

As administrators in organizations with systems of shared governance and elaborate processes incorporating many constituencies—boards, faculties, students and their parents, alumni, public authorities, and local communities, to name just a few—we are mindful that how we do things is as important as what we do. We hope that fair and just processes necessarily yield fair and just outcomes. But what if they do not? What if fidelity to the process results in an outcome that is anything but fair and just? It is the classically difficult case of doing the wrong thing the right way or the right thing the wrong way.

Billy Budd, Melville's complex novella, presents this in it starkest terms. The youthful, angelic Billy Budd is impressed into service aboard a British ship during the late 1700s when Britain is at war on the sea, and stories of mutiny abound. The evil Claggart, envious of the admiration Budd received from his shipmates, wrongly accuses Budd of plotting a mutiny. Captain Vere arranges for the accuser to confront the accused, and the innocent Budd, incapable of comprehending the inexplicable charge and the character of the person making it, is left speechless. He lashes out physically at Claggart, who falls, strikes his head, and dies. In a moment, as Melville puts it, the good and the evil have seemingly switched from one person to another. The captain, though he knows Budd is innocent, feels duty bound to follow the military procedures—which, when all proper forms and processes are scrupulously maintained, tragically lead to Budd's hanging.

Vere faced the choice between a just process or a just outcome. He could not have both.

My point is not that literature provides the answers to the challenges we face. The decision when to step outside the process to avoid an unjust outcome is intensely difficult, derived from the particular circumstances and the ineffable quality of judgment required of any good leader.

Nor is it to make the case that we should read for pleasure. These are not books one necessarily reads for "fun."

Nor is it to make the case for the virtues of immersive reading or what some have called the "power of the narrative" and "moral imagination." The lesson I want to draw is consistent with those others, but different.

As administrators and leaders within complex organizations, we need to have the capacity, the willingness, and the means to see our worlds from a different perspective.

This is not a call for idle contemplation, or clearing one's mind, or—especially—escaping from the world around us. It is about engaging the issues even more deeply but with the widened or adjusted angles that come from stepping away from it.

There are costs as well as benefits that come with our brave new hyper-connected, Twitter-based, Instagram-fixated, cell-phone obsessed, Linked-In world. The quality of argumentation diminishes in direct proportion to the ease of transmitting opinions. The ability to persuade through reason and evidence diminishes in direct proportion to the convenience of reading and seeing only what we want to.

The world we live in grows ever more complex, yet our angle of perspective grows smaller and smaller, and our vision shrinks accordingly. Unless, that is, we find ways to scale a House Mountain from time to time, and widen our views.

Colleges and universities also are deeply connected to the world around them. That's a good thing, and one of the admirable developments of modern academic is its ever-expanding engagement in its communities and in addressing and solving some of society's most pressing problems. Engagement is not to be disparaged; being connected does indeed have benefits.

My call is for retaining some balance, some equilibrium in the tension between immersing ourselves in the world around us and occasionally detaching ourselves to see the reality critically and more expansively, which is not to get away from it. It is a lesson for the organizations we are a part of. It is a leadership lesson for us personally as well.

Chapter Eight

When to Lead How

*The Stylistic Challenges of
Administrative Leadership*

Robert J. Sternberg

The toughest part of administrative leadership is knowing when to lead how. Styles of leadership for academic administrators can be divided roughly into four categories. These four categories are summarized in table 8.1.

A successful administrator needs to lead in different ways in different situations. Administrators who have a rigid style of leadership are at a disadvantage in their work.

Problem Formulation ➡ Problem Solving ⬇	*Top-Down*	*Bottom-Up*
Top-Down	I Authoritarian	III Faculty-based Authoritative
Bottom-Up	II Administratively-based Authoritative	IV Laissez-Faire

Table 8.1

There are two distinct aspects of leadership style: problem formulation (or definition) and problem solving. We tend, in our educational experience, to get more instruction and practice in problem solving than in problem formulation. But both are important to administration, lest we end up either solving the wrong problem (inadequate problem formulation) or solving the right problem the wrong way (inadequate problem solving). Therefore, as educational leaders, we need to focus both on how we solve (and prevent) problems and on ensuring we are solving (or preventing) the problems that truly need to be solved (or prevented). We will combine discussion of problem solving and problem prevention because preventing a problem is a problem to be solved in itself.

THE FOUR STYLES OF LEADERSHIP

I. Authoritarian Leadership

Style I, or *authoritarian* leadership (upper left cell of the table), involves an administrator's taking primary responsibility for both formulating or posing problems and for solving them. Educational leaders with a strong vision and a strong sense of how to implement that vision are most likely to utilize this style.

This style is particularly useful in three kinds of situations: when you need to act quickly and can't wait for faculty committees to be formed and come up with solutions that may or may not work; when you need to ensure that you are getting a solution to the problem you have posed rather than some other problem; and when you need to show who's the boss, which sometimes is necessary when one's authority is being tested. This style leaves no doubt as to who is running the show.

There are, however, three potential drawbacks to this style: First, some, and perhaps many, faculty members are likely to feel disempowered. Second, faculty members who feel cut out may end up—overtly or covertly—sabotaging the outcome so that it becomes very difficult to implement over an extended period of time. Third, if faculty members end up distrusting you, it may be hard ever to get their trust back.

Here is an example of where Style I leadership is needed. A president starts his term, only to discover that the previous president has hidden serious financial problems at the institution. The institution, which had appeared to be doing reasonably well financially, is actually on the brink of insolvency. The president does not believe he has a year, or even six months, to form a broadly representative committee to figure out what to do: In six months, the institution will be bankrupt unless something drastic changes. The president thus decides that he needs to take rapid action with regard to dubious programs, tuition levels, and financial aid. He knows that his actions will create a storm, but he feels he has no choice. Thus, after discussing the matter with his board of trustees, he informs the university community of the situation and takes rapid action.

II. Administratively Based Authoritative Leadership

Style II, *administratively based authoritative* leadership (lower left cell of the table), involves the administrator's taking primary responsibility for formulating, posing, or otherwise defining problems but involves delegating much of the responsibility for solving the problems to faculty, ideally working in collaboration with administration. This style does not signify that the administrator poses problems without listening to faculty. On the contrary, it is impossible to gain a sense of the important problems facing an institution without active, careful, and mindful listening. Rather, it confers on the administrator the primary responsibility for deciding which problems to tackle, when to tackle them, and how extensive the resources should be that are allocated to them.

There are three kinds of situations in which this style of leadership is particularly appropriate: when administration believes that the faculty and perhaps other constituent groups have been dragging their feet on needed, but perhaps painful, reforms; when there is a strong culture of shared governance in the university and decisions made unilaterally are viewed as illegitimate; and when faculty acceptance is key and nonparticipation by faculty in the decision-making process will result in large pockets of resistance.

The style has three potential drawbacks: First, the outcome of the faculty-driven committee or task force is likely to be different, in some degree, from what the administrative leader hoped for, or even a clearly suboptimal solution. Second, the rate of implementation of change may be relatively slow. The third is the possibility that a task force may drift and produce a report that addresses a problem other than the one the administrator hoped it would solve.

In my experience, this style usually is successful, empowering both faculty and administration to work together for a common good. But it requires patience and a willingness to accept outcomes that are not quite what the administrator initially sought.

A successful use of Style II leadership would be a provost who wants more stringent evaluations of teaching than are currently used in her university but who recognizes that if she introduces a new, more rigorous evaluation procedure, faculty members are likely to rebel, believing that evaluation of teaching is their responsibility. She believes that faculty members know that more rigorous evaluation of teaching is needed in the university but that they have been reluctant to institute it because of a belief that such evaluations will be used to deny tenure or promotion to faculty members. She forms a faculty-based task force that includes students and administrators, asking them to recommend a procedure. The students, in particular, are adamant that faculty members be more rigorously evaluated for their teaching. The committee recommends new procedures, which are passed after much debate by the faculty senate and then are implemented.

III. Faculty-Authoritative Leadership

Style III leadership, which I refer to as *faculty-based authoritative* (upper right cell of table), essentially reverses the roles in Style II leadership. The administrator draws heavily on faculty leaders, perhaps through a faculty senate or similar body, to set the agenda for change, and then takes it on him or herself to figure out how the change should take place. Educational leaders who follow this style are likely to want major faculty participation in agenda setting but feel that unless they, as administrators, take charge of implementation, little will actually get done with any deliberate speed.

This style of leadership is particularly advantageous under three conditions: when an administrator wishes to send a message of empowerment to faculty members by letting them set the agenda on issues that affect them; when the administrator wants to show she prefers to work with faculty, not in opposition to them; and when the administrator needs to set the pace of implementation to make sure things get done.

The style has three potential drawbacks, however. First, administration cedes primary responsibility for setting the agenda of the institution to the faculty, who may not have a broad view of the university's needs. Second, some stakeholders, especially trustees or regents, may see agenda setting as an administrative prerogative. Third, problems that an administrator really would like to solve may never even be addressed.

A successful example of the use of this style would be when faculty members decide that their procedures for awarding tenure are not well specified and generally unclear and bring up this problem with a department head (chair), dean, or provost. The administrator then takes responsibility for formulating more rigorous procedures and presents them to the faculty as a package. The faculty senate or equivalent unit may or may not get to vote on the procedures.

IV. Laissez-Faire Leadership

Style IV, *laissez-faire* leadership (lower right of table), involves assigning primary responsibility for both problem formulation and problem solution to faculty. The main responsibilities of the administrator are to allocate resources, to serve as a resource, and to guide the faculty in its leadership over academic matters.

This style of leadership is particularly useful under three conditions: when a matter is entirely a faculty matter, such as curriculum, and the administrator believes she has no role in intervening; when, perhaps due to past feelings of learned helplessness on the part of faculty, it is important to maximally empower faculty members to guide the institution and its future; and when, to generate goodwill on the part of the faculty, they are, to the extent possible, given control of their own destiny.

The potential disadvantages of this style are threefold. First, the administrator might be seen by some as abrogating his role as an academic leader, leaving it to others to do what he was hired to do. Second, it may put faculty in a position of greater power than they may be prepared to assume, given that their perspective on the institution often is somewhat limited by their role as faculty members. Third, supervisors above the administrator may begin to question whether they have hired someone with the leadership skills to do the job for which he was hired.

A successful example of this style would occur when a dean realizes that she has a structural deficit, and the central administration tells her that she will have to cut her budget in order to deal with it. The dean empowers a faculty committee to recommend to the faculty senate how to deal with the deficit. She makes no suggestions to the committee on the origins of the cuts, leaving it in their hands. They suggest cutting several programs, something she never could have done without instigating howls of protest. Of course, implementation of the recommendations may present a whole new set of problems.

CONCLUSION

There is no one style of leadership that will always produce (a) an optimal educational outcome (b) with the greatest possible speed and (c) to the satisfaction of all relevant stakeholders. In my experience, faculty tend to care a lot about process, so Style I (authoritarian) may lead to faculty members being unwilling to accept the outcomes, even if they are positive, because of what the faculty view as an inadequacy of process. Style IV (laissez-faire) may lead to maximum acceptance on the part of faculty but may produce results that are skewed in favor of faculty interests because of the lack of bird's-eye perspective that administrators and others have to contribute to the process. I believe Style III (faculty-based authoritative) can work but that the agenda may be limited in scope by faculty's tending to pose problems that are primarily relevant to their own interests. In my experience, Style II (administrator-based authoritative) works best, on average, although it certainly is not without risks or shortcomings. It lets administrators lead but also lets faculty have an active part in governance.

In the end, it may be that different styles work better not only for different situations and at different times, but also for different administrators. An administrator may find that alternating among styles works best, depending upon the situation and the set of problems at hand. For example, at one extreme, if a problem is particularly urgent and simply does not allow for a long, deliberative process, Style I may be the only alternative. At the other extreme, if a problem is not urgent or is clearly most directly relevant to faculty—such as revising faculty-governance procedures—Style IV may be appropriate. Style III may be appropriate for a faculty-driven issue in which there are irreconcilable differences among factions of faculty and it is useful for an authority, such as a dean or provost, to settle the matter.

Although Style I might seem as though it would be most damaging, on average, to faculty morale, Style IV can be equally damaging. In the case of Style I, faculty may feel disenfranchised and left without a meaningful voice in matters that vitally concern them. But in the case of Style IV, many faculty members may come to feel adrift, as if they are floating in a boat with no clear destination or even direction.

Style II may work best, on average, with complementation as needed by Styles I, III, and IV. Administrators all have to decide what style or styles of leadership will contribute toward achieving optimal outcomes, given the circumstances encountered in their daily work.

III

Provosts and Past Provosts

Chapter Nine

Developing Mentors on the Path to Leadership

A Case Study and Conversation

Jennifer P. Bott and Michele Wheatly

As university administrators, we are accustomed to employing mentors to assist our students in discovering and engaging with careers throughout their collegiate experience. We know the value mentors bring: candid and practical advice, establishment of context, and the development of specific skills, often in a risk-reduced environment. We often encourage mentorship in our career centers and have mentored students throughout our time in the classroom. In the professional arena, mentorship has been deployed successfully to encourage women to aspire to leadership positions in business and industry, positions that tend to be filled predominantly by men.

Higher education administration is no different; mentorship, either formal or informal, can be leveraged to provide exposure to aspirant leaders. This exposure and expectation-setting process is especially important for women leaders in higher education administration.

SETTING CONTEXT

Since 1986, the American Council on Education (ACE) has gathered data nationally that provide a profile of the president across all types of institutions of higher education; the most recent update to this longitudinal study was published in 2012 (data were collected in 2011).[1] Every four years, these data generate comparisons across types of degree-granting institutions in traditional demographic categories (like gender and age). Some relevant data from the most recent study include the following statistics:

- Twenty-six percent of college or university presidents are women, up from 23 percent in 2006.
- The highest percentage of female presidents serve at associate degree-granting institutions (33 percent, including both public and private institutions).
- A smaller percentage of male presidents are currently unmarried or childless (10 percent versus 28 percent), as compared to their female counterparts.

These data demonstrate the challenges for women aspiring to the presidencies of colleges and universities. An analysis of the trend of female presidents indicates a slow and steady increase in their number since 1998 (19.3 percent). However, the women who are presidents differ from men in the role in that a greater percentage are currently unmarried and/or haven't had children. What do these data mean for aspiring women leaders? How can mentorship empower women to successfully reach the presidency?

A CASE STUDY AND CONVERSATION

Much can be learned through case studies of successful women leaders who have both received and given mentorship. What follows is a case study and conversation with Dr. Michele Wheatly, provost and chief academic officer at West Virginia University, conducted by Dr. Jennifer Bott, American Council on Education Fellow at West Virginia University and associate provost for Learning Initiatives at Ball State University. Questions used to stimulate this conversation reflect several themes specific to women's leadership and were generated by surveying aspiring women leaders.

Background. When Michele Wheatly, currently provost at West Virginia University, discusses her path to senior leadership, she easily identifies those people she credits as mentors. Dr. David Evans hired Wheatly, a biologist, as an assistant professor at the University of Florida. Dr. Evans, a male chair in a closely related subdiscipline, served as a remarkable mentor and exemplified true work/life balance, maintaining a long-term committed marriage and a daily presence in the lives of his children.

Wheatly also benefited from her own identification of another woman further along in her career as a role model for her own potential path. "The first female role model I had at the University of Florida was Dr. Karen Holbrook, Vice President for Research and Dean of the Graduate School. Her academic background was in a related field and I remember observing her professionalism and translating my own career aspirations onto her, even though our personal interactions were minimal."

After a successful period of leadership of the Association of Women Faculty and the Provost's Committee on Faculty Enhancement Activities, and having attained full professorship at the University of Florida, Wheatly moved to Wright State University to serve as chair of the Department of Biological Sciences and later as dean of the College of Science and Mathematics before moving to West Virginia University as provost.

At WVU, Wheatly has made the mentoring of both established and aspiring women leaders a focus of her own leadership. Shortly after she arrived on campus, she spearheaded WVU's successful pursuit of a $3.2 million, five-year National Science Foundation ADVANCE grant. She has since reinforced the work done under the auspices of that grant by providing funds from the provost's office to expand its mentoring program to include other faculty who are underrepresented in non-STEM disciplines. In 2011, Wheatly created the Women's Leadership Initiative in partnership with the dean of the Reed College of Media, Maryanne Reed. The WLI has provided executive coaching and leadership mentoring to twenty-five women in 2011–2012. The current membership of the group is 117 women, an example of exponential growth.

Jennifer Bott interviewed Dr. Wheatly in the spring of 2014 to discuss mentorship, the notion of work/life balance, and the future for female leaders in higher education. What follows is a transcript of that interview, followed by summative conclusions.

Developing mentors: Michele, how many mentors are necessary to achieve your goals? How are mentors selected, and when do you transition to new mentors?

I don't believe there is a magical number of mentors, so possibly the best answer would be, "as many as it takes"! Mentors may serve very specific purposes (e.g., "female with a family") or may be enduring across many years (e.g., "working in the same research field"). These relationships are often quite fluid, not formally documented, and may mean more to the mentee than the mentor.

Let me give you two examples, one in which I gave mentorship, another in which I received it. When I was an active researcher, a young woman approached me at a meeting one day. She had seen me present at an international symposium and that I had been the only woman on the platform. Several years later, she told me that she stayed in the research field because she had viewed me as a role model. I keep warning faculty that they are being watched by the next generation all the time!

Lately, I have been studying several STEM women who are presidents of research universities. There are two, in particular, whom I have met at professional meetings but only in a most cursory way. I recently approached these two women for some help on an issue and both jumped at the chance to assist me. I would imagine that they have been in a similar situation in their past and they know that mentorship relationships that we hope to find the higher we climb can occur spontaneously.

Expectations of others, specifically family issues: As a mother of three, did you find yourself making others comfortable with your gender? Your family choices? What expectations do you feel women must meet that don't apply to men?

This came very naturally to me. I have always brought my "whole self" to work and so I have freely spoken about my husband and children. Early in my career, I did encounter male faculty who gave me advice on whether I should have children before tenure and if so, how many. I politely listened, unsure whether they were proffering the same advice to their male colleagues. Also, I do remember not mentioning my pregnancies until they were through the first trimester. This became increasingly hard with my second pregnancy which turned out to be twins! Being a wife and mother was very important to me and so I never based my personal decisions on input from professional colleagues.

Aspirations and "work/life balance": How did your aspirations influence your family life (e.g., timing of children, work/life balance of your spouse)? How do you protect time with your family and perform a life-consuming job?

I had a faculty appointment at the age of 28. The British educational system is accelerated, with many doctorates earned at 24. I married at 31 and had my children when I was 36 (already tenured) and 38 (the year I went up for promotion to full professor). This timing meant that I was tenured and had scholarly momentum by the time I had small children. I was fortunate to marry a man who created flexibility in his own professional life to accommodate the needs of our growing family. We are partners in every sense of the word and have done whatever it took to help each other and to create a stable home environment for our children. It probably helped that he was 8 years my senior and well into his 40s when the children arrived. Since all the extended family was at considerable distance, we had to rely on each other exclusively.

As any parent will attest, it requires more than 100 percent from each parent to raise a family. We both absorbed a lot of extra work. I was climbing the administrative ladder the entire time that my children were young. I did not beat myself up about the impact of my aspirations on the day-to-day lives of our children, because I knew that they had two very involved parents and were experiencing opportunities (like travel) that were not available to their friends.

Women have an amazing ability to quilt their lives from pieces of fabric that blend when stitched together. When my children were smaller, I would find opportunities to take them to events with me with the result that they did a lot of very cool things! Now that they are all in college at the institution I serve, it is even easier to do this. Bottom line is that I have never separated the day into "family" time versus "work" time. While I am at home, or cooking and cleaning for my family, I am often solving university problems and vice versa. I am not sure that "balance" is a very good word because it connotes that if one bucket becomes heavier, the other becomes lighter. I think it would behoove us to talk about career and life integration. After all, you have one life to live, not two!

Overall status of women's leadership in academia: In conclusion, Michele, what is your perspective on the status of women leaders in higher education? How can programs like the WLI at WVU impact the pipeline for future leaders?

In general, I feel optimistic about the future of women in higher education leadership. Among APLU provosts for example, many are women. Also, one often sees male/female university leadership teams these days. Having said that, I think we clearly have a ways to go with women being appropriately represented as presidents of prestigious universities.

One such approach to developing women leaders for all levels of higher education is through formal training and mentorship programs. We created the Women's Leadership Initiative at WVU to provide programs on key issues (like negotiation) to emerging women leaders from across the institution, many of whom have no other women in their immediate work environment. The group is encouraged to meet both formally and informally to discuss issues and provide one another with support and encouragement.

The WLI is creating, artificially, the scaffold that already exists for the success of men. The fundamental premise—appreciative inquiry and framing conversation around a leadership issue—can be broadly utilized by any group at the university, including students. Both qualitative and quantitative results indicate that this program has been successful in empowering women on campus to more confidently seek leadership positions. In fact, we recently published an article on the WLI documenting the data-supported success of the program.[2] Based on survey responses from the women who participated, not only is the WLI having an impact at WVU, but the "home grown" version of the program—in which women from within the university mentor other women at WVU—is both well-received and valuable. This is significant because a program like this one can be more easily replicated elsewhere than an expensive program relying either on having executive coaches brought in or on having the participants sent out for their coaching.

CONCLUSION

Dr. Wheatly's case study offers perspective on several key issues researched and debated in the women's leadership area, namely work/life balance and attainment of career goals:

- *Developing a mentoring relationship* is a fluid process, based on needs. Mentors can provide specific help at a singular time (think more role model than mentor, as Wheatly explained above) or can be a relatively constant source of support, advice, and perspective. For example, Wheatly developed a relationship with Dr. Mary Ellen Mazey when they were both deans at Wright State University. Both Mazey and Wheatly have transitioned to new roles (Mazey is now president at Bowling Green University), and their relationship has evolved with them.
- *Asking those you respect to assist you with a problem can be a powerful way to begin a mentorship relationship.* Keep in mind, however, that mentoring relationships are additional work for both the mentor and mentee, and establishing expectations of commitment up front will generate greater satisfaction with the relationship over time.
- *Seeking work/life balance* may be an outdated notion; expecting to leave work at the end of the day to focus solely on family is more difficult for women (and men) in higher-level positions. The expectation of constant availability and connectedness from multiple constituencies makes this even more difficult. Developing realistic expectations with your partner/ spouse are critical to a woman leader's success in meeting all of her responsibilities. Further, acknowledging your role as a parent, as a caregiver to an elderly parent, and/or as a spouse/partner will help those around you understand the responsibilities you maintain outside of work.
- The women's leadership literature and books in the popular press discuss a woman's ability to "*have it all*." This competitive framing can create the perception that "having it all" comes at the expense of others (such as a colleague or spouse). Organizations, especially academic organizations founded on the principle of shared governance, are highly interrelated and interdependent, which could be considered at odds with a "having it all" perspective. Rather, we should consider creating greater support mechanisms and scaffolding to allow for the development of women leaders in a context of shared success in the work and home environments.
- Successful developmental programs are more than connections and mentorship. Research evidence indicates women approach leadership experiences differently from men; *creating programs* that target areas in which women self-sacrifice and self-limit are critical to addressing the leadership shortage. Creating skills and generating confidence through evidence-based training is an important component of developing women leaders.

Developing leaders for higher education is of critical importance today, especially in light of the changing demographics of university presidents. According to a 2012 ACE report examining retirement trends,[3] 52 percent of university presidents plan to step out of their positions in the next five years, and another 21 percent plan to do the same in the next six to nine years. Developing a pipeline of leaders is critical to fill these vacancies with qualified, competent leaders. Acknowledging the differences in leadership perceptions, opportunities, and experiences between genders, and building capacity to address these differences, will be of paramount importance to meet this challenge of leadership in higher education.

NOTES

1. Cook, B. and Kim, Y. (2012). *The American College President 2012*. American Council on Education.

2. DeFrank-Cole, Latimer, Reed, and Wheatly. (2014). The Women's Leadership Initiative: One university's attempt to empower females on campus. *Journal of Leadership, Accountability, and Ethics* 11(1).

3. McLaughlin, J. (2013). *Retirement transitions in higher education*. American Council on Education.

Chapter Ten

My Life in Administration

From Accident to Career

Ana Mari Cauce

Until quite recently, I thought of myself as an "accidental administrator." I assumed that when the time came, I'd do my duty, take my turn as department chair, then return to the faculty. As to fulltime "career" administration, like too many faculty members, I did not think it was wholly honorable. Indeed, during my early years, more than a few of my colleagues would have described me as a hothead. I had an intrinsic distrust of authority, disdain for bureaucracy, and distaste for process, not exactly the trifecta of traits suitable for academic leadership. Yet, as I review my academic career, I can't help but note that I have been involved in some level of administration for virtually all of it.

I began doing administrative work when I became director of clinical training (DCT) within the Psychology department, a position I took immediately after achieving tenure. The University of Washington clinical graduate program is a relatively large one, encompassing both research and professional training. Hence, the job involved directing a PhD program (appproximately fourteen faculty members, sixty-plus graduate students) with a clinic serving about one hundred community clients a week. The program also requires outside accreditation, by the American Psychological Association, and so is somewhat more separate and independent from the overall department than most other subspecialties within the field. I guided the program through an accreditation visit and through major curricular and programmatic changes, while learning about the virtues of compromise, patience, and impulse control.

But, despite the many administrative aspects of my job as DCT, I did not think of myself as an administrator, nor as headed toward an administrative career. I continued to teach all along (with a reduced load) and my research thrived. I was heading up two NIH projects focusing on at-risk youth, one on normative development of minority youth, which was my primary research focus, and another on homeless, street youth, which was still a relatively new area for me. So, I was ready, and looking forward to, rejoining the faculty at the end of my five-year term. However, I was convinced to stay on until I could identify, and convince, a suitable replacement to sign on. After two more years, that was done, and I was in conversations with my chair about taking a sabbatical before my return when, rather unexpectedly, the dean of Arts and Sciences asked me to serve as chair of American ethnic studies (AES), where I had held a joint appointment for less than a year. This time the challenge was not to bring an already good program to a higher level, it was to take over a department that, in spite of good faculty, staff, and students, was in very visible distress.

It would be impossible to adequately convey the sense of AES's disarray. There was a lack of consensus as to the direction of the program. The faculty was polarized, making new hires impossible. There was also a great deal of student unrest, and it was playing out very publicly in the media. Things had gotten to the point that the problems in this relatively small department were affecting morale, and hiring, of faculty of color across campus. The search for an outside chair had failed, and at least one other faculty member had turned down the dean's offer. Inspired by my academic mentor, Edmund W. Gordon, who came out of retirement to chair City College's Black Studies Department during times of turbulence I thought if not me, who? It seemed the right thing to do.

I didn't expect it to be a walk in the park, but I was pretty clueless as to what awaited me. While few students in AES knew me, as a representative of the administration and someone who did not belong to any of the ethnicities represented in the program content (I am Cuban, and AES consists of African American, Chicano, and Asian-American Studies), I was viewed as suspect from the get-go. The fact that my research and teaching fit squarely within program parameters was beside the point, at least under these circumstances.

Far from having a honeymoon period, it seemed like my every word, look, and action were scrutinized. My first day on the job, I walked to my office down a hall papered with my picture from the cover of the student newspaper. Superimposed on a picture of my face was a gun sight, and the title "Under Fire" was emblazoned across my forehead. In protest of my appointment, students staged a sit-in during a board of regents meeting, shutting down the administration building for an afternoon. It was all a bit surreal for someone used to being on the side of the protestors.

Those first few weeks, I had to dig deep within myself to find my center. But, by focusing on student well-being and trying to understand their perspective, we were able to slowly move forward. Within a month, I visited every AES class to talk to students and hand out a survey that tapped their satisfaction or dissatisfaction with various aspects of the program. The results of that survey, which had an astounding 70 percent response rate, provided the framework for forging common goals across faculty and for uniting faculty and students.

By year's end, the student demonstrators awarded me a certificate as "Rookie of the Year." We also made the first of what would be three consensus hires, the first in over a decade. We formally adopted a set of priorities and goals. An outside review committee that visited during the end of my three-year term gave the department a positive review and commended my leadership. It felt better than I could have imagined. Although I did not realize it at the time, I had become hooked on administration—the ability to bring disparate groups to the table, the satisfaction of building a program or department, or helping one to change, the adrenaline rush that comes from decision making under pressure.

I have held various administrative positions since then, directing the university-wide honors program, chairing the Department of Psychology, serving as the executive vice provost, then dean of Arts and Sciences, and now provost, all within the same university where I started as an assistant professor. Each position has had its own set of unique challenges and rewards, and each has given me a slightly different perspective on my university and how universities work (or don't) more generally. Through my work with these diverse sets of units, I have learned some important lessons that apply to any administrative job.

One should work hard to build consensus, but not let the need for unanimous agreement lead to paralysis. One must examine problems and issues from the perspectives of the various parties involved, gathering data and insights from multiple sources to inform decision making. One cannot shrink from difficult decisions, but it's always best to anticipate and plan for the blowback. The job of an academic leader is to be strategic and to forge a clear sense of direction for the unit, but it is equally important for him or her to inspire, listen to, and support the vision and efforts of others. Indeed, the biggest satisfaction in my job comes in the form of reflected glory. It is all about taking pleasure in the success of others and knowing that their success is yours.

Of course, this is easier said than done. One of the toughest parts of the job is that mistakes are very visible, and all too often, because of stereotypes about administrators, they are attributed less to incomplete information, miscalculation, or just plain ignorance, than to malice, chicanery, bad intentions, or a lust for power. Sometimes I feel as though there is me and "the Provost," a bureaucrat that isn't even a close approximation of who I am or where I came from. More than once I've joked that when I write my memoirs it will be under the title "Confessions of an Academic Administrator: How I Became a Straight White Man." (I am none of the three.)

For those of us who grew up wielding whatever power we had from the margins, the move to the center can be especially jarring. It is for that reason that I have found it especially important for me to "administer" in a place where I have long-term friends and colleagues to provide grounding and perspective, and, when needed, comfort. It can be a lonely job and I've found the best antidote to the isolation is creating spaces for close interaction with students and faculty colleagues on a continuous basis, not only when there are problems.

In academia, as I suspect is the case in most enterprises, the higher up the food chain you are, the more you end up dealing with the messiest problems. If they were easier, they would have been resolved at lower levels. Hence, you spend much of your time dealing with the worst of your faculty, staff, and students. Or, at the very least, with faculty, staff, and students when they are at their very worst. I've seen some longtime academic administrators engage in some fairly unseemly faculty, staff, or student bashing because they begin to generalize unpleasant encounters with difficult individuals to the group more generally. It's something that can only be avoided by building in regular points of positive contact.

I've never gone for more than a year without teaching a course; it reminds me why I became an academic in the first place. I also work closely with two advisory groups, the Provost's Advisory Committee for Students (PACS) that I spend a few hours with every Friday, and the (faculty) Senate Committee on Planning and Budgeting (SCPB), which meets on Monday afternoons. Thus my week is bookended by venues in which budget issues are discussed, where policies are challenged and set, and where together we search for common ground and develop common goals. These meetings, and the relationships forged by this close contact, have been invaluable both to the work, and to the soul.

I find it hard to give generic advice about academic leadership. I can only recount what's worked for me, which is why I've focused on my own story, struggles, and successes. I've talked little about budgets or planning or fundraising because that's the easy part of the job; you may get the credit but it's others who set you up for success. And academics are generally smart people and good problem solvers. We are good at learning. It's the "me" part, and the dealing with other people, that are hard.

When I used to do clinical supervision, I'd tell my students to remember that "they" were the tool they used and they had to learn how to use it. That meant watching their videotaped interactions with clients and discussing them with a supervisor to better learn how their mannerisms, body language, idiomatic expressions, and even their voice and intonation, affected their communications and how those were experienced and received. The first thing you need to know to become an effective therapist is yourself. I find myself falling back on my own training in this regard, more than occasionally. I know that the best way for me to tamp down my impulse to speak, when I should be listening, is to literally sit on my hands. (Joke: How do you get a Cuban to shut up? Handcuff them.) I talk very slowly and in a very quiet voice when I need to control my temper. I've learned that sometimes it's best to find an excuse to exit a meeting because I'm about to say something I'll later regret. And I know the people I should meet with when I need to feel refreshed.

Self-monitoring is essential to a job where you are constantly with people in high-stakes situations. People look to you to see how they should react. If you look panicked when you talk about budget cuts, others will panic right along with you. If you appear calm and confident, others are more apt to stay grounded and join you in problem-solving mode. Your behavior sets the tone. But we each do that in ways that are very individual and that reflect our own personal style. I've seen other academic leaders carry out their work very differently from the way I do, yet equally effectively if not more so.

There really are no general rules that I am aware of about how to do it right. I've found leadership books that try to impart rules to be pretty useless. I do many things they suggest are wrong, and they work for me. Other things they suggest you should do just don't come naturally and make me feel inauthentic. That said, there are three pieces of advice I that I believe apply across the board: (1) Make sure you have first-rate senior staff. In any university, it is the vice presidents, vice provosts, and deans who do the heavy lifting when it comes to management. Never settle for less than a good fit for your institution and for your own leadership style. Searches need to last as long as it takes to find the right person. (2) Never underestimate the importance of top-rate professional staff throughout the upper echelons of budgeting and finance, information technology, human resources, legal advice, and research and administrative support. Professional staff provide continuity from one academic leader to the next. They are the bearers of institutional knowledge and they know where the bodies are buried. Chances are good they will outlast you. (3) Never work for someone you do not truly respect and who does not respect you. If their values are not consonant with yours, it will not be a good partnership.

Much has been said and written about how academics know little about management and are ill prepared to lead today's increasingly complex academic institutions, most especially large research universities, like my own. Some say that with the new challenges facing academia, it is time to hire professionals who have been trained to manage and who have experience outside of the ivory tower. I've spent my entire adult life in universities, taking my first academic position in my twenties. I've found that my work leading a lab, doing grant writing and budgeting, and conducting research in community settings, along with my experience as a teacher and mentor, guiding others to success, have given me both the credibility and the skill set I've needed to be successful in the various leadership positions I've held. That doesn't mean that at times the learning curve hasn't been steep or that I've never felt overwhelmed or in over my head. The latter happens quite regularly.

Diversity in all things, including the vocational backgrounds of those in academic leadership, is welcome. Those who enter these positions with backgrounds in politics or industry have much to offer and can provide fresh perspectives. In this same vein, those who become academic administrators in institutions where they did not serve first as "regular" faculty bring fresh ideas and new skill sets to their new institutions. An outside leader may be best suited to pushing the reset button when that's called for. But love of place and intimate knowledge of its people and practices have been key to my ability to get things done. Though academic administration will continue to become more specialized and demanding, I hope there will always be room for some of us to rise through the ranks of our own institutions. It is neither necessary nor sufficient for success, but, for me, it has made the experience immensely more meaningful and enjoyable.

Chapter Eleven

The Art of "No"

Elizabeth Davis

I don't like "no," despite what my children say. I'm much more motivated by a "yes, if," a "yes, and," or even a "yes, but." And I try to use such phrases as much as possible whenever an outright "yes" is not warranted. Nevertheless, saying "no" is part of my job, and given that you are reading this chapter, it's likely part of yours. Unless you have an outsized need to be liked, it's not that hard to tell someone "no." It might be unpleasant, but not hard. If you do have a need to be liked, then you will have a hard time saying "no." But that's a subject for a different chapter.

The hard part of getting to "no" is the deliberation that precedes the decision, not the actual delivery. Clarity in (at least) three areas can facilitate the deliberation and help the receiver of the news understand the rationale. These three areas are institutional, strategic, and procedural clarity.

Institutional clarity requires shared understanding of the mission of the university. Land-grant universities, liberal arts colleges, community colleges, faith-based institutions, and the many other types of institutions of higher education have different purposes. What is right for a public land-grant university isn't necessarily right for a private university. However, without clarity of institutional purpose, it's difficult to justify why, say, one program or faculty hire should be privileged over another.

Baylor University, where I spent the vast majority of my academic career, is a faith-based, national research university. Advancing academic excellence while affirming and deepening Christian commitment adds a dimension to decision making that nonsectarian institutions don't face. For example, faculty hires must be outstanding teachers, scholars, and committed Christians or observant Jews. Outstanding scholars who are supportive of the mission, though not active church or synagogue attenders, are not acceptable faculty hires. Neither are committed Christians who do not demonstrate an ability to produce scholarship at the highest levels. Early on in my tenure as provost, I occasionally said "no" to a department's request to hire department chairs and faculty because either the faith commitment was missing or because evidence of scholarly productivity/outstanding teaching was missing. Does this make faculty hiring more difficult? Yes. Adding one more criterion shrinks the applicant pool. Nevertheless, the university has an institutional identity that requires care and patience in faculty hiring. Clarity of institutional mission guides the hiring process and sometimes leads to saying "not this candidate."

Institutional clarity is as important as ever, given the current state of national conversations about the value of a college degree. Various high-demand or online programs are often suggested as the cure-alls for the high cost of education and the need for post-graduation employment. Such options make sense for some institutions, but not for all. Without institutional clarity that is shared by the governing board, administration, faculty, staff, parents, alumni, community, and other interested parties, any new gimmick or solution can seem to make sense. Creating shared institutional clarity is the hard part. Saying "no" to new programs that don't support the institution's mission is not.

While institutional identity does not change for decades (or maybe ever), strategic clarity represents the current means by which the institution's mission is carried out. Often such clarity is articulated through a strategic plan or five- to ten-year institutional goals. Baylor's most recent strategic vision calls for the university to approach the Carnegie classification of "Very High Research Activity." For the next several years, investments will be made in academic programs that increase research funding and doctoral productivity. More specifically, those investments will be made in the sciences and engineering. That doesn't mean the humanities and social sciences aren't important at Baylor. In fact, the doctoral programs in the humanities and social sciences are much stronger, as a whole, than the programs in the sciences and engineering. And these programs contribute significantly to the institutional mission of the university. However, at this particular point in the life of the university, a request for additional funding from the operating budget to enhance a program in the humanities and social sciences is likely to be met with a "no." Does that mean Baylor will never again invest in the humanities? Absolutely not. But the strategic vision and five-year institutional goals provide clarity as to what programs will be enhanced during this particular period at the university.

The third kind of clarity is procedural clarity. Procedural clarity can be formal, in the case of institutional policies, or informal through the practices that make day-to-day operations easier. If you have ever had the opportunity to teach, you've likely had practice delivering a disappointing "no" to your students. Consider the plea from a student at the eleventh hour for extra credit to pull up a failing grade. I don't give extra credit to students unless it is available to all students. How do I support such a decision? It's in my syllabus. My students know my practices, but that doesn't stop them from asking. After thirty-plus years in academia, it still doesn't feel good to tell a failing student "no." It's unpleasant, but given my syllabus, it's not hard.

Not everyone is attuned to all of the relevant university policies and practices at all times. As an administrator, I'm more conversant regarding policies than the average faculty or staff member. And if your institution is like mine, there are a lot of policies on the books. Lack of familiarity is not often regarded as an excuse for noncompliance with policies. However, as administrators, we can make it easier on our faculty and staff if we provide opportunities for easy access to the policies or seminars at strategic times to reinforce the policies that exist. For example, every fall Baylor offers mentoring sessions for new faculty. Those faculty members who are on the tenure track will attend a session explaining the university's tenure policies and procedures. Each year, the tenure-track faculty member meets with the tenured faculty and the dean (or dean's representative) to assess progress toward tenure. And in the fall of the fifth year, the tenure-track candidates and their department chairs will meet with a representative from the provost's office to review the requirements for the tenure dossier. Expectations for a successful tenure review should be clear by the time the faculty member is up for tenure. Nevertheless, occasions will arise when a negative tenure decision will be rendered by the department, dean, or the provost, to the dismay of the candidate (and potentially some members of the department). Clarity of procedures and expectations along the way justify the decision, even though such clarity cannot dispel profound disappointment for all.

Institutional, strategic, and procedural clarity can help the decision maker arrive at "yes" or "no." The message, then, must be delivered. If the news has the potential to be received unfavorably, the conversation is likely to be unpleasant. Here are six strategies I have found to facilitate the conversation, serving the interests of the institution and the recipient of the news.

Be timely. As soon as you know the correct answer is "no," deliver the message. Don't wait for someone else to do it or for the recipient to figure it out. Especially in the case of unacceptable behavior, failing to deliver the news may be construed as tacit acceptance. Leaving the job to your successor is unfair and will likely exacerbate the problem. In the case of requests for resources, waiting for your response may leave the requestor in limbo, failing to work on other projects that add value to the university.

Be transparent. Explain your rationale for arriving at "no." You may have impeccable institutional, strategic, or procedural clarity, but that doesn't mean others do. It goes without saying that a necessary condition of transparency is honesty. I know of a decision maker who used to turn down requests for funding by saying that no money was available. That was not true, but in his mind, it was easier for the proposer to hear. Unfortunately, that message created other kinds of tensions on campus. Honesty in why a proposal is turned down or what might make the proposal stronger has the potential to improve the quality of work across campus.

Be self-reflective. Use the occasion of saying "no" to reflect on how you can better communicate the reasons for why you responded "no." Why would anyone spend months on a proposal that is ultimately rejected? Perhaps the criteria for a successful proposal were unclear. Or perhaps the realities facing the university are not well understood. If either of these is true, greater communication across campus is necessary. It could be, too, that as the institution continues to grow and advance, a decision made in one year is no longer reasonable years later.

Be consistent/fair/reasonable. Except in the case of unusual circumstances (and as a provost, I seemed to have a lot of those), your decision making should be somewhat predictable or at least follow predictable decision rules. Favoritism is not an acceptable decision rule. You are the leader of your entire unit, and you need to advance the unit in a way that is free from personal biases or preferences. Occasionally, you will need to vary from your normal decision-making practices. As an example, I follow a very strict attendance policy for my undergraduate courses. Too many absences and the student fails the class. One semester, a student who had been warned that one more absence would result in a failing grade missed another class. Turns out, his sister was a student at Columbine High School in Colorado. When he heard of the shooting, he didn't know if his sister was alive or dead. He missed my class waiting to hear. That excuse seemed worthy of reconsidering my policy. The student experienced other consequences, but he didn't fail on absences.

Be willing to own a bad decision. You will make a bad decision. I can guarantee it. Even given institutional, strategic, and procedural clarity. Why? Because the hardest decisions involve judgment. If all decisions were formulaic, based on the execution of institutional policies, we would have no need for decision makers. But that is not the case. You will make decisions with which others don't agree, but that doesn't make them bad. However, when you do make a bad decision, you will know it. How you handle the bad decision will affect your relationship with your campus constituency. As difficult as it might be, immediately accept responsibility for the decision, and begin to remedy the situation. It is only human to make an occasional mistake; just be sure yours are new mistakes, rather than repetitions of old ones.

Be compassionate. I have two thoughts here. First, give the request its full hearing. Don't use "no" as an easy way to stop the conversation. Whether it's a department making a request for a new program or a student appealing a failing grade, situations that you see frequently are not so frequent for others. Take the time to consider the merits of each request. And second, when delivering bad news, if at all practical (and consistent with institutional policies), do so in person. Certain decisions change the course of someone's life. You are an institutional decision maker, and you must act in the best interest of the institution. At the same time, you are also a human being, dealing with individuals' lives. If it means anything to be human, it means walking through difficult times alongside our colleagues. Not sugarcoating a decision, delaying it, or making the wrong one, but also not dismissing the decision as inconsequential.

Where is the art in saying "no"? When it is thoughtfully used, when the recipient understands the rationale even if she doesn't agree, and when it is not used to avoid a difficult "yes." Our responses—"yes," "no," "not yet," and so on—should be the result of deliberate, transparent, fair, and consistent decision-making processes. While I argue that reaching the decision is the hard part, careful consideration should be given in how the news is delivered. Surprisingly enough, I've found that a thoughtful hearing followed by a reasoned "no" can actually strengthen relationships and create a greater level of shared commitment among colleagues. Such practices create trust across campus, and that can make all the difference in a successful or unsuccessful administrative tenure.

Chapter Twelve

Leadership Advice

Enlarging the Coin of the Realm

Donald J. Foss

Advice, n. The smallest current coin.

—Ambrose Bierce, *The Devil's Dictionary.*

"The man was in such deep distress,"
Said Tom, "that I could do no less
Than give him good advice." Said Jim:
"If less could have been done for him
I know you well enough, my son,
To know that's what you would have done."

—Jebel Jocordy

My university library has about fifty to sixty linear feet of books on leadership, not even counting books on management and cognate topics. And in just the last ten years the PsycInfo database has added over a thousand books and ten thousand articles with "leadership," "leader," or "leaders" in the title. That's a big realm! So, to say the least, there is plenty of advice readily at hand; and some of it is backed by more than bitcoin. It's not surprising that doing some reading can spark fruitful reflection, self-assessment, and planning; but where to cast one's line in this vast river of possibilities? I'll start by mentioning two specific sources other than this book that give good value, and then I'll offer five suggestions that stem from my quarter-century experience as chair, dean, and provost.

It's useful to remember that good leaders lead with a purpose. Long ago I spent thirty-five cents to buy a now dog-eared paperback copy of Alfred North Whitehead's, *The Aims of Education*, originally published in 1929 (a used copy is about two dollars on current websites). I don't agree with everything Whitehead said, but it's got a lot of bang for two bucks. For example, I've often returned to this inspirational passage:

> The universities are schools of education and schools of research. But the primary reason for their existence is not to be found in either the mere knowledge conveyed or in the mere opportunities for research afforded members of the faculty. . . .
>
> The justification for a university is that it preserves the connection between knowledge and the zest for life by uniting the young and the old in the imaginative consideration of learning. (p. 97)

Expanding your knowledge and maintaining your zest for life are good things. So, too, is leading with the purpose of helping others do the same.

Second, and from a more data-oriented perspective, is John Campbell's splendid chapter, "Leadership, the Old, the New, and the Timeless: A Commentary." It's in the *Oxford Handbook of Leadership*, edited by M. G. Rumsey. Distilling twenty-five years of taxonomic research on leadership and management, Campbell describes fundamental factors comprising leadership performance spanning interpersonal, communication, and goal-directed topics, among others. His two tables listing core factors of good leadership and good management are well worth copying and using as both aspirational and practical reminders of what you are trying to do and how to do it. Highly recommended.

Good leadership/management choices take into account both context and one's role in it. Thus, under similar circumstances, what constitutes a wise move for, say, a department chair or for a dean may differ somewhat. It also matters whether one is dealing with an individual, a group, or an institutional unit. Again, thoughtful people have written books or other guides that take context and scope of responsibility into account. So in addition to the two recommendations above, I suggest typing "academic department chair" or "academic dean" into a search engine or a site like Amazon.com; that will yield useful hits and, if a couple of other books are read, useful hints.

YOUR NEW ROLE

If we were chatting over lunch, though, I'd mention five topics that are helpful in the transition to leadership roles and in carrying them out. First, the duties and role expectations of chairs, deans, provosts, and presidents are different from those of "regular" faculty members, and nothing you can do will change that. Accepting a leadership role means you now are "different." So you have to adapt and get used to your modified role. For me, one odd result was that I had to sharply reduce my tendency to engage in intellectual debate for its own sake. It sometimes led a tea leaf–reading colleague to overinterpret an offhand remark. In addition, even though academic leaders typically come from the faculty and are almost invariably recommended by a faculty committee (what other workplace gets such input about its leaders in this way?), some faculty members consistently conclude that their leaders have lost their academic bearings. Of course it does happen: there definitely are, for example, some narcissistic leaders, an example of a factor that Campbell dubs "counterproductive work behavior"; but in my experience they are not the norm. Even so, you may hear that you've "gone bad."

YOUR NEW TIME ZONE

Second is how you spend your time. Among the toughest adjustments I had to make when I first became a department chair was the hit on "my" time. At the end of the day, I commonly felt I had accomplished nothing—no new research ideas, no new words on manuscripts, not enough time to work on teaching, and so on. I finally realized that I had to change my reward tokens. For example, I had the practice of taking manuscripts to the post office and personally dropping them in the mail (it's a dated example, I know). My brain's reward center popped and fizzed any time I did that. Now it appeared there were going to be fewer trips to the mailbox, and my reward center was fizzling rather than fizzing.

To cope with that problem, I talked myself into believing that I could take a small fraction of credit for the successes of colleagues and students. (I did it without talking about it lest I be seen as a raging narcissist or credit plagiarist.) Given that change, it followed that I would benefit by developing the department such that the rate of others' successes—including those of staff members—would grow. This was an important adjustment; it was like flipping a light switch, though admittedly it phased in more like a dimmer. I started to feel like myself again.

SHAPING AND SHARPENING YOUR GOALS

Third, it is good to reflect on one's leadership "philosophy" or criteria for "success." As just suggested, for a time I conceived of myself as a "servant leader," one who wants to help others and to make them feel that they are meeting their goals. As it says in the Gospel According to St. Mark: "Whoever wants to be first must be servant of all." That seems noble and a way to be effective. But, not to be blasphemous, it isn't fully possible or even desirable to do it. For example, when I was a department chair, a couple of colleagues wanted to carve out as much time as possible to spend in off-campus activities for private gain. I certainly could not, nor more importantly should not, have helped them reach their goals. And more generally, since there are always limited resources, leaders need some standards by which to apportion them. It follows that we need a set of commonly acknowledged goals, and that the leader should help clarify them, help provide resources to reach them, and help reward those who do the best job of it.

To a first approximation, it's easy to state the goals of academic institutions; they are hugely similar across thousands of colleges and universities: to develop the human resources of society; to contribute to the advancement of knowledge; and to be productive members of our academic, professional, and regional communities. The relative importance of these goals will differ depending upon the particular institution and its mission. However, it's at the next level of specificity where things get dicey. How do we decide on teaching assignments, on the areas of scholarship and teaching to emphasize in our next hire, on who will do the needed committee work, on who (or which unit) gets the resources of time and money that we may be able to disperse? And, importantly, what processes will we use to get to those decisions? In other words, how can we effectively set and "sell" the goals?

In *The Creation of the Future: The Role of the American University*, former Cornell University president Frank H. T. Rhodes says, "Behind much of the success of the American university lies the steady leadership and vision of generations of deans who have nudged the aspirations and nurtured the creativity of their colleagues" (p. 15). In my view, such "nudging" means getting those responsible for carrying out the mission to agree on it and on what steps are needed to accomplish it. In academia, that more effectively occurs via a transaction rather than a decree. Transactions can lead to transformations. You, as leader, have the goals roughly sketched out in your mind, but you then must have conversations with those responsible for putting them into practice. Many new leaders go on the equivalent of a "listening tour" soon after they take office. That's wise because it conveys an interest in the opinions of others, provides a chance to hear about immediate concerns, and starts some real give-and-take. Such tours can be rebooked on a semester or annual basis. I found these visits useful in part because I could also question my colleagues about how their resource requests would contribute to the outcomes we agreed upon, which was a satisfactory substitute for the intellectual debate I mentioned earlier.

Midlevel leaders eventually need to buy in to the president's and dean's goals, and in turn they can help shape those goals and the implementation strategies via the transactional process. Do we want upper-division semester-credit hours increased, more first-year students returning for the spring semester, more grant proposals submitted? Let's talk about it and how to do it. When I had common goals with those who worked with me, I didn't have to worry excessively about monitoring how they accomplished them. They owned the goals as much as I did, and we could genuinely work together—

though I always understood my job as, in part, helping to get resources for my unit, and I knew that those reporting to me had the same aim.

DEVELOPING NEW LEADERS

Fourth, I'd like to share a couple of tips about developing academic leaders who have a good chance of succeeding. New leaders, especially department chairs, should insist on getting appropriate training. And deans and provosts should ensure that such training is available. I've written about the consequences of not being properly trained to take up a leadership role; it's not always pretty.

Wise department chairs also look ahead and try to pick out the likely next leaders. They should then arrange to provide those prospective leaders with some of the knowledge that can help them be successful if they eventually take such a role. For example, one very helpful experience is to serve on the college promotion and tenure committee. That gives prospective future chairs a feel for what a successful candidate has to have accomplished; it provides practical examples of the institution's P&T (promotion and tenure) standards. I had that experience and learned a ton, especially from a distinguished colleague in the Classics Department. He had very high standards about what he wanted to see in both the scholarly and teaching dossiers, and he didn't like excuses.

CHATing ABOUT FUND RAISING

Fifth is the issue of private fundraising (yes, sorry, this is getting to be a long lunch). Many academics are good at writing memos that request resources from their chair or dean, or from internal committees; and many faculty members, especially in the sciences, are good at writing proposals to federal or state agencies. However, they typically have very little experience asking individuals or foundations for money. But nowadays, academic leaders are typically expected to do so.

The first thing is to get over the sense that you are asking for yourself—that you are trying to feather your own nest. That's how I felt when I first entertained the notion that I had to be a fundraiser—almost like a beggar. I wasn't sure I could take that role. But ask yourself: Do you believe in the institutional mission? Do you believe your students deserve and need support? Do you believe that your faculty members are doing good work? Yes? Well remember that you are asking for them, not for yourself. In this role you are close to being a servant leader. I was taught that lesson in one conversation over dinner with a well-known colleague, and it made a tremendous impression on me. In an hour I changed from being anxious about asking for money to being proud to do it. Fundraising can be fun. Yes, it requires alertness and being on one's toes. Those lunches and dinners are not times to relax. Even so, I took it as almost R&R relative to the day-to-day rigors of administration—it certainly is different. Too, the people I met were almost invariably interesting and had fascinating life stories.

Over time, I developed a four-factor "theory" of successful fundraising. Some of its components can be carried out by staff members, at least in part, but some definitely require your personal attention. I call my approach the "CHAT theory of fundraising." I can only outline here; each component requires considerable unpacking to make it truly practical, but the basic ideas are simple. Each of these four components must be present if you are to have substantial success raising private money. Here are my CHAT points:

C = Capability. Almost any adult you come in contact with can give a gift to your institution, and a surprising fraction will give if you ask them. But you should not ask until you have an idea of how much to ask for. In other words, you need to figure out the person's capability to give. Staff can help because there are publicly available cues (e.g., one's zip code, to take a very simple example). But there is more to it. Some people have an expensive house but are "house poor." Others live modestly but have substantial net worth. It takes skill to determine the sweet spot—what should I ask for? It's a good idea to have a list of gift levels at the ready in case your first assessment misses the mark.

H = Heart. By which I mean philanthropic heart. Some people have substantial resources along with the goal of dying with the most toys. They are not good donor prospects. In conversation, web searches, or by looking at the plaques on the home or office walls, you often can discover whether the donor prospect is public spirited and what some of his or her interests are. Does the individual have the "life force": a concern about future generations, the health of society or of the planet? If so, you can keep going. If not, you should expect at most a relatively small gift relative to capability. Your time is valuable, so you need to focus on people who meet both the C and H criteria.

A = Appeal. (I used to call this "Interest," but the CHIT theory too often got misheard!) Up to a point you can raise money for your priorities, for what appeals to you; but that point is very limited. People give to support what appeals to them, not to what appeals to you. There is an exception when it comes to support for students, because that appeals to nearly everyone. If student support is your priority, you'll get a lot of easy buy-in. But if you are trying to raise money for some other cause, say to support the history of World War II, you will have a hard time finding donors. It lacks appeal for the vast majority of them.

A key part of the fundraiser's job is to determine what the prospective donor cares about, or could readily be "converted" to care about. Then your task is to find something in your portfolio that is close enough to the person's interests such that it will appeal to them. That is a creative aspect of fundraising. For deans with large scope, this is relatively easy. When I was dean of an arts and sciences college I had mental health, some aspects of education, climate change, creative writing, the social history of World War II, and many, many other topics in my portfolio. I was able to find an appealing project for many—but not all—prospective donors. The main lesson here is not to jump too quickly to a conclusion about what you are asking the donor to support. This is a mistake made by a lot of development officers; they try to raise money for the president's priorities. That's okay up to a point, of course, but raising money in the service of the institution is more important—especially if you are successful. This task requires someone who knows the unit very well and so can be creative during conversations. I think it needs the leader. There is a corollary: if the donor's heart is in, say, the history of World War II, and history is not in your unit, then you must pass him or her on to your colleague responsible for that department. This is also true for deans whose units have a narrower scope. One's biggest loyalty is to the institution.

T = Trust. I saved the most important one for last. Donors absolutely must trust and like the person they are dealing with. They must trust that you will follow up to ensure that the gift is put to work in the way you agreed upon. They must see you as a fine representative of the institution they care about. Therefore, you must take your time in cultivating donors. Get to know them and let them get to know you. Don't succumb to pressures that you must ask for a gift because some arbitrary deadline (e.g., the end of a fiscal year) is upon you. Big gifts don't come to individuals, but they do come through individuals. While you are building trust, you obviously are building a relationship, one that may last for years beyond the time when you are in the job. Clearly, this is not a task for anyone else but you. I know a lot of chairs and deans who thought they could raise money by delegating it to a fundraiser. That won't get to the finish line. You cannot see yourself as just a closer; you must also be a builder.

In sum, being a leader has both aspirational and hard-nosed managerial aspects. I think leaders are successful if, when they leave the position, the institution continues to improve because of some things they've brought to it—which might include a lot of valuable coins. You won't enjoy every day, but you can enjoy every year.

Chapter Thirteen

In Search of a New Language of Leadership

Pamela Martin Fry

The Roman poet Ovid (43 BC to 17 or 18 AD) provided an early concept of leadership: "A ruler should be slow to punish and swift to reward." This foundational idea of leading people in a highly controlled manner frames leadership primarily as a power differential between the leader and the follower; that is, the leader directs (hopefully in a thoughtful manner as Ovid suggests), followers obey, and consequences—as determined by the ruler/leader—occur. Further, the word "ruler" as translated from Ovid's writings in Latin illustrates a metaphor that evolved from the notion of a wooden stick used to "rule, straighten, guide" (see dictionary.reference.com/browse/rule). The comparison accomplishes a metaphor's mission to compare something to be defined (a word for one who is in power) to an existing concept (a straight, wooden stick that sets a standard of measurement). A clear and underlying value for leaders, expressed by this metaphor, is a high degree of control of others in an organization.

The primary argument of this chapter will be that our thinking about leadership is framed and possibly restricted by this powerful and, for most people, unconscious root metaphor that portrays leaders as individuals who are expected to exert a high degree of control. A secondary argument will be that a new language, that is, new metaphors for leadership, are needed to express new approaches that value group members, their contributions to the organization, and their development as leaders in organizations.

THE PARADOXICAL POWER OF METAPHORS

Lakoff and Johnson (1980) describe structural or basic metaphors as presenting one concept "metaphorically structured in terms of another" (p. 7). For example, "Time is money" (p. 7). This basic metaphor spawns corollary metaphorical expressions:

> "You're *wasting* my time."
> "This gadget will *save* you hours."
> "I don't have the time to *give* you."
> "How do you *spend* your time these days?" (p. 8)

Such systematicity of metaphoric thought, according to Lakoff and Johnson, can limit our ability to question the inconsistencies or absurdities of the metaphor: "In allowing us to focus on one aspect of a concept, . . . a metaphorical concept can keep us from focusing on other aspects of the concept that are inconsistent with that metaphor" (p. 10). Can "time" literally be saved, wasted, spent, and/or given away like money?

On one hand, metaphors provide a means to express new ideas by comparing an unknown to a known and, in doing so, create new perspectives, concepts, and meanings. In this process of metaphorical thought, new conceptions of reality can be formed. The paradoxical power of metaphor is that we simultaneously can become constrained in our thinking while generating a novel comparison. For example, consider a common metaphor to describe the brain (the unknown to be explained) as a computer (the known, a familiar machine). We often use words such as *memory*, *networks*, and *processing* to describe both the brain and a computer. At the same time, many argue that the comparison limits our thinking about the complexities and human uniqueness of the brain.

Some metaphors can be considered "root metaphors" or fundamental metaphors that assist in organizing ontological orientations to the world and thereby in creating paradigms of thought that often go unquestioned. The Newtonian view of a clocklike universe is a common example of an ontological metaphor that guided scientific inquiry for centuries. Similarly, the fundamental concept of "leader as ruler"—consciously or not—appears to have guided a technocratic, behaviorist approach to our thinking about leaders.

MODERN CONCEPTIONS OF LEADERSHIP

Many modern expressions of leadership reflect a ruler-leader paradigm of thought. These views of leadership are rooted in conceiving leadership as a power differential—the ruler or boss and the leader are one and the same. At its extreme, the leader is the "all knowing" entity who directs and evaluates the standards for the organization. Consider these more recent quotes about leadership that exemplify this point.

"Lead me, follow me, or get out of my way."

—General George Patton

(Commentary: *A leader is the person who assertively takes charge of the situation and keeps others in line. In following a highly assertive approach to leadership, have organizations unthinkingly adopted a military paradigm for leadership to apply to their nonmilitary organizations?*)

"A leader is one who knows the way, goes the way, and shows the way."

—John Maxwell

(Commentary: *Leaders lead, and followers follow because leaders know where the group should be going and how to get there. A corollary metaphor associated with the systematicity of a high-control leadership paradigm is "leader as trailblazer or pathfinder."*)

"A leader takes people where they want to go. A great leader takes people where they don't necessarily want to go, but ought to be."

—Rosalynn Carter

(Commentary: *Similarly to the previous quote, a leader is viewed as a pathfinder. In addition, a "great leader" is one who influences others who may resist following. Important questions that should be considered by this view: How does a leader know that his or her way is the right way, especially when the followers do not want to go there? What means does he or she use to get people to go where they do not want to go? What happens when the leader is no longer in the organization?*)

For almost three decades, an increasingly popular metaphor for leadership is *servant leadership*, a concept originating with an AT&T executive, Robert Greenleaf, in the 1970s. The primary thesis of servant leadership, according to Greenleaf (2002) is that "*the great leader is seen as servant first*, and that simple fact is the key to his greatness" (p. 21). Greenleaf further writes:

A new moral principle is emerging, which holds that the only authority deserving one's allegiance is that which is freely and knowingly granted by the led to the leader in response to, and in proportion to, the clearly evident servant stature of the leader. Those who choose to follow this principle will not casually accept the authority of existing institutions. *Rather, they will freely respond only to individuals who are chosen as leaders because they are proven and trusted servants.* (p. 24)

While the servant leader concept moves well beyond the traditional ruler or boss-leader metaphor to emphasize the role of humility, the development of knowledge and the experience to lead, and the role of moral conscience that should guide one's actions, leadership remains framed by language evoking a differential power relationship between the follower (servant) to leader (former servant). Building on the values that underpin a servant leader approach, the final section of this chapter will present alternate language that may better reflect the relationship between the leader and others in the group, as related to the leader's control over and concern about members of the organization.

TOWARD A NEW LANGUAGE OF LEADERSHIP

Following the assumption that a given organization of people desires and needs a leader, approaches to leadership can be differentiated by many factors. For the purposes of this discussion, two of the most significant factors will serve as the foci: the degree that the leader exerts control over the organization and the degree that the leader cares about the organization and the individuals in the organization. (See figure 13.1.)

Leaders who exert high control/low care can be characterized as having a dictatorial style and typically lead through directives. In contrast, leaders who exert high control/high care often adopt a parenting style based on nurturing individuals in the group. As shown on the lower right quadrant of figure 13.1, a leader who has low control/low care is disconnected and inattentive, allowing members of the group to navigate the organization which may be in a haphazard, directionless manner. Finally, the top right quadrant represents a leader who maintains an approach of low control/high care with the goal of inspiring others to develop as leaders. In fact, the consistent and integral involvement of the organization's members in decision making and in growth as leaders themselves is the primary goal of this leader's style. Further, this leader is connected to the group and makes decisions that are purposeful, in the best interest of the group and of the organization, and in accordance with principles that reflect a concern for the common good. This approach can be characterized as "conscientious leader" to capture these qualities. The essential shift in language relates to the quality of a leader's consciousness or, more specifically, "conscientiousness" to guide thoughtful, ethical, purposeful action in contrast to action of leaders framed in the language of differentiated power.

Note, too, that the roles of others in the organization shift among the quadrants from follower, child, survivor, to professional. Another consideration in this model is the level of functioning of the group as noted by the dashed line from high control/high care to low control/high care: if the group functions poorly, a leader may indeed need to adopt a more directive approach, although the ultimate goal is to move the group toward professional

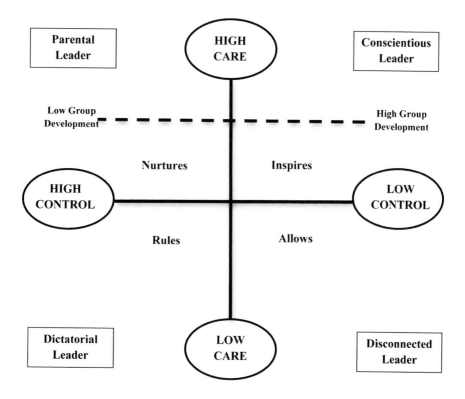

Figure 13.1.

autonomy as leadership capacity is developed among the members of the organization.

CONCLUSION

The goal of this chapter is to provoke reflection about our conscious and, more importantly, our unconscious frames of reference that underpin taken-for-granted conceptions about leadership. New approaches to leadership that value purposeful action and ethical concern for others and for the greater, common good require creative language to express these perspectives. The concept of "conscientious leadership" illustrates such an attempt. The language of leadership is much more than merely words that describe roles and dynamics in an organization. Instead, this language frames our thinking about the nature of leadership; reflects particular values and expectations we hold about control, caring, and other aspects of leaders and leadership; and creates particular realities that come to life in every organization.

REFERENCES

Greenleaf, R. K. (2002). *Servant Leadership*. Mahwah, NJ: Paulist Press.
Lakoff, G. and M. Johnson (1980). *Metaphors we live by*. Chicago: University of Chicago Press.

Chapter Fourteen

Changing for Excellence

Finding Resources to Enable KU's
Bold Aspirations

Diane H. Goddard

University leaders all across the country are working hard to transform, strategically position, and competitively strengthen their institutions in order to improve the ability to attract and retain top students, faculty, and staff as well as to protect and improve their brand and ranking. The University of Kansas is no different. KU is in the third year of implementing the six goals contained in our ambitious strategic plan, aptly named *Bold Aspirations.*[1] The plan provides the roadmap, strategies, and action steps needed to successfully bring the university community together in its efforts to transform itself to meet the needs of the future. The six goals will look familiar to most university leaders, but what sets KU apart is the leadership recognition of how important change management, communication, transparency, community inclusion, accountability, and focused attention to detail are for the success of reaching the goals.

In order to reach the full potential of *Bold Aspirations,* the university realized significant resources would be required and organizational structures had to be transformed to make the university business and administrative operations more effective and efficient. KU's *Changing for Excellence* (CFE) initiative generated a number of programs designed to deliver maximum effectiveness and designed to generate savings to be reallocated to the higher level priorities.

For six months, the entire university, with assistance from an external consultant, worked to identify areas of opportunity and then to develop business cases and implementation plans. The decision was made to implement all ten CFE initiatives (see textbox 14.1 below) concurrently with the implementation of the strategic plan. These initiatives would impact every unit on campus so thorough planning and careful coordination was a high priority.

The keys to success when undertaking transformational change of this magnitude include coordinating many different, overlapping, and at times competing activities, including those listed below:

- Support and commitment of top leadership is imperative.
- Build the team and identify all stakeholders.
- Create a communication plan.
- Develop change management capability across the institution.
- Develop and choreograph individual and overall project plans and timelines.
- Create accountability with weekly and monthly check-in and report-out meetings and document, document, document.
- Listen to what is NOT being said along with all other feedback.
- Live the plan every day and all day.

Careful focus on the above bullet points can set the stage for the difficult task of transformation.

Strong, visible support of all the top leaders in the institution serves to motivate not only those working directly on the various initiatives but also helps everyone in the community understand the importance of transformation. Communication from the KU chancellor and provost in their weekly newsletters to faculty, staff, and students almost always includes information about *Bold Aspirations* and/or *Changing for Excellence*. These frequent reminders about why we are undertaking so much important change at this time, acknowledging the challenges, and celebrating the successes helps everyone accept the turmoil created by the change process.

In the early months of the process, it is critical to pick leaders and team members for each of the initiatives who are credible, believe in the initiatives, and are trusted by their colleagues. Identifying and involving as many stakeholders as possible in each phase of the process is both necessary and very time-consuming. The campus community is made up of three basic groups: people who are excited about the proposed changes and want to be part of the process, people who are simply not ever going to agree with the changes, and a fairly large group of people who are somewhere in the middle. This third, large group is where energy needs to be directed, as these are the people you can and need to bring along in a positive manner.

A robust communication plan, developed early in the process, pays dividends throughout the entire process. Early in our process we held many town hall meetings and focus-group meetings to explain the various initiatives and outcomes we hoped to achieve. At KU we included a marketing and communications staff person who attended as many meetings as possible, helped design and provide content for the project website, authored much of the communications from the chancellor, provost, and team leaders, provided guidance on best communication practices, and assisted each initiative leader to develop a communication strategy. This meant our communication across all sectors of the university would be consistent and deliver the same message. A primary goal of KU's communication plan is transparency. KU's CFE website contains detailed information for each initiative, including sections on opportunities, goals, challenges, stakeholders, project resources, and project news. All meeting agendas and notes, timelines, calendars, reports, updates, FAQs, videos, and survey results are posted, providing the campus community up-to-date information on each initiative.

One successful innovation was the creation of a Change Facilitators Committee charged to build the capacity for organizational change at KU by applying knowledge from a variety of academic fields and by providing educational materials and facilitation assistance to campus leaders and teams. This committee, led by the KU faculty member who directs the School of Public Affairs and Administration, developed training for team facilitators who were then assigned to various initiative teams to provide assistance. The training sessions and workshops included general information on facilitation and the skills involved, on how to plan the facilitated session, on guidelines for skillful discussion and handling difficult dialogues, on group process and how to read a group, on common participant/group behaviors and interventions, and on a robust toolbox of change management tools and methods. This training was open to anyone in the KU community who wanted to be involved in the change process.

Building a project plan and timeline for a standalone project is fairly straightforward and familiar to most of our project teams. However, when you are implementing ten initiatives, most of which have major system upgrades as part of their charge and all of which have dependencies and prerequisites from other initiatives, you can quickly end up with something that looks like the convoluted diagram in figure 14.1.[2]

At KU, in the Office of Administration and Finance, my staff and I have the responsibility for coordinating and choreographing all CFE project plans to keep every aspect of each project moving forward at the appropriate pace and with the appropriate level of resources. Whoever assumes this role must live the plan all day, every day—but more on that later.

Carefully scheduled and planned meetings assist tremendously in providing the structure and accountability for all initiative teams. Team leaders meet together weekly for a detailed status update, advisory groups typically meet monthly, stakeholder groups meet as needed, and the executive committee, which used to meet monthly, now meets on a quarterly basis for updates on all initiatives. Each team leader rotates through the executive

Changing for Excellence: Project Cross-Functional Relationships

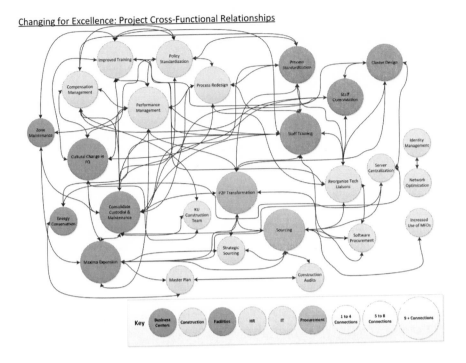

Figure 14.1.

committee meetings in order to give an in-depth update once a year. Team leaders also provide biweekly updates which are posted on the CFE website.

Managing ten initiatives concurrently provides leadership with a never-ending flow of feedback. Encouraging constant feedback provides many great ideas and a sense of the pulse of the campus community and alerts leadership to where the hot spots are. An example of leveraging feedback in a timely manner is how our dean of the College of Liberal Arts and Sciences utilized monthly surveys at his department chairs' meeting while we were implementing shared service centers for the college. The college is the largest academic unit at KU, so its shared service centers were implemented over twelve months and in four phases. These monthly surveys allowed the team to address issues immediately and to monitor overall acceptance and service levels.

Managing the constant feedback can be challenging, but at times leadership needs to pay very close attention to what is NOT being said. One of the first initiatives we kicked off was the merger of the custodial and maintenance staffs on campus. We chose this particular initiative because we wanted a quick win and a success story early in the process. What we encountered instead was impacted staff coming to town hall meetings to express, without exception, that this merger should not take place. Hundreds of reasons to not merge were delivered by very passionate, and at times emotional, staff. The reasons presented did not explain the passion and emotion. Clearly something was not being said, and clearly this was not looking like a quick win. A two-part strategy emerged: conducting a climate survey and then meeting individually with all forty-eight workgroups to discuss the results of the survey. As vice provost for administration and finance, I personally met with all workgroups on all shifts to listen to their concerns, which uncovered unexpected and serious management problems within the unit. Addressing those management issues and putting new leaders in place quickly set the project on course and provided the quick win we needed. This approach allowed us to dramatically improve the workplace climate, address nonexistent safety training, and empower the new leadership to transform that unit.

Transformational change takes leadership courage. It requires changing the institutional culture without sacrificing what makes it great. It requires leadership to live the plan all day, every day. Every activity we choose to undertake has to contribute to the successful implementation of our strategic plan. It also requires leadership to care deeply about providing the resources and support to the staff working to make it a reality.

Textbox 14.1 CHANGING FOR EXCELLENCE INITIATIVES AND GOALS

Budgeting Process

- Redesign the annual budget process to encompass all sources of funding
- Use cost drivers and quality metrics to enable comprehensive budget understanding and budget transparency

Shared Service Centers

- Create regional shared service centers across campus to streamline staff around job functions and increase training effectiveness for business processes
- Decrease risks and increase compliance
- Improve career paths for staff
- Better customer service for end user

Construction

- Create a construction specific strategic sourcing capability
- Embed audit language in all construction contracts and create an audit group to enhance due diligence and financial control

Enrollment Management

- Create a robust first-year experience
- Design a new core curriculum
- Strengthen the recruiting pipeline
- Enhance transfer student recruitment and retention
- Increase student enrollment through enlarged applicant pool and yield management
- Increase applicant pool through more coordinated approach to branding and outreach

Facilities

- Consolidate individual custodial and maintenance operations and develop service level agreements among clients
- Increase maintenance worker productivity by establishing six regional zones
- Improve internal operations and procedures to provide better service to customers and increase work productivity
- Institute a comprehensive utility reduction plan and incentivize faculty and staff to decrease utility usage
- Fully implement the Maximo facilities management system

Human Resources

- Create a strategic role for HR
- Redesign the organization chart to include all critical HR functions
- Streamline processes and increase workflow implementation across HR
- Implement a performance management and learning management system
- Standardize job descriptions and create salary bands

Libraries

- Reassess library staffing and key service levels in accordance with the strategic initiatives

- Monitor and analyze the annual impact on collections and services resulting from demand driven acquisitions

Procurement and Sourcing

- Develop commodity specialists to more actively manage supplier relationships and performance
- Standardize procurement processes to drive university spend to KUPPS to ensure contract pricing and provide visibility to all purchasing activities
- Complete KUPPS implementation and streamline the approval and settlement process to address the low utilization and efficiencies of procure to pay technologies

Research Administration

- Strengthen operations, processes and overall effectiveness from PI initial concept to close-out of projects
- Implement systems for Conflict of Interest, Institutional Review Board protocol, Institutional Animal Care and Use Committee protocol, Accounts Receivable/Billing, proposal development and electronic submission

Information Technology

- Server centralization
- Reorganize and redefine IT staff through centralization
- Increase MFD usage
- Implement a Single Identity Management System
- Network optimization
- Leverage software purchasing

NOTES

1. In the chapter *"Bold Aspirations—A* Community Effort," Provost Jeff Vitter articulates the campus-wide process that created the KU strategic plan.

2. Huron Education, presentation for "How Much Change Can a University Absorb at Once," NACUBO, July 21, 2014.

Chapter Fifteen

Academic Strategic Planning

How Can It Mean Something?

April C. Mason

The strategic planning process of Kansas State University in 2010 had to be different. A new president after twenty-three years set an overall goal of becoming a top-fifty public research university by 2025. K-State 2025 is the name adopted for the plan (www.k-state.edu/2025/). The plan represents a fifteen-year planning window with an aggressive goal received on campus and off with both excitement and disbelief. How were we to get there? By our own admission, based on Arizona State University's Measuring University Performance, *The Top American Research Universities*, we were in the mid-70s to mid-80s, depending on benchmark. How would people from all the communities of the university see themselves as involved in achieving this goal?

Even describing the university as a public research university had sparked questions and concern that the "new" administration was abandoning the solid undergraduate educational experience of the university for a new direction. Reminding all that the university was a doctoral-granting, Carnegie-classified Research University—High Research Activity did little to dispel this concern.

Nearly five years later the university is preparing for the evaluation of short-term outcomes (one to five years). College and departmental plans are in place and specific metrics are used to monitor progress. The Kansas Board of Regents is updated annually on university progress and is in full support of the plan. A visiting Higher Learning Commission accreditation team in 2012 complimented the administration on the strong strategic plan and how well-informed of the plan the campus members they spoke to were. Campus naysayers are still concerned, but the goal remains the same and the plan is front and center of campus decision making and communications.

THE STRATEGIC PLANNING PROCESS

Eight benchmarks were chosen in collaboration with the president's cabinet to measure progress toward the top-fifty public research university goal. There are no surprises in this list of benchmarks.

- Total Research and Development Expenditures
- Total Endowment
- Number of National Academy Members
- Number of Faculty Awards
- Number of Doctorates Awarded
- Freshman-to-Sophomore Retention Ratio
- Six-Year Graduation Rate
- Percentage of Undergraduates Involved in Formalized Research Experience

Focus groups facilitated by cabinet-level administrators were held to explain the overall goal of the plan to alumni, faculty, community stakeholders, elected officials, and students and to ask what they thought of the goal and what challenges we needed to address related to the goal. Focus group reports were evaluated, and seven themes were identified to be addressed as the university moved forward in its goal attainment.

- Research
- Undergraduate education
- Graduate education
- Engagement, outreach
- Faculty/staff
- Infrastructure
- Athletics

The Office of Education Innovation and Evaluation at Kansas State University (oeie.k-state.edu/) was retained to facilitate discussion around each theme. At an initial planning meeting, the topic of the Logic Model was raised. This was embraced as the framework for preparing and presenting the university's strategic plan. The Logic Model or Program Action Plan looks at the inputs needed, the outputs or activities done, and the outcomes or impacts to be achieved (www.wkkf.org/resource-directory/resource/2006/02/wk-kellogg-foundation-logic-model-development-guide). This framework fit our planning perfectly. What did we want to achieve? What will we need to do to accomplish these achievements? What strategies will we use to get there?

Committees were assembled around each theme. Each theme committee had subject-matter experts, faculty, alumni, classified staff, and graduate and undergraduate student representation. Each committee was cochaired by a dean and a member of the Faculty Senate Committee on University Planning. The committees met formally three times for two hours with two facilitators and were taken through the Logic Model planning to identify what was needed, what would be done to address the needs, and what outcomes or impact was to be achieved. Only a few of the many members of the seven themes had even heard of the Logic Model, and none had used it in this manner.

The strategic planning process at Kansas State University was met with the same "wild enthusiasm" all academic strategic planning processes seem to receive: "Why are we doing this? They will never use the stuff we come up with anyway." We have all heard these comments many times. I have been involved in strategic planning at two other universities. I heard the same comments there.

The process for K-State 2025 was different. Theme committees were charged by the provost and the process began. Initial reports from the facilitators indicated things were moving along well. Enthusiasm was building. Committees were meeting between work sessions to discuss and add ideas and materials to the mix. The two facilitators assisted in the process and synthesis of ideas, but the ideas were the committees' own.

After initial Logic Models for each theme were drafted, a website was set up to share drafts, and input was received on each theme for a set period of time through open Web entry. From a start time of February 2010 to April of 2011, a university strategic plan was written and communicated to all of the university, community, and the board of regents governing body. A celebration for all the members of the theme committees was held and comments were heard like, "I didn't think this would work, but I actually enjoyed the process." Requests were made to the Office of Education Innovation and Evaluation to do similar facilitations with the Logic Model for other purposes all over the university.

In a fall 2011 report to the campus on the K-State 2025 Strategic Plan, the president reported over five hundred people participating in the process including eighty-four theme committee members and fourteen cochairs. Forty-nine focus groups were conducted, twenty-one formal theme committee meetings were held, hundreds of hours were invested, thousands of comments were made, and three different open comment periods with Web input capability were conducted. The process was open, interactive, and inclusive.

The next academic year, colleges and major units were asked to use the same process and put together their strategic plans. Plans needed to align with the university plan, but not completely encompass it, and to identify which benchmarks were addressed as well as indicate resources of people and money needed to achieve success. Plans were posted to the K-State 2025 website for all to see. A crosswalk of all the college plans to see the connectedness was done. Diversity and internationalization were already identified as common elements in the planning process, and indeed they were reflected in all the plans submitted.

It had worked very well. Departments within colleges and major units were next to write their plans. The same format and open process was requested. What could go wrong?

Spring of 2013. A divided session of the legislature. A June 2 adjournment and a 4 percent total cut to the university budget, that is what could go wrong. The strategic plan in many people's minds had died with the signing of the fiscal year 2014 legislative budget. Budget reallocations had to be made.

REALITY CHECK

Analysis of the college strategic plans showed they had a great deal of "wish list" quality. "We will grow this with new resources." Both the president and provost asked that budget reallocations be made with the strategic plan firmly in mind.

Our absolute conviction was that strategic plans are to be used in building and adding as well as to restructuring and subtracting at the unit level and the university level. A budget cut is a license to stop doing some low priority (nonstrategic) things. The decision making should be made easier with a carefully constructed strategic plan in place.

We had missed the mark by not realizing that faculty and staff were positively engaged in the planning process as long as it meant new resources. When resources needed to be reallocated, or cut entirely, plans were abandoned and retrenchment was immediate.

The air came right out of the optimistic balloon of the strategic planning process. It is indeed more exciting to add to budget building programs, than to restructuring and subtracting. The new era of higher education is not one of building whole scale, but of specific program investment and strategic decision making. These decisions are difficult to make and unpopular.

Over the last thirty years of my participation in public higher education the pattern has been of escalating tuition rates, diminishing public support from states, and the changing environment of federal research funding and accountability. Increased dependence on philanthropic giving and corporate support have partially replaced state support for education.

During that same period, institutions of higher education have expanded their disciplinary offerings, expanded the array of extracurricular and extramural activities, and changed the on-campus living environment. Student-success programming from tutoring to intentional advising has also increased with some gains in persistence and graduation rates but, in the opinion of the author, not enough.

The profile of expectations on university campuses has increased exponentially. Faculty complain, with good reason, that expectations on them continue to rise. The strategic planning that was done set a course for the university and for allowing colleges and departments to decide what part they would each play in advancing the university toward its goal. To continue to be competitive, universities need to identify what can be done well and need to not spread efforts too widely with too lean staffing and resources, which leads to not doing anything well.

Although given license to prioritize and eliminate, faculty are concerned that they will be held responsible for areas they set as lower priority and/or decide to discontinue. There is a lack of confidence with administration, and faculty members still exhibit much cynicism.

LIVING WITH THE STRATEGIC PLAN: THROUGH THICK AND THIN

Staying the course was difficult in the environment, but staying the course was what had to happen. A very careful and conscious decision was communicated to campus in all talks and written pieces that the K-State 2025 Strategic Plan would move forward. A cultural shift of truly identifying as a research-intensive university had begun and was not to be abandoned. A main theme of all communications was that K-State 2025 was now! Strategic planning for diversity, sustainability, and internationalization, common elements of the university plan, went forward using similar representative groups, with open, all-university requests for input.

At the same time, the faculty senate called for a more transparent budget process for the university, and a university budget advisory committee was set up and charged by the president. The committee has representation from faculty senate, classified senate, student government and administration and is chaired by the provost.

Messaging of any important situation is important. At this critical juncture, the president tied his annual goals set for the board of regents and communicated them with the campus, linking each goal to strategic plan themes and their outcomes. All university budget spreadsheets had an additional column added to align the budget revenue or expenditure with a strategic plan theme area.

COMMUNICATION

As the strategic planning and use moved forward, a concept was formed that ties the plan to the university budget, the comprehensive campaign (also being planned), and measurement of progress. We adopted an approach of four pillars: strategic plan, university budget, comprehensive campaign plan, and progress reporting. The overall strategy is to follow the strategic plan, tie it to the comprehensive campaign plan, make budget decisions with the plan, and measure progress on the plan—all broadly communicated to diverse stakeholders on campus and off.

PLAN FATIGUE?

A valued member of the provost's office carefully inquired if there might be some K-State 2025 "fatigue" on campus. There may well be some who are hearing the plan's name often enough to be a bit tired of it. However, I don't see this as a bad thing. The plan, and what it stands for, must be a part of the daily fabric of the university. I interviewed a department head candidate recently, and the main reason they considered applying (after nomination, calls, and recruitment) was that they saw the strategic plan on the Web, felt the university knew where it was going, saw planning was in place to help it get there, and wanted to be a part of it. The number of interviews that included this same conversation reinforces to me the importance of the plan, the planning process, and its consistency. Is it K-State 2025 fatigue, or has the plan been put into the fabric of the university? I think it is part of the fabric. Like the land grant mission, our research, teaching, and engagement areas, our strategic plan distinguishes the university, distinguishes the people here, and sets a course for the future—whatever that future might be.

Chapter Sixteen

University Leadership

A View from the Dark Side

Richard McCarty

For most of my academic career, I have been involved in some form of academic administration at the departmental, school, and provostial levels at two research-intensive universities, the University of Virginia and Vanderbilt University. These positions have included stints as associate chair (two years), interim chair (one year) and department chair (eight and one-half years) at the University of Virginia and dean of the College of Arts and Science (seven years) and provost and vice chancellor for academic affairs (six years) at Vanderbilt University. Sandwiched between Virginia and Vanderbilt was a three-and-one-half-year stint as executive director for science at the American Psychological Association in Washington, DC. My experiences in each of these positions have shaped my approach to academic administration—for better or worse, I might add. In this brief overview, I will focus most of my attention on my views relating to the role of provost, or chief academic officer, at a private research-intensive university like Vanderbilt, although I believe many of these views are generalizable to other settings.

THE IMPORTANCE OF A ROLE MODEL(S)

Without doubt, one person shaped my interest in academic administration soon after I was promoted to associate professor of psychology with tenure at the University of Virginia. In July 1985, Hugh P. Kelly, Commonwealth Professor of Physics, was selected as the dean of the Faculty of Arts and Sciences at the University of Virginia. The two deans prior to Hugh, both distinguished scholars, did little, in my opinion, to engage directly with faculty or students or to promote the centrality of the liberal arts in the life of the university. Almost overnight, Hugh seemed to be everywhere on the campus, and he elevated the critical role played by faculty to a new high. He brought great energy and a wonderful sense of humor to everything he did, and he always deflected credit for any good things that happened to others—most notably, faculty. He played an active role in faculty recruitment and retention efforts across all of the liberal arts disciplines and had a keen eye for talent.

Hugh also recognized the need to establish a success-development effort to support the exciting vision that he was shaping for the College of Arts and Sciences. He devoted himself to meeting with prospective donors in a way that no previous dean had done, and his personal qualities often won the day in securing additional support for faculty and students. He also did the little things, like sending handwritten notes and personally signing hundreds of letters of appreciation, which conveyed in a clear manner his sincerity and his commitment to the mission of his college.

Not surprisingly, Hugh was so successful as dean of the faculty that he was named provost of the university. As university provost, he was now in a position to effect positive change on a much larger scale, and he did so with his characteristically high levels of energy, enthusiasm, and personal charm. Unfortunately, within a few years of being named university provost, Hugh died from complications of prostate cancer. His death in 1992 at age sixty-one was a tragic loss for all whose lives had been touched so powerfully by this kind, generous, and immensely talented man.

I will be the first to say that I am no Hugh Kelly, even when comparing his worst day to my best day. But that isn't the point. I learned a great deal from my primary role model, and my challenge was to infuse as many of his qualities into my efforts as a leader as I could. In nine years, I would have that chance.

Decanal Challenges. When I came to Vanderbilt University in July 2001, I was the fifth dean of the College of Arts and Science in nine years due to a series of tragic circumstances. A major challenge I faced as an externally appointed dean was to learn as much as I could as quickly as I could about the university in general and the College of Arts and Science in particular. Who were the faculty, where were the pockets of existing scholarly strength, where were the opportunities for building stronger departments and programs, what were the sources of frustration among the faculty, what were the students like, how did Arts and Science fit in the overall strategic plans of the university, and so on. With the advice and support of several talented colleagues in the dean's office, we were able to work through a number of these issues in my first year as dean. I also had to convey my long-term commitment to Vanderbilt as often as I could, given the lack of stability in the dean's office prior to my arrival.

The most impactful decisions of any dean are those related to promotion and tenure. In my first semester, I instituted a more rigorous system of review of promotion files that centered on a new faculty-based promotion and tenure committee. Several years later, a committee of recently tenured associate professors was established to evaluate fourth-year faculty reappointment files. Both of these committees remain in place and have contributed in significant ways over the past decade to the quality and integrity of the reappointment and promotion and tenure recommendations that are advanced by the dean to the provost.

A major challenge for the College of Arts and Science when I arrived was an outdated undergraduate curriculum that was originally put into place in the early 1980s. Two previous efforts to revise the curriculum failed to receive a positive faculty vote. I delayed tackling this problem for several years until I had a deeper understanding of the College of Arts and Science and the difficulties that resulted in the two previous failed votes. I established an *ad hoc* curriculum committee made up exclusively of tenured associate professors who represented the humanities, the social sciences, and the natural sciences. Only one of the committee members had played a significant role in the previous efforts, and his institutional knowledge was invaluable to his colleagues. The committee did an outstanding job of formulating a strong initial draft proposal and then made appropriate changes as feedback was received from various constituencies, including faculty, current students, and alumni. It was a very satisfying moment for all when the curriculum received a strongly positive faculty vote and was implemented soon thereafter. That same curriculum, *Achieving Excellence in a Liberal Education* (*AXLE*), has benefited from several tweaks but is still in place a decade later. To the extent that my leadership contributed to the success of having a new curriculum, it was due to frequent one-on-one conversations with faculty leaders at all levels, engagement with students and alumni, and frequent mentions of the process with department chairs and program directors. I also spent time, as did the committee members, in asking key faculty why the two previous efforts had failed. Addressing these shortcomings played an essential role in the success of the effort.

TRANSITION TO THE PROVOST'S OFFICE

After seven years as dean of Arts and Science, I was named provost and vice chancellor for academic affairs in July 2008, following an internal search. Over the past six years, I have expanded my knowledge of higher education significantly, especially in the areas of student life, finance, and academic medical center administration. As I prepare to return to the faculty after thirteen wonderful years in academic administration, I wish to share in the space that remains ten of my most memorable lessons learned.

1. The demands on the provost's time are such that it is very easy to remain in one's office and meet constantly with a small circle of direct reports and other vice chancellors or vice presidents. It is critical that the provost be visible on campus and known to student leaders and the faculty. This requires managing one's schedule carefully to insure that adequate time is available to engage with students and faculty around the campus. Advising students or teaching a class also facilitates that strong connection to the ebb and flow of the academic year. Another simple activity is to go to the cafeteria for lunch several times each week. You will have many opportunities to converse with faculty, staff, and students while there, and it is amazing what you will pick up.

2. Playing a direct role in fundraising activities is important for the provost. Some donors have interests beyond the scope of a single department or school and the provost is well positioned to engage in those conversations for the benefit of the broader institution. These interests may include the freshman experience, undergraduate financial aid, enhancement of the residential experience, interdisciplinary research programs that cross school boundaries, graduate education, or faculty chairs that connect to the experiences of multiple faculty members and across schools.

3. If a provost has a goal of "knowing everything," it is a recipe for disaster. The amount of information that comes into a provost's office on a daily basis is considerable and one needs to decide what to work on directly and what to hand off to a colleague within the office. Having a strong team of vice/associate provosts is critical to the success of any provost, and allowing them decision-making authority is vital to the provision of timely responses to inquiries. Knowing when to manage a given issue versus when to delegate it to a colleague becomes easier with time and the pain of a few mistakes along the way. In the end, the buck stops with the provost, so updates on those items that are delegated are critical.

4. Being as transparent as possible with all direct reports is essential to a provost's success. No one likes a surprise, and, to the extent that one can avoid surprises with frequent communications, being transparent gives everyone the sense of being a part of the decision-making process. Regular meetings with deans and provost office staff, monthly one-on-one meetings with direct reports, e-mail communications, and old-fashioned telephone calls all aid in the flow of information. School

deans are much more effective in leading their schools when they are fully briefed on critical issues as they arise.

5. Managing e-mail is an eternal challenge, especially for a provost. I have an internal rule that I don't leave my office until there are fewer than twenty-five messages in my inbox that have not been resolved. I have a deeply held belief that a prompt answer, especially if it is a relatively straightforward one, is appreciated and allows others to move ahead promptly rather than being held in limbo until the answer arrives. I realize that some e-mails require significant time for analysis and research before an answer can be formulated. However, timeliness is a virtue in my eyes and an important way to convey appreciation for the efforts of others.

6. The provost is the final individual to review promotion and tenure files before they move to the chancellor or president and then on to the trustees. The provost must plan ahead to have the time required to review promotion and tenure files carefully prior to making recommendations to the chancellor or president. There are times when a provost must go against the recommendation of a school dean or even the promotion and tenure review committee at the provost's level, and such decisions are vital to the commitment to excellence that all universities espouse. These decisions can generate controversy, but they must be made.

7. As the complexity of the regulatory environment increases, the provost will often be asked to make decisions that affect the risk profile of the university. Developing a clear sense of when to request support from the Office of General Counsel is another skill that develops with time. A safe rule of thumb is to ask for advice and counsel if there is any doubt. Having clear policies and following those policies is essential to having difficult or controversial decisions sustained.

8. The budget for academic affairs is often developed in and managed by the office of the provost. The provost must focus carefully on the revenue and expense drivers of the budget, with support from the chief financial officer and the provost's budget officer. If a budgeted bottom line is not achieved at the end of a fiscal year, there is nowhere to hide, and the buck stops with the provost. The provost is often presented with opportunities to invest in retention of faculty, cost sharing on a critical piece of equipment, recruitment of new faculty, target-of-opportunity faculty hiring, developing new programs, or addressing an unmet need in student affairs. These opportunities require a balance between fiscal discipline and enhancement of the educational mission of the university, and striking the right balance is more art than science.

9. At Vanderbilt, the office of the dean of students (DoS) reports directly to the provost and is responsible for the student experience outside of the classroom. I have been fortunate to work with a remarkable dean of students, Mark Bandas, who has been a mentor and teacher to me for all of my time at Vanderbilt. Areas of responsibility for the DoS include student government, leadership development, Greek life, campus housing, academic integrity, the Women's Center, Project Safe (sexual assault prevention and support services for survivors), LGBTQI Life, community service activities, multicultural education, religious life, and so on. Staff members in this office and others like it at colleges and universities throughout the United States are available twenty-four hours per day, seven days per week. They often assist students during times of greatest need, and they provide a critical interface to schools and departments so that students are able to remain on track academically.

I have chosen to be an active partner with the DoS, and I have communicated to my direct reports a clear expectation that academic units and student affairs units will work cooperatively for the benefit of our students. I am well aware that, in general, most faculty members have limited knowledge of the work of the DoS, and there are times when I can elevate the work of this office through communications with faculty, staff, and students.

In the past six years as provost, I have been actively involved in two major issues on campus that are connected to the DoS but that have had ramifications across the campus. The first issue involved a challenge to our university's nondiscrimination policy by Christian groups that sought to either restrict membership in their organizations or to prohibit some members from holding leadership positions within the organization. As an example, consider a Christian student organization that is open to all students but would only allow Christian members to run for leadership positions. I was the lead spokesperson on campus for the university's nondiscrimination policy and I met with numerous student and faculty groups and many individuals and small groups to explain the policy and to work toward accommodations when possible. And of course, there was heavy e-mail traffic and telephone calls from alumni and "interested" individuals who viewed our actions as an attack on the freedom of religious expression of our students. This was not a time to delegate; rather, it was a time for me to express publically and through various media the university's position in a calm and clear manner. With the benefit of several years of hindsight, I believe we handled this situation as fairly as we could but, most importantly, we never wavered from the principles of our nondiscrimination policy.

A second issue occurred more recently and involved a possible gang rape of an unconscious female student in a residential hall on the Vanderbilt campus during a summer session. Once again, the DoS was involved from the first moments that this possible sexual assault occurred by providing support services to the survivor and reviewing evidence against the four students who were charged with rape. I have worked closely with the university's general counsel, Audrey Anderson, to ensure that our current policies and procedures are consistent with federal requirements and that we are doing everything possible to prevent sexual assaults from occurring. Ms. Anderson and I made presentations to the faculty members of all schools at the university to begin conversations about how we address the broader issue of sexual assaults on our campus. We also held town hall meetings for faculty, staff, and students to make clear our position on sexual assaults and to ask for the active engagement of the entire university community to confront this issue.

As I prepare this chapter, the trials of the four students are scheduled to occur in two months. But our efforts on campus to support and expand services to prevent sexual violence continue. This is a national challenge of the highest order, and we hope to contribute in positive ways to the unique challenges that exist on college and university campuses.

10. Having a support network of other provosts was very important to me and I strongly encourage others to build such a network. I benefited greatly from colleagues in meetings of the Association of American Universities (AAU), a small offshoot of the AAU provosts' group (The 10 Provosts Group), SECU (Southeastern Conference Academic Consortium), as well as in other irregular meetings. Having a small group of colleagues, who over time become friends, can provide a source of clarity and support during difficult times.

In summary, as I conclude six years of service as provost and seven years of service as dean, I believe more strongly than ever that leadership matters at colleges and universities. How that leadership is expressed varies from person to person and situation to situation. Colleges and universities must constantly develop leadership capacities of the faculty, and occasionally one of those faculty members may be asked to move over to the dark side and take on an academic leadership position. Such an opportunity allows one to effect change at a broader level with the organization. In the end, provosts are often most successful when they serve their faculty colleagues by being catalysts for change. And to the cynics, I submit that a great deal of light and relatively little heat are generated on the dark side.

Chapter Seventeen

Success in Central Administration

Intentionality, Listening, and Optimism

Sally M. Reis

Having spent almost a decade as a university administrator, I enjoyed the opportunity to reflect on the experiences and lessons leading to the ideas discussed in this chapter. I hope that these reflections are helpful without appearing to be self-serving. My intention was to share observations that were not at all obvious to me when I became a central office administrator.

REMEMBERING WHY AM I HERE

After three years, I still need to regularly remind myself why I am in this position (vice provost for academic affairs at the University of Connecticut). After a successful run as a professor, endowed chair holder, and department head, two pivotal events led me to consider the position of vice provost for academic affairs and administration, which I had been offered previously. First, my grant funding was abruptly eliminated after massive federal budget cuts, and I found myself without the funds to continue what had been a very exciting line of research that had resulted in the formation of a top-notch research team and some notable and personally satisfying publications. The second was my continued unhappiness with the lack of progress in a few critical areas at our university, such as innovative online initiatives and research support.

This discontent, coupled with the arrival of a new and innovative president and vibrant central office administrative team, sent a clear signal that change was about to happen. Having been invited to be part of it, I gracefully accepted a new role. That is why, after three years in my current position, I still consider myself fortunate to work for a thoughtful and intelligent president and a dynamic and diligent provost whom I respect. Both have created a work climate that stimulates and engages me.

Any successful central administrator understands that this job is not about her. During my twenty-five years as a professor, my scholarly interests and choice of work came first, or at least first after my students. I published widely, accepted invited keynotes and presentations, had lucrative consulting opportunities, and essentially absorbed myself in my discipline and my own interests. Retrospectively, I have come to understand how little I observed about what happened around me at my university. Any challenge was filtered by how it affected my work, my department, and my research agenda. In my current role, my own research and scholarly interests still surface occasionally but as a secondary pursuit to my service to others; the betterment of my institution is my focus, and my own work is done in stolen hours, a rare morning, or evening. While I unreservedly believe that the best administrators at research institutions maintain their scholarship, the practicality of finding time and focus remains a challenge.

Gone are the days when I had the luxury of a day working on an invited chapter or having a long conversation with my colleagues or graduate students about a creative idea. My efforts are largely devoted to the betterment of my university, our students, and my faculty colleagues; each day's activities are about making things a better university for these essential groups. In many ways, I see my current role as enhancing opportunities and eliminating unnecessary obstructions to faculty and student academic life. This does not mean I don't regularly miss my former life; it just means that I need to understand that that was then and this is now and now is not about me—it is about service to others. I have also begun to understand that giving back has made me feel both happy and satisfied, another unexpected insight about this position.

Another unexpected pleasure that has occurred during the last few years is the feeling of humility I have experienced from knowing more of our faculty than I did when I was a professor or department head. I work with, and for, such intelligent and talented people from whom I have learned so much and for whom I have so much respect. On any given day, I interact with poets, mathematicians, philosophers, nutritionists, doctors, lawyers, social workers, scientists, chemists, art historians, artists, directors, writers, and psychologists. One of the joys of working at a comprehensive research university like UConn is the interaction with so many talented stars, many of whom are world renowned. And it takes so little time to acknowledge others' good work. Taking ten minutes each day to write notes to those who have published books or garnered important grants and giving credit to those who work diligently is a hallmark of good leadership. Showing appreciation for others' good work has been an important lesson in my administrative career and one that I have learned from the best leaders for whom I have worked.

ENJOYING PROBLEM SOLVING

I find it difficult to believe this, but I have come to enjoy the creative process that accompanies effective problem solving with routine problems that our faculty and department heads encounter. Trouble with travel policies? Difficulty with online assessment of teaching? Challenges with veterans' transfer credits? Mission creep? Regional campus resources? Cognitive dissonance? Academic power struggles? The diverse issues encountered in my position require constant study to understand the many challenges associated with a large public research university.

Initially, I spent hours each night reading and learning about programs, policies, centers, programs, procedures, and all the complexities of running the institution at which I had worked for over two decades. After three years of learning, I still find chance encounters with areas about which I know little and therefore need to delve into unanticipated contextual material and the personalities that frequently accompany complex issues. My background in educational psychology and training in creative problem solving has also helped. The steps in effective problem solving, that is, the need to gather information and identify the real problem, find ideas and solutions to solve the problem, and then seek acceptance of a solution have helped me in my current position. Working with the talented people around me and understanding the myriad ways in which they contribute to problem solving has also been gratifying. When my colleagues and I are able to solve a problem that makes life easier for our faculty or students, I often feel a sense of satisfaction similar to when learning an article has been accepted in a competitive journal—go figure!

LISTENING AND THEN LISTENING SOME MORE

Effective administrating, at least in my style, requires the practiced skill of listening well. Some administrators with whom I have worked violate this essential skill—they interrupt, talk too much, or show impatience with others who are not as facile with words or able to synthesize as quickly as might be hoped for. I have learned to listen intently, even when I already know some of the information that is being conveyed. Learning not to interrupt (and remembering to thank my parents for the demands placed on me for good manners that were a requirement of my childhood) has led to effective outcomes for me. Becoming a good listener and enabling those who tell me their ideas or problems without interrupting has actually saved me time and resulted in the identification of ideas to resolve problems as the story unfolds. Active listening makes a difference as it encourages quiet and attentive rephrasing of what my colleagues have said, which often avoids misunderstandings. In active listening, I learn the details, which often produces better problem solving opportunities.

When Howard Baker died recently, an NPR reporter called him one of the greatest politicians in the United States, someone who achieved compromises across the aisle. The reporter credited his talents as an eloquent listener. In academe, an administrator who is an eloquent listener is more able to accomplish tasks and does not have to worry about always having to say the right thing. Too many administrators feel the need to be the smartest person in the room, or at least to appear that way. I have learned to listen and continue to strive to listen more eloquently each year and have come to believe that more administrators should take the time to listen more carefully to the faculty they serve.

ASKING THE RIGHT QUESTIONS AND COLLECTING THE RIGHT DATA

Regardless of what administrative position one holds, the power of making decisions and planning new initiatives based on data is becoming increasingly obvious. The role of using data to research background information and make decisions will become even more important as the federal government raises tougher questions for higher education. How many students graduate and in how many years, and do we have a gap among those who are first-generation college students? Scrutiny about how carefully we use our resources is becoming more of a daily grind, and this will only increase in public institutions as both parents and political leaders ask us to provide even more information and statistics about conditions in higher education. Understanding data and what data you need to effectively understand a problem and, more importantly, utilizing data to engage in higher level and more informed conversations saves time and creates a more scholarly tone to conversations about the ways we invest our resources and how we measure the impact of those investments. It is also one of the most intriguing and promising ways to provide other administrators, faculty, and staff with an understanding of how we can measure whether something has worked or not worked, leading to better results.

I ask for relevant, pertinent data on a regular basis and share it widely—before, during, and even after decisions have been made so those in positions of making change can know the impact of the decisions that have been made. I particularly like data gathering that demonstrates outcomes that occur before we chose one path instead of another. Making decisions based on sound data demonstrates careful decision making and problem solving and is appreciated by those who care about both of these traits in administrators.

OPERATING WITH HONESTY AND RESPECT

Another important lesson I have learned is to tell the truth—as painful and difficult as it can be to do so. Telling colleagues that they have not been effective in their position, or that it is time for new leadership, or that they are being terminated is one of the most demanding and necessary tasks that administrators have. I have learned to deliver bad news with compassion but to do it directly and with candor. No one wants to give this kind of news and certainly no one wants to hear it, either, so it is better to give the news quietly, kindly, and move on. The first few times I had to terminate someone's employment were among my most difficult tasks but I have learned that kindness and compassion can make a difficult situation better. Telling the truth also made a difference in those situations.

Creating a culture of honesty also means that those around you are more honest with you, and this exchange of honesty seems to breed a culture of respect. The most effective higher education leaders are those who tell the truth and who want to work well with faculty and gain and keep their colleagues' trust and confidence. When I need advice, I seek it from those deans and department heads with whom I have worked who are the most respected at our university. Those who have lasted but also have done things—created programs, changed directions—are wise colleagues who provide valuable lessons.

PROJECTING OPTIMISM AND HUMOR

I have learned another trite but true rule for success in central administration—no one wants to work with someone who is pessimistic, controlling, and/or negative. When I take the time to reflect about leaders who have personally inspired me, each was optimistic and praised those around them who had done well or succeeded at some task. At the end of a day of meetings, I have to remind myself that the fifth group I am meeting with does not care if I am tired or how busy I am—they care that they have a window of time to tell me about their initiatives and remind me of the importance of the work they are doing and how important it is to them. An optimistic leader can convince others that they have the capacity to achieve at higher levels, can portray an optimistic future in which individuals can attain success, and can change conversations from what is wrong with the current situation to how to improve it and how we can improve both personally and professionally. While pessimistic leaders see the world as a narrow tunnel with limited turns and entrances, positive and optimistic leaders view it as an open landscape, filled with different paths and possibilities.

Having a sense of humor helps in all high-stress positions. I try to approach tense situations with humor and bring levity to my interactions with the highly professional staff and other vice provosts with whom I work. I try to lighten the mood when difficult situations arise. Laughter is an excellent antidote to stress, and despite the daily challenges we confront, I work to inject some humor into each day. Bad stuff happens daily, and the way that we react to stress often makes a difference in how problems are solved. If we approach a big problem as solvable and remain optimistic in the face of challenges, issues are resolved. Even if we can't, the team of folks working on the problem remains optimistic and hopeful and continues trying to solve it. If we approach any problem with anger or cynicism or a negative attitude, we are more likely to create the conditions that perpetuate, rather than ameliorate, the problem.

BUILDING A TEAM

Any successes I have experienced over the last few years have occurred when someone I have selected for a leadership opportunity has been able to build his or her own team. In this time period, we have made some very big changes in several areas that report to me and each has required a new leader who created a new group. To make the changes that I believed were necessary required new attitudes and change. Each new leader was able to move to a new level of success by creating his or her own group. Whether it was a new Honors director, a new e-campus or career development leader, or a new assistant vice provost for institutional support, each new position led to positive changes.

Creating new energy in old systems required me to find new people who understood and supported a new vision for their sphere of influence as well as giving them encouragement and support to make the changes needed. A quote I love by Franklin D. Roosevelt says, "It is a terrible thing to look over your shoulder when you are trying to lead—and find no one there." I took the time to find good people, and when I looked over my shoulder, they were working just as diligently as I would have expected. I think that leadership is a creative process—and that good leaders need to simultaneously give freedom as well as time to focus and, at times, some direction.

But one thing I know for sure—people who work for me feel free to take ownership and be innovative. They are not afraid to make decisions and challenge outmoded policies and rules that no longer work. They feel free to innovate, and they work with pride, knowing that I am behind them—not the other way around. A core value that I believe each member of my group knows is that I place a high value on their ideas and that I understand that it takes time to create a strong product and to foster creativity and build on strengths. These traits are very important to me, in fact, as important as anything I believe in: giving time for creativity to occur, looking for strengths, and trusting good people to do good work.

EXPLORING WOMEN'S LEADERSHIP STYLES

Perhaps due to some of the research that I have conducted on eminent women, I am often asked whether I believe female leaders' styles and traits differ from men's. During the last few years, my views on this have solidified. Although I have noticed some differences in the style of high-level female administrators, I have also perceived differences in the ways that people react to various male and female leaders. As has been noted in some academic research and popular-press books about gender differences and communications, John Gray and Deborah Tannen have suggested that men and women communicate differently, as men use conversations to establish status and control in relationships, and women use their communication skills to create bonds and strong relationships with others. Generalizations cannot explain the complicated individual traits that underlie the communication and leadership styles of male and female leaders. Some women establish their status and administrative roles immediately, and others are much less obvious. Some male leaders take the time to create the relationships for which female leaders are known. The best of these leaders, regardless of their gender, seem to treat others the way they would like to be treated, with compassion, openness, and interest. The best leaders relate well to those who work for them, give meaningful praise when it is deserved, and serve as mentors and role models for positive action.

CONCLUSION

The most successful administrators I have known in academe practice intentional respect, listening, and optimism. They make others want to do their best. They don't waste time with unnecessary meetings, and they are not focused on themselves, but rather on others. My most successful colleagues consistently tell me they enjoy their work because they believe they can make a positive difference for the faculty and students for whom they work.

Some things make the environment you work in a better fit for you than others. For example, I believe it is easier to be successful at an institution that is a good fit for your interests and talents—for example, understanding the need for time for one's own research makes an administrator at a research university more aware of the need to make others' research an institutional priority. Trying to stay research active is also a way to remain in touch with your colleagues and earn the respect of the faculty that you represent.

As administrators, we can't control very much, but we can control our optimism. Each day, I try to remember that for the small number of problems with faculty I face, hundreds of other excellent faculty members work diligently and produce at high levels. Given the small number of problems with students that cross my desk, thousands of students cause no problems whatsoever.

To create positive administrative changes, my role is pretty straightforward. I try to rally a group of creative, smart people, put incentives in place, and establish opportunities for them to work with me to create something new and innovative. Together, those of us who have chosen to work in central administration have to remember that we can't make too many changes at once, have to trust and respect those around us who do important work, treat people well, and give creative opportunities to others. When we do that, we remain open to creative solutions, keep our eyes on the future, and remember to accomplish what we know is in the best interests of our students and our university, for, ultimately, any changes we are trying to make will only be successful if they benefit both.

Chapter Eighteen

Where You Stand Is Where You Sit

Moving Up and Down the
Academic Administrative Ladder

Robert V. Smith

Where you stand depends on where you sit. . . . The first lesson of Miles' Law
is that when a person changes positions organizationally, he or she changes
both perspective and responsibility.

—Rufus E. Miles, Jr. (1910–1996)
(Examiner, U.S. Bureau of the Budget; Assistant Secretary,
Department of Health Education and Welfare; Senior Fellow,
Woodrow Wilson School of Public and International Affairs,
Princeton University)

The wisdom of Miles' Law—that your perspective, advocacy, and preparation for a new administrative post requires thoughtful planning and execution—is at the heart of this book. In this chapter, I offer a roadmap for the
journey from faculty member to first administrative assignment (e.g., chair)
to central administrative posts. At the end, I offer some suggestions for post-
career opportunities.

IS THE JOURNEY FOR YOU?

Academic administration is not for everyone, and initial forays into the administrative world ideally should be pursued only after one has developed a
solid reputation as an academic scholar with notable accomplishments in
teaching, research, and outreach. Indeed, some of the best academic adminis-

135

trators are those who see synergy in the three roles and have a record of integrated scholarship. Thus, with the "arrogance of confidence" to succeed, as noted by the eminent sociologist William Julius Wilson, the well-established academic may launch an administrative career—with one critical caveat. Administrative work is more about service to the institution and its faculty, students, and staff than about self-advancement. So, unless you are capable of subsuming personal ambitions for others and an institution—think twice about an administrative life.

There is one rejoinder to the above advice: Don't give up research and scholarship as an academic administrator. In fact, there are examples of faculty members who have maintained major scientific laboratory-based programs while contributing broadly to administrative operations. But, most often, those who serve in more traditional academic administrative posts find it difficult to maintain major disciplinary research programs. However, this is not to say that administrative assignments are devoid of scholarly challenges and opportunities. To the contrary, some of the most effective academic administrators are those who weave their scholarly efforts into the needs of academic administration. Thus, we find accomplished department chairs and deans writing books on "being chairs or deans."

Provosts and presidents who have authored chapters in this work are also authors of major works on the challenges and vicissitudes of administrative life. Accordingly, no one should remove his or her scholarly cap when becoming an administrator. Indeed, there are internal papers, reports, and communiqués to craft in creative and persuasive ways that test the limits of scholarly talents. As importantly, with appropriate dedication, skill, and experience, you'll find that people outside of your institution will become interested in your thoughts as well. Journeying forth, consider how this scholarly approach may begin with an interview for a first administrative post.

INTERVIEWS

An interview is improved by gathering extensive background information about the new institution and position, from institutional or unit strategic plans and programs to people who may become future colleagues. Google™, or equivalent "image searches," helps with the identification and recognition of names and faces of people that are likely to participate in the interview process.

A formal presentation, typically required and well prepared with Power-Point or equivalent technology, assists with prompts for presentation comments. Take the opportunity to imbed images of the new unit or institution with imagery of programs or units that you have previously led, perhaps with examples of ideas that might be imported into the new "position."

During the interview, practice the advice of philosopher Harold Rosen, "to seek what others need" through good listening and drawing out the thoughts of others. Remember that an interview—especially for administrative posts—is a two-way interaction, with opportunities not only to exhibit skills and experiences but also to demonstrate interest in the needs and aspirations of those you may serve or work with in a new post.

After an interview, consider following up with e-mail notes to key people met during the process—indicating gratitude for the opportunity to share some time and perhaps with a specific point or two. Few things are more impressive than the simple follow-up note—poignantly demonstrating thoughtfulness and kindness.

"PROMISE OF A NEW POSITION" PAPER

Once an administrative post is offered and accepted, consider the promise it offers to you and the unit or institution you will be serving. The double entendre of the word "promise" offers an opportunity to prepare a paper that allows you to not only reflect on your joy in accepting a new challenge but also what you intend to promise the people you will be serving—in new and special ways. Politicians are fond of preparing "position papers," which outline their views on policy and other matters. The idea of "position papers" also has merit for nonpolitical professionals and is enhanced by use of the intriguing title of "The Promise of a New Position."

In the paper, be sure to comment on the position as a meaningful leadership opportunity—an opportunity to help make a difference in the future of the institution being served. While noting the promises you intend to make to the people who report to you, describe anticipated hopes for the unit you will be serving along with the values you will embrace while carrying out your responsibilities. This part is tricky. On the one hand, you have ideas on where you would like the relevant unit to go (vision), what milestones the vision will require to become reality (goals and objectives), and how it can all be accomplished (action steps and initiatives). But how do you convey these ideas without leaving the impression that you are going to take your colleagues someplace without their input? A way to avoid this negative assessment is to pose a set of hypothetical questions that provide clues to your thinking without your being perceived as getting too "far out in front" of the people you will be serving.

The questions should be customized according to your current understanding of the unit. However, the questioning signals that you do not have all the answers. The questions can also be crafted to suggest that you will be seeking answers through the unit's faculty members, students, and staff.

The questioning portion of the paper can be used to segue into a section on ideas of how the answers and further information will be gathered. Here, you can signal intent to meet with individuals and groups following a commitment to reading previous planning documents and reports that may pertain to the future operations of the unit. Consider coupling the latter allusions with a preliminary outline of your anticipated communication strategies.

DEVELOPING AND MAINTAINING
A WRITTEN LEGACY

People in academic leadership positions commonly develop newsletters or similar vehicles for keeping their constituents informed. My purpose in developing Web-based journals, however, went beyond the mere sharing of information. Thus, as provost at the University of Arkansas (UA), All Things Academic (ATA; libinfo.uark.edu/ata/) was developed and published on the University Libraries website four times annually during 2000–2008. An analogous journal (All Things Texas Tech [ATTT]; www.depts.ttu.edu/provost/attt/) was published twice yearly for four years when I was provost at Texas Tech University. I used both ATA and ATTT to discuss positions, policies, and possible academic initiatives through articles (at least one per issue) that were solo-authored or coauthored with other leaders in the university (e.g., president, vice president for research, dean).

Besides providing vehicles for keeping the university communities informed about "views from provost office," ATA and ATTT were used to engage the academic communities, offering opportunities for serious contributions from faculty members, students, and staff. The contributions, in turn, were referenced when developing presentations for meetings with shared governance organizations (e.g., faculty and staff senates) and in conducting all-university forums on matters of general importance.

CONSIDERING CHAIR, DIRECTOR, AND DEAN POSTS

A person appointed as chair or head is charged with administering an academic department. But fewer academics are familiar with perceptions about the differences between chairs and heads.

A "chair" is often perceived as a choice of the faculty and in some cases may actually be designated through a faculty vote, but chairs are either clearly appointed by a dean or with significant involvement of a dean. A "head," on the other hand, may be perceived as principally the appointee of the dean, but deans will note that department heads would not be appointed without input from relevant faculty. The literature on departmental leadership tends to focus exclusively on the terminology of the "department chair." Regardless of working title, chairs typically assume a set of roles and responsibilities that place them "in the middle"—between faculty and deans. Thus, they face challenges parallel to those of deans, but with more focused responsibilities.

Books on chairing academic departments tend to focus on chairs' primary roles and responsibilities in managing, leading, developing faculty, and studying (i.e., personal research and scholarship), with the caveat that faculty members contemplating the assumption of chairs' positions may be least prepared to assume leadership and faculty development roles.

"Director," as an academic administrative title, applies to myriad responsibilities, from research centers or institutes to interdisciplinary academic units to administrative services units to heads of schools that are often imbedded in collegiate units. The title and position of "dean," on the other hand, is generally reserved exclusively for the head of a school or college in which the unit head reports to the institution's chief academic officer. Dean-led academic units are usually larger and more complex units, including colleges of arts and sciences, which may have dozens of departments and hundreds of faculty members. Thus, deans often assume responsibilities for very broad academic landscapes and all that that implies relative to strategic planning, policy development, and budget management. Deans also have the added responsibilities of appointing significant numbers of chairs and administrative staff along with fundraising.

MOVING UP TO VICE PROVOST, VICE PRESIDENT, OR PROVOST

As one moves from a dean-level post to positions at the vice provost, vice president, and provost levels, the landscape gets broader and deeper. Problems become more complex and more nettlesome relative to overall institutional liabilities. Compliance matters alone (e.g., animal and human-subjects research, auditing, safety, sexual harassment) can occupy extraordinary blocks of time and effort, often with teams of players including university counsel. Thus, one comes to work each day anticipating that something new and different may turn up on the horizon. The incidences and stories may at times be disconcerting, but rarely dull.

The closer one comes to the executive office (e.g., president or chancellor), the more one becomes enveloped in planning and policy making decisions that help—at once—to keep institutions moving forward and out of trouble. Thus, it takes a sense of adventure, curiosity, and a willingness to deal with ambiguity to survive initially and fare well in the long term.

ACADEMIC EXECUTIVE OFFICER POSITIONS

Presidents and chancellors of single institutions or university systems may come under the rubric of academic executive officers (AEOs), with roles and responsibilities that are in many ways unique to higher education. The uniqueness stems in part from reporting responsibilities—typically to boards of laypersons referred to variously as *governors, regents, trustees,* or *visitors.* Herein lies an additional layer of complexity and political vicariousness because state governors frequently appoint boards of public institutions, which carries the baggage of political partisanship and patronage since board members are frequently appointed from among significant donors to a governor's campaign fund. Election of board members doesn't solve all difficulties, as partisan electioneering and maneuvering may place politics at a higher priority than the overall good of institutions. In private institutions—religiously affiliated or not—self-perpetuating boards may be subject to favoritism or cronyism in the appointment and reappointment of board members. The analysis is a way of signaling how political the appointment of an AEO can be in a major university or university system.

Despite professional antecedents, newly appointed AEOs need to understand the political landscape defined by board members and citizens in a given state and region of the country. This understanding includes attempts to divine how all major decisions will be read politically as well as for their soundness in terms of an institution's mission and cultural ethos. The university or system AEO is also the 24/7 spokesperson and public relations and front line development officer for the institution. Thus, great portions of her or his time will be devoted to efforts external to the institution—whether they involve local chambers of commerce, editorial advisory boards, benefactors or prominent alumni, and not least of all, the students, faculty, and staff. In short, a job well done allows for little down time or "fatigue."

Despite the AEO demands alluded to above, many academics enjoy the challenges and edginess of the AEO role, which clearly requires the broadest possible view of the landscape. The job also affords opportunities to meet not only the boorish, but also some of the brightest and most entertaining personalities that have ties to higher education institutions. The experiences therefore can be heady—at least at times.

Because of the inherent risks and liabilities associated with AEO positions, exit strategies are more often than not negotiated along with the acceptance of posts. The strategies may include severance and development leaves or delayed payment options—sometimes tied to performance or longevity in a position. These matters need attending to along with realistic assessments of potential outcomes.

The higher one rises in the academic chain of command, the harder and faster one may fall, for reasons that may have little or no relationship to one's performance. Such scenarios are understandable, given the nature of boards and their typical remoteness from higher education. Thus, AEOs, provosts, and other administrators need to be philosophical in terms of their fates, recalling always that they serve at the pleasure of their supervisors, so caveat emptor!

POST-CAREER OPPORTUNITIES

Whether a dean, provost, or AEO steps down or is asked to step down, or decides to retire, the following question might be considered: Is there life after posts in academic administration, especially at the terminus of a career? At one time, we thought of sixty-five as a magic retiring age. Now, we find individuals working well beyond seventy and the options have broadened.

Of course, the majority of academic administrators hold tenure in a unit related to their disciplinary expertise so they may "go back to teaching." This is not always as easy as it sounds, as expectations for teaching, research, and service may exceed what the seasoned administrator is prepared for or feels comfortable with. Thus, some former AEOs and provosts, for example, may find "niches" as heads of specialty programs or centers.

Fortunately, opportunities have expanded for the "retired" academic administrator, including (1) search consultant; (2) interim post or posts at other colleges and universities; (3) higher education consulting.

Academic search firms often hire former academic administrators to provide search-consulting services to colleges and universities. The work is often done out of one's home and requires considerable time on the telephone locating and speaking with prospective candidates for academic jobs at various levels. The search consultant will also spend time at off-campus interviews, making arrangements for interviews, scheduling, and having conversations with search committees and job candidates. The work includes the satisfaction of making a difference, getting to know intelligent and interesting people throughout the world, and travel to different parts of the country.

The second option of serving in interim academic administrative posts may be facilitated by a number of firms, including the Registry for College and University Presidents (www.registry-online.org), which has a listing of over four hundred retired senior academic officers and has been placing members in interim CEO positions for over twenty years and other interim posts (e.g., deans, vice presidents, provosts) for more than ten years. The postings may last from three months to three years and typically offer exciting challenges for transitional leadership in institutions of various missions and sizes.

The third option, academic consulting, typically involves contracting as an independent agent with a firm that has been engaged by a college or university for various purposes (e.g., strategic planning, organizational re-configuration, federal compliance matters).

In conclusion, I hope that this short essay has brought some joy, some insight, some good information, and possibly some sage advice that may be useful in your work and academic administrative career. *Bon voyage et bonne chance*!

Chapter Nineteen

Bold Aspirations

A Community Effort

Jeffrey S. Vitter

The field of higher education today faces unprecedented challenges and opportunities—involving issues of student access and affordability, timely graduation and graduation rates, the financial viability of universities, state and federal budget reductions, and public questioning of the intrinsic value of higher education. Disruptive innovations—such as MOOCs, competency-based education, and ubiquitous computing—are challenging traditional business models and opening up new ways of educating students.[1] Those universities that strategically navigate these swirling waters will position themselves among the leading universities of tomorrow.

A challenge many universities face is that, culturally, they are relatively slow to change. That feature of stability has served them well in the past. In fact, some of the world's most enduring institutions are universities, tracing their origins back several centuries. While most members of a university community would acknowledge a number of the looming challenges on the horizon, relatively few might see significant change as urgent.

At the University of Kansas (or KU, as we call it), we are engaged in sweeping change to transform the university. In this chapter, I discuss the framework for our transformation, which we call *Bold Aspirations: The Strategic Plan for the University of Kansas, 2012–2017*.[2] The underlying subtext is about how comprehensive campus dialog and engagement can lead to meaningful change in the short term and position the university for long-term success.

STRUCTURING THE PLANNING PROCESS

We launched *Bold Aspirations* in October 2011, after spending the preceding 2010–2011 academic year in a vigorous campus-wide strategic planning effort. Over 160 individuals—representing thought leaders from faculty, staff, students, alumni, and the surrounding community—took part in either the steering committee, its four work groups, or the four strategic initiative summit planning groups. During the prior year, three task forces of faculty and staff appointed by Chancellor Bernadette Gray-Little conducted a preparatory study of important issues in improving research, admissions, and retention and graduation.

The strategic plan steering committee, which I co-chaired along with Merrill Distinguished Professor Mabel Rice, first convened in October 2010. The fifty-plus members of the committee began with a frank, data-driven analysis of KU's strengths, weaknesses, opportunities, and threats that created an immediate sense of urgency and excitement. We compared KU with its peer universities and fellow members in the Association of American Universities in areas such as federal research expenditures, faculty awards, first-year retention, six-year graduation rates, and graduate research support.

A telling comparison was the finding that the general education requirement of seventy-two credit hours for the BA degree in our College of Liberal Arts and Sciences was far more than typical requirements, which were in the range of thirty to forty-five hours at peer universities. As a result, our undergraduate students lacked the flexibility to avail themselves fully of the potentially life-changing experiences that KU offers, such as study abroad, undergraduate research, internships, and experiential learning. The requirements were complex and lacked a compelling rationale. There was no common and coherent university curriculum, and as a result, retention and graduation rates suffered. In fact, nearly 20 percent of undergraduates who applied for degrees were turned down because one or more of their general education requirements remained unmet.

As the steering committee proceeded, it formulated six key goals based upon its discussions and the data presented. Goals 1–4 focused upon undergraduate education, doctoral education, research, and engaged scholarship. Goals 5 and 6—revolving around developing people and resources—served as enablers of the preceding four.

For the important work of developing the strategies and action steps for achieving the first four goals, the steering committee formed cross-campus work groups, entitled

1. Energizing the (Undergraduate) Educational Environment (EEE);
2. Elevating Doctoral Education (EDE);
3. Driving Discovery and Innovation (DDI); and

4. Engaging Scholarship for Public Impact (ESPI).

With widespread interaction by the KU community, the EEE work group formulated strategies and action steps for goal 1 around key issues in undergraduate education, such as establishing a vibrant outcomes-based curriculum, how to improve student recruiting, and helping students advance through KU. For goals 2, 3, and 4, the other three work groups likewise developed strategies and action steps in their respective domains.

The steering committee as a whole developed the strategies and action steps for the remaining two goals—goals 5 and 6—about enabling people and building resources. The resulting six goals and the twenty-two strategies of *Bold Aspirations* are summarized in figures 19.1 and 19.2.

DIRECT INVOLVEMENT OF THE KU COMMUNITY

A distinguishing feature of KU's strategic planning effort was its remarkable level of transparency. At the start of the process, we publicized to the entire KU community—for the first time in the university's history—the comparative statistics and assessment that the steering committee had just grappled with during its first meeting.[3] By doing so, we signaled to one and all that this great university encouraged active self-examination and a culture of excellence.

Most important was the engagement of the KU leadership and the entire KU community in the planning process. The fact that we would do something significant was determined by KU leadership and the steering committee. How we would do it was determined by the entire KU community. From the very beginning, the clear message went out that this strategic planning exercise would be different from those prior. We were serious about doing what it takes for KU to excel and advance to the next level. We encouraged the KU community to participate actively in the process and contribute their ideas and expertise. In essence, we created a structured process, as represented by the six overarching goals, and a mechanism for bottom-up input to develop the strategies and action steps to realize those goals as part of a coherent, shared vision.[4]

For example, in addressing the issue of undergraduate curriculum, the EEE work group started from scratch and asked the simple question, "What educational goals should every KU student achieve by the time of graduation?" In order to set the desired tone for involvement, the work group solicited nominations from across campus, and over seven hundred people responded. After combining like entries, they then asked each department (or school, for those without departments) to prioritize the submitted list of educational goals by convening one or more faculty meetings so that every

Jeffrey S. Vitter

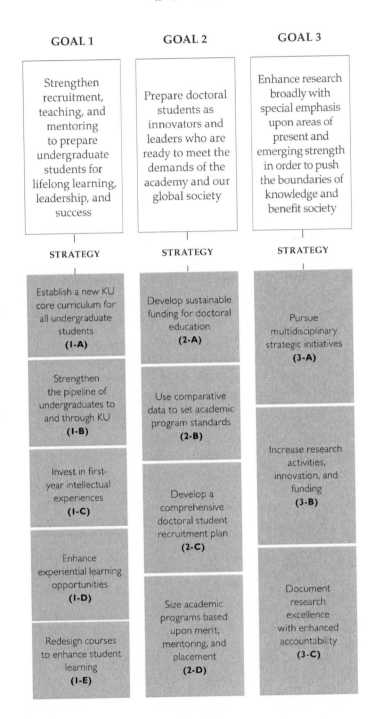

Figure 19.1.

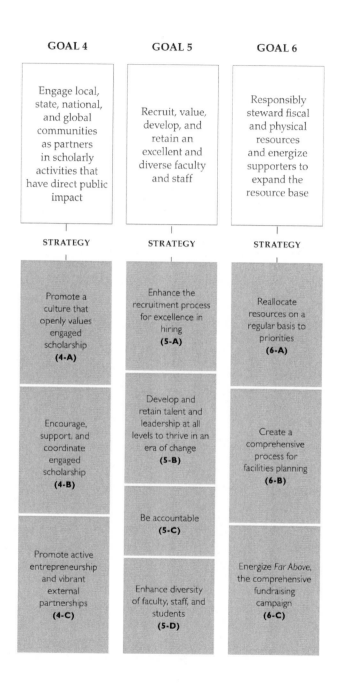

Figure 19.2.

single faculty member could individually weigh in. The work group similarly conducted focus groups with students and alumni to gather their prioritizations.

What emerged from that input was a strong consensus of six educational goals to be the basis of a new curriculum. After *Bold Aspirations* was launched, further engagement with campus led to learning outcomes and options for how to meet those educational goals. A new university curriculum committee, with input from university governance, encapsulated the educational goals, learning outcomes, and paths to completion into what has now become KU's first-ever common curriculum, the KU Core. The individual schools mapped their school-wide requirements to the KU Core, and the KU Core successfully went into effect in August 2013.

Other forms of involvement and input in the planning process took the form of surveys, blogs, departmental visits, and town hall meetings. For example, as the steering committee worked on the "people" enablers of goal 5, it used the results of a survey with 1,664 responses, and the annual Staff Leadership Summit provided additional input. For goal 3, each department designated a representative to determine which data should be collected and to advise on the design and implementation of what became our faculty activity reporting system, PRO.

As provost, I make it a priority to visit departmental faculty meetings and unit staff meetings on a regular basis, which during the planning process permitted me to interact directly with over a thousand individuals on a variety of planning matters. We held focus groups with hundreds of faculty, staff, students, alumni, and external partners. Campus-wide town hall meetings, also viewable on the web, provided regular opportunities for input and updates.

The goal was for every individual who wanted to give meaningful input to have the opportunity to do so—and in multiple ways. That sort of inclusive approach brings forward the best ideas, and in every instance it has led to tangible improvements in the plan. Even more importantly, broad engagement reassures people that their ideas have been heard and carefully considered, which in turn promotes the buy-in and trust necessary for successful implementation.

STRATEGIC INITIATIVES—CAMPUS-WIDE MULTIDISCIPLINARY RESEARCH PRIORITIES

A unique component of *Bold Aspirations* is its focus on big, bold research initiatives that harness KU expertise and address some of the world's compelling grand challenges. By their nature, such challenges are too complex to be solved by any single discipline and necessarily must draw upon multiple perspectives working in synergy. The DDI work group launched a process in fall 2010 to identify campus-wide research priorities that build upon KU's intellectual strengths, tap into additional funding resources, and make the world a better place. The resulting priorities became KU's four strategic initiative themes:

1. Sustaining the Planet, Powering the World;
2. Promoting Well-Being, Finding Cures;
3. Building Communities, Expanding Opportunities; and
4. Harnessing Information, Multiplying Knowledge.

What was especially significant was how we determined them—with transparency and bottom-up input. We issued a campus-wide call for proposals with clear criteria and vetting process. The resulting conversations and collaborations by faculty, staff, and students across campus were truly energizing. To help inform those conversations, the college and every school, as well as several research centers, publicized a list of their areas of emphasis and expertise.

By the February 28, 2011, due date, the DDI work group received 104 proposals, which were then posted publicly for review and comment. Over nine hundred individuals took part as authors, on average each participating in two and one-half proposals. National experts and deans reviewed the proposals and combined the most promising ones into the themes that form our four strategic initiatives.

In the months following the fall 2011 launch of *Bold Aspirations*, we organized all-day university-wide summits around each of the four initiatives—each drawing full crowds of over 225 participants. Many of the original proposals, as well as those put together as a result of the summits, have since gone on to garner significant research funding and results. A regular seed funding mechanism continues to encourage collaboration. We also initiated a series of faculty cluster hires revolving around the four themes, building upon funding provided by the state of Kansas for a dozen distinguished professors, to bring further intellectual strength to KU.

FUNDING BOLD ASPIRATIONS

A practical consideration in implementing a strategic plan is how to fund it—the topic of goal 6 in *Bold Aspirations*. We were fortunate at KU to receive two consecutive influxes of recurring funding from the state for growing our engineering student body and for hiring distinguished professors in support of strategic initiatives. However, for the most part, we knew that significant additional state funding would be hard to come by. As a result, KU is undertaking a pair of major initiatives concurrently with *Bold Aspirations* that were incorporated into goal 6.

In April 2012, KU publicly launched its $1.2 billion comprehensive capital campaign, *Far Above: The Campaign for Kansas.* And in the chapter "Changing for Excellence," Diane Goddard, vice provost for administration and finance, outlines our initiative to do more with less and reallocate freed-up resources to strategic goals. She does a fine job of articulating the many challenges in identifying and implementing administrative efficiencies. Undertaking three major initiatives at once increases the sheer amount of change at the university, but achieving our strategic goals would not be possible without key resources.

IMPLEMENTATION MOVING FORWARD

The implementation of *Bold Aspirations*, now nearing the end of year 3, has followed a similar path of feedback, inclusion, and accountability. The implementation committee chaired by Sara Rosen, senior vice provost for academic affairs, measures and reports on our progress, adjusts strategies as needed, and solicits input for how to "phase in" the action steps.

Each year as part of the Provost Retreat, deans weigh in on immediate next priorities and how to manage the pace of change. Components we need to flesh out further become topics of focused working groups, as the case with doctoral funding, course redesign, and advising.

LESSONS LEARNED

The main lesson learned—which forms the subtext for this chapter—is how crucially important it is to engage the broader community, seek input, and communicate transparently. By doing so, we developed trust, buy-in, and a sense of shared ownership among the various stakeholder groups, which enabled a successful launch and implementation.

Another key lesson is focus. We focused the plan on particular priorities where we really wanted to move the needle. In five years, after significant progress, focus may well shift to a different set of priorities. Focus is also crucial for the implementation. Even though our plan is more narrowly focused than some plans, we are committed to implementing all that we said we would do, and we have made progress on each of the sixty-one specific action steps. For that reason, we must be careful to "phase in" our action steps so as not to overwhelm deans, department chairs, faculty, and staff with the pace of change. In this arena, input and communication again come to the fore. In fact, in those instances when we interjected too much change at one time, it tended to be because we were not sufficiently mindful of the pulse of the community, and the fix has been to reengage the various stakeholders to prioritize actions and focus more appropriately. Generally, we have found that the components of our plan that are most focused tended to be the easiest to implement successfully.

Change is often difficult to deal with, and when the pace of change is high, it is important to utilize tested principles of change management—such as frequent and transparent communication, strong leadership support, and building upon small wins. As part of Changing for Excellence, we formed a change management committee that trained facilitators to assist units throughout the process by helping them understand the dynamics of change. It served as a unique and important addition to our process, helping to manage the emotional roadblocks to change that could derail the work at hand.

Ultimately, the proof of the pudding is in the eating—how the plan is implemented. Input, communication, transparency, and accountability remain crucial aspects to achieving long-term success. The will of an institution to transform itself is powerful. When done in a way that embraces a shared vision and preserves core strengths, the institution can and will position itself for long-term success.

ACKNOWLEDGMENTS

Thanks go to Linda Luckey, Jack Martin, Sara Rosen, and Gavin Young for their advice and feedback.

NOTES

1. Dean Ann Brill describes educational disruption and recent initiatives in the field of journalism and new media in the chapter "Disruption, Innovation, and Journalism Education."

2. Available on the KU web pages at www.provost.ku.edu/strategic-plan. A wealth of materials used by the committee and its work groups, including input from the KU community, can be accessed via the archive link.

3. *Provost eNews*, November 2, 2010. Numerous issues of *Provost eNews* were devoted to strategic planning updates and activities. All past issues are archived on the KU web pages at www.provost.ku.edu.

4. A list of many of the mechanisms for engagement with the KU community during the planning process appears at www.provost.ku.edu/strategic-plan/inclusion-communication.

IV

Deans and Past Deans

Chapter Twenty

Disruption, Innovation, and Journalism Education

Ann M. Brill

In his book *The Innovator's Dilemma*, Harvard professor Clayton Christensen introduced the phrase "disruptive innovation." The last few decades of journalism and journalism higher education would provide an excellent example of what Christensen saw as change affecting every aspect of an industry as well as the academic preparation for careers in that industry.

That's certainly been the case at the University of Kansas School of Journalism and Mass Communications. We are named after William Allen White, a Kansas newspaper editor who won a Pulitzer Prize for editorial writing almost one hundred years ago. We have a long tradition and reputation for excellence in journalism education. We pride ourselves in teaching what has been termed "transferable skills" while complementing our curriculum with liberal arts courses. Journalism graduates use their reporting, writing, editing, presentation, and critical thinking skills in a wide variety of careers. That's as true today as it was one hundred years ago. But so much else has changed.

Thirty-five years ago, when I began my career, journalism schools were flourishing across the country. Riding on the waves of an interest fostered by Woodward and Bernstein's Watergate investigation and popular sitcoms such as *The Mary Tyler Moore Show*, teenagers and their parents saw the media as glamorous, fun, well paying, and having a positive impact on society. They also saw newsrooms with typewriters, large pages of type being set, and presses running at breakneck speed until someone yelled, "stop the press" for an exciting last-minute story. Readers waited with anticipation for the morning or afternoon newspaper to be tossed onto their lawns by a twelve-year-old boy with bad aim. Television viewers saw Walter Cronkite and his serious broadcasters report on the evening news, with the entire family sitting down together to watch. Viewers had habits of media consumption controlled by radio, newspapers, and televisions. And all this was supported by advertising dollars. There were few companies that employed public relations people and the media were trusted, respected, and, to some extent, taken for granted. Journalism graduates reported having two or more job offers without much effort. At schools such as the University of Kansas, having a journalism degree meant going to work for one of these traditional media companies.

If Christensen was studying the journalism industry in those days, he would have characterized it as traditional, dominating a niche market, having costly production techniques, labor intensive, in touch with customers, and respected in the marketplace. And, even more so than most industries, media managers were expected to know the latest innovations. Reporters, after all, were trained to report and write about new companies, innovative ideas, and trends in the community. Certainly, both industries and journalism educators thought their traditional skills of reporting, writing, editing, communicating via broadcast media to the public, and delivering not only news but advertising to the public would continue to be the model for a long time.

Then along came the Internet. Talk about a disruptive technology! Journalism educators knew about the Internet and the use the military and a few other industries were making of it. Programmers had figured out how to send and receive e-mail but there were only a few media-based adopters in the early days of the Internet. It wasn't until Tim Berners-Lee and his team at a Swiss laboratory invented the graphic user interfaces that led to the World Wide Web, that journalism and journalism education began to take notice of the technology.

At first, newspapers and educators thought the Web might just be another way to deliver their traditional formats. Broadcasters didn't really see how the Web might impact their work and people in radio assumed, since it had survived the coming of television, it would survive the web just fine. Few in traditional media were prepared for just how disruptive the Web would turn out to be. Journalism education saw those early days as fodder for a few classes in "new media" and as a research novelty.

By the mid 1990s, the Web became ubiquitous, and traditional media realized the critical need to not just have websites, but to begin to think in terms of digital technology. As Nicholas Negroponte and his team at the MIT Media Lab learned, the miniaturization and digitization of information technology was exponentially changing how information would be processed and consumed.

Journalism educators began to pay more attention. Some programs tried to teach the traditional "print and broadcast" majors together but eventually returned to a more "silo-based" approach. And some smaller programs around the country held combined classes that were really more about efficiency than multimedia. Meanwhile, most media jobs were still in traditional media.

However, at the journalism school at the University of Kansas, it was not business as usual.

In the late 1990s, the faculty voted to revise the entire curriculum and reconstruct the program around the skills needed to produce students who could work in traditional and new media. By 2000, the entire curriculum was based on the premise that the Web was no longer an "add-on" but a major player in the media industry. The other top-tier journalism education programs around the country watched the University of Kansas experiment with a mixture of awe and horror. We became the "go to" place to see how these courses could be taught for some; for others, we were a harbinger of all that could go wrong.

We heard the kudos and the criticism. There were a lot of risks involved. Few places were hiring multimedia journalists, and some in the industry expressed concern that KU students would no longer have the skills they needed to put out their newspapers, produce their broadcasts, or create their advertising. Faculty members who were well trained in traditional journalism were not prepared to teach multimedia, much less courses in e-commerce or online journalism. And, while journalism labs had long ago replaced typewriters with computers that used a host of pagination and production software, no one was quite sure what new software and hardware would be used to produce Web-based content. We also realized that the Internet and the Web were only the beginning of the cascade of new technologies, culture changes, and audience expectations that we would encounter. With each development, we stayed grounded in those original transferable skills while remodeling curriculum to include the innovations. We no longer teach the typesetting classes of the 1970s but do teach students the impact of fonts in visual storytelling.

Faced with uncertainty, the innovators at the University of Kansas adopted classic change tactics. Faculty opinion leaders were the first to spend summers as "interns," at the industries that were adopting the Web. Places like the *Chicago Tribune*, the *New York Times*, the *Kansas City Star*, and other newspapers had formed teams of journalists and tasked them with developing strategies for using the Web. For the most part, these teams were not led by reporters and writers, but by the photo or design staffs of these newspapers. Those journalists had made the transition from film to digital cameras. They literally came out of their darkrooms and were using software to create electronic images that would soon be the basis for websites. Those faculty opinion leaders returned to KU with the conviction that multimedia should be the basis for the revised curriculum. We also decided to have some fun along the way and created a new course in information gathering and verification and called it "Infomania." Our new oral presentation skills course became "Stand and Deliver."

And, of course, the role of faculty members includes bringing their own research discoveries into the classroom. Research agendas broadened to include the new technologies and at Kansas, we looked beyond our own discipline to form partnerships with schools of business, engineering, and medicine, as well as our traditional partnerships in liberal arts. At Kansas, we have a Media Innovations Lab that partners with the School of Engineering. And the Interdisciplinary Computing Degree at KU has an option to focus on journalism. It's those kinds of partnerships that create opportunities for faculty and students and help us all become innovators.

It also became clear to journalism educators throughout the country that the technology was changing much more than in the way information would be produced and consumed. The Web was "open" 24/7. No longer would people wait for the newspaper to be delivered or the nightly newscast to appear. The Web was always available and for the first time, people could access information when and how they wanted. The audience had taken control. Educators looked to what places like the Associated Press were doing—get it fast, get it right, and get it out to the audience. In addition to all the technological change, a cultural change was taking place.

And, this wasn't just happening in the news industries. Advertisers took note that they could create their own websites. No longer did they have to rely on news media to deliver their ads. Many journalism schools had already added "mass communications" to their titles. And the disruptive innovation of the Web was felt on that side of the aisle as well. Now advertising and public relations faculty were forced to learn about how to use the Web in their teaching as well as in educating students about how to produce online strategic messages. Advertisers no longer needed the newspaper or television to create a brand or get their message to the public.

The disruptive technology of the World Wide Web has impacted every aspect of what we teach these days in journalism education. It's also disrupted the economic models of media industries. Internships, entry-level jobs, and mid-career opportunities are changing.

It's imperative that schools create on-campus, hands-on experiences for students. The era when students worked on the daily campus newspaper, radio, or television station is over. Today's students need to work in various media outlets. At KU, we've used the business model of the *University Daily Kansan* to create opportunities for all students. Our student media today encompasses five multimedia companies. In addition to the four-day-a-week print product, the *UDK* has an award-winning website, an app, a video production company, an interdisciplinary television production company, and a strategic communication agency. We have formed partnerships with athletics, our performing arts center, the Dole Institute of Politics, schools of engineering, business, medicine, and others, and worked with investing partners to create our strategic communication agency. Our students are writing news stories, live streaming events, creating apps, designing websites, and producing shows ranging from news/sports/weather to the general morning show to hip-hop culture to Greek life. Those students also are learning to pitch ideas to management, sell advertising and underwriting, and create and maintain social media accounts for clients and eventually they will be paid by the student media company.

There is one constant in all that we have done and when all the change seemed overwhelming, we reminded ourselves of our mission—to be student centered. Students. Fulfilling their need for an innovative and thoughtful curriculum and creating experiences to enhance the classroom experience have been our guiding principles.

Disruptive? Yes. Innovative? Yes. That is the tradition, the present, and the future of journalism education at the University of Kansas.

Chapter Twenty-One

Academic Leadership through Strategic Planning

A Dean's Perspective

John D. Floros

THE AUTHOR'S EXPERIENCE IN ACADEMIC LEADERSHIP THROUGH STRATEGIC PLANNING

My first experience in shaping the future of an academic unit dates back to the mid-1980s, when I was a graduate student at the University of Georgia. Although it was not called strategic planning at the time, looking back at the experience now, it was indeed planning in a very strategic way. Later on, as a member of the faculty at Purdue University and as a leader of graduate programs, I had several opportunities to participate and strategically shape the future of the department and the college. At the Pennsylvania State University, as department head, I led the department's efforts in strategic planning, chaired the committee that developed the college's strategic plan, and contributed to the university's plan in significant ways. Finally, as dean of the large and complex College of Agriculture at Kansas State University, I have been responsible not only for developing and implementing the college's strategic plan, but also for aligning it to the university's plan, and using it as a tool to lead the college through tough financial times. Thus, the perspective, thoughts, ideas, recommendations, and examples about strategic planning presented in this chapter stem from my experience in the above academic institutions. All four are large, public, land grant universities known for their comprehensive undergraduate and graduate academic programs, their significant research activities, and their heavy involvement in extension, outreach, and public service.

INTRODUCTION

It is universally expected that great leaders have high ethical standards, honor all people, follow through on commitments, and inspire trust. Effective leaders must also be able to "see the Big Picture" and understand the entire perspective on a given issue. They must maintain open lines of communication in every direction, seek broad input from many groups and individuals, share information with others on a regular basis, assemble effective and powerful teams to get the job done, and work well with others to execute the planned activities. The best leaders not only understand the situation at hand broadly, deeply, and clearly, but also use such profound insights to develop a compelling vision and then translate that vision into concrete plans to improve the situation.

Additionally, in academic institutions, leadership must take place within the framework of "shared governance," where faculty, staff, and students exercise their rights with a powerful voice. To be effective, the academic leader must genuinely seek input before planning and implementing changes. One of the best tools to seek such broad input, understand the current state of affairs, articulate a compelling vision, develop clear plans, implement positive changes, raise awareness, promote buy-in, and achieve continuous improvement is strategic planning.

The process of strategic planning requires a set of skills that must be honed and sharpened constantly. Just as with many things in life, when it comes to developing and implementing an effective strategic plan, hands-on experience counts. My experience with developing and implementing strategic plans, and then using them to lead academic units, spans four decades and four and grant institutions—the University of Georgia, Purdue University, Pennsylvania State University, and Kansas State University.

This chapter provides my perspective on how to lead a college through strategic planning, and addresses questions such as: Why do we need strategic planning in academic institutions? How does one develop an effective strategic plan for a college or university? How do we implement it successfully? How do we connect it to budgetary and/or other important decisions? How do we use it to lead and improve an academic unit? How do we keep it front and center in everybody's mind?

WHY STRATEGIC PLANNING?

For most organizations, particularly academic institutions, strategic planning is the key to gaining control of their future and their destiny in a collective and cooperative manner. For leaders, strategic planning affords the personal satisfaction of taking charge of the institution's future. Strategic planning:

1. forces a look into the future;
2. provides an opportunity to influence the future;
3. results in better awareness of needs, issues, and environment;
4. helps define the overall mission of the institution;
5. focuses people and resources on the objectives;
6. delivers a sense of direction and continuity;
7. contributes to effective staffing and better leadership;
8. brings everyone into the system and the process;
9. creates metrics and standards of accountability for people and programs; and
10. offers a basis to allocate resources. [1]

The process of developing a draft strategic plan, receiving feedback, making changes, finalizing the plan, publicizing and implementing it, is as important as the plan itself. The process involves scores of people and takes a lot of effort, time, and energy. As a result, most people contribute meaningfully to the development of the strategic plan, and thus they feel a sense of ownership of the plan. It is the leader's responsibility to ensure that a sound planning process occurs and that the budget follows the plan. The ultimate role for the leader is to create the structure for planning strategically and to fully participate in the process.

BEGINNING IS IMPORTANT: THE PROCESS OF DEVELOPING A STRATEGIC PLAN

Plato said it best: "Beginning is the most important part of the work." When it comes to strategic planning, how a leader starts the process of developing a plan is critical. The most important first step is to choose the appropriate people who will lead the effort and write the first draft. This steering team or committee and the strategic planning subcommittees formed under it will influence everything that follows and will, or will not, deliver a great plan.

In our case, the steering team and the subcommittees were representative of the diversity in the college. They included a balance of instructors, assistant, associate, and full professors, staff members, graduate and undergraduate students, department heads, other administrators, and a few external stakeholders. The balance also accounted for expertise in teaching, research, extension and outreach, appointments of people from the main campus as well as from other sites throughout the state, and a few other considerations. The one common thread of all the people appointed was that they were all well-respected thought leaders, known for their significant contributions in their respective fields and having a passion for the common good. Each member of the steering team, except the chair and co-chair, led one subcom-

mittee and participated in a second as members. This assured that two different perspectives came forward to the steering team from each subcommittee
that addressed one important topic: undergraduate teaching, graduate teaching, research, extension, facilities, and so on.

In addition to appointing the right people to planning teams and committees, other essential elements for an effective strategic planning process are:
adequate preparation, a well-structured process, good data, and sufficient
resources.

Adequate preparation for everybody planning the future of a department,
college, or university is imperative. Examples of preparation may include
talks by futurists, book reviews and discussions about change, training in
alternative future directions, or visits to other institutions for ideas on what
worked successfully elsewhere. Preparation that expands the team's perception of what is possible and desirable leads to innovative and bold strategic
plans.

A well-structured process should be maintained by a knowledgeable and
experienced facilitator, who should make it possible for everyone in attendance to participate, while discouraging domination by anyone. Structured
processes normally include activities such as brainstorming, small group
work, listing, prioritizing, summarizing, and SWOT (strengths, weaknesses,
opportunities, and threats) analysis.

Strategic planning must be based on good data to drive sound decision
making and continuous quality improvement. For example, data on quantity
and quality of student programs (i.e., recruitment, retention, graduation rates,
placement figures, etc.), teaching and learning outcomes, research activities
(extramural funding, expenditures, publications, impact, awards, etc.), and
stakeholder needs and their evaluation of existing services are required for
the planning process. The more data available to describe the current situation, the better the plan will be.

Sufficient resources in terms of people, time, space, and money are required for optimal planning. Bringing together a large number of people,
training them adequately, asking them to meet several times in facilitated
sessions to produce a first draft and then to receive feedback before finalizing
the plan require significant amounts of money and time. However, spending
either insufficient or excessive time during the strategic planning process
could be detrimental to the quality of the final plan.

The process of developing a college strategic plan is summarized on
Kansas State University's Web page for the 2013 College of Agriculture and
K-State Research and Extension Strategic Plan as follows:

1. Steering committee and subcommittees are appointed and meet to
   discuss:

a. Where we are
b. Where we need to go
c. What we need to do to get there

2. Preliminary input is received from faculty, staff, students, and stake-holders through meetings and/or web surveys.
3. Preliminary plan is developed by the steering committee and sub-committees.
4. Leadership team reviews and comments on the preliminary plan.
5. Comments are compiled and the draft strategic plan is released.
6. Internal and external feedback on the draft strategic plan is sought.
7. Comments are compiled and the final strategic plan is released.
8. Individual departments and other units use the college's plan as a base to develop their own strategic plans.

ESSENTIAL ELEMENTS OF AN EFFECTIVE STRATEGIC PLAN

Once the appropriate people have been appointed to the planning teams, adequate preparation and training have taken place, a well-structured process has been outlined, good data have been found or collected, and sufficient resources have been allocated, the development of the plan begins. To develop an effective strategic plan, certain essential elements must be incorporated into the plan at the appropriate time.

First, the planning committees must review, refine, clarify, reaffirm, or create the unit's **Mission**. A mission statement considers questions such as: Why do we exist? What are our primary functions? Who is affected by our work? What are their needs? A well-crafted mission statement defines the organization's essential reason for existence and establishes the scope of its business. It also reflects stakeholders' needs and other similar fundamental issues that underscore the **Core Purpose** of the unit, which does not change often over time. This "constancy of purpose," as W. Edwards Deming articulated it, is one of the basic requirements for continuous quality improvement. The mission statement then becomes the foundation upon which all subsequent parts of a plan are built.

With the mission statement clearly stated, the group is ready to define the unit's **Organizational Values** and operating principles. Values are the core of what the unit—department, college, university—is and what it cherishes. Values are beliefs that manifest how faculty, staff, students, and stakeholders interact. Values are behaviors we live by, reward others for, and find most important in life. As with the mission statement, values are long lasting and are not changed often.

Another equally important part of any strategic plan is the early articulation of a bold **Vision**. The vision is an aspirational statement that mostly answers the question: Where do we want to be in three, five, or ten years? The vision statement defines the unit's strategic position in the future and the specific elements of that position with respect to the mission statement. In some cases, the vision is provided by the leader, such as the president for the university, the dean for the college, or the head for the department. However, the vision is usually reviewed and revised by members of the strategic planning team.

The vision statement normally assumes that knowledge of and data about the unit's current position exist. If not, a **Situational Analysis** should be performed and integrated throughout the planning process to answer questions such as: Where are we now? What are our stakeholders' needs? What do our assessment data tell us? What are we doing well? What can we improve? What are the external trends, opportunities, and threats? What else is happening in the external environment?

Finding answers to the above questions and collecting the relevant data will also help to establish the unit's **Strategic Priorities and Goals.** These big strategic priorities and overall direction should be based on an honest evaluation of the unit's strengths, weaknesses, and opportunities. They must be articulated as long-term lofty initiatives (not always measurable) that will transform the institution over the next ten or more years. These strategic initiatives will guide the construction of short-term, mid-term, and long-term measurable goals, and will help establish funding priorities.

A set of specific **Tactics** and **Metrics** must then be clearly defined. They are precise and measurable actions designed to accomplish the goals established. Examples of such actions may include the creation, continuation, change, or elimination of programs. The result is a number of **Outcomes** that can be measured to show progress toward targets.

SUCCESSFUL IMPLEMENTATION OF
THE STRATEGIC PLAN

Turning strategies, priorities, goals, and objectives into desired outcomes in a suitable timeframe is messy work and the function of the Implementation Plan. This part of the strategic planning process is a working plan not usually available widely to the public, mainly because it is frequently revised, amended, and changed in response to environmental factors. Successful implementation of the strategic plan requires commitment, proper resource allocation, and communication. Everybody within the institution—leaders, faculty and staff—must candidly commit to change and implementation of the strategies recommended by the strategic planning committee.

The leaders—president, provost, dean, and department head—should implement actions and programs, and commit resources to meet the goals of the strategic plan at a level that is attainable for the organization and the unit. The ultimate purpose of a strategic plan is to drive resource allocation—people, time, space, technology, and funding. Thus, leaders must use the strategic plan to set funding priorities, respond to funding requests, direct grant writing, and plot fundraising targets. If the unit's vision requires additional resources, securing such appropriate resources to make it all happen becomes imperative, and the plan must be implemented in phases over time.

Leaders must also communicate clearly and often during this implementation phase to ensure widespread awareness of progress. Regular presentations by the leader (i.e., state of the university, college, or department address); a dedicated strategic planning website; a special internal communication campaign, including electronic bulletins, e-mail circulation of documents; and upbeat notes of major accomplishments or milestones will all promote buy-in and maximize the likelihood of success. To solidify campus-wide awareness and ensure successful implementation, all units must be carefully trained to create unit-based strategic plans using a standard format. Leadership should provide adequate support as the units move through the planning process and allow ample time to complete and implement their plans.

In addition, each unit leader must hold everybody below them responsible for adhering to and implementing the strategic plan. Through periodic reviews, annual evaluations, and other similar instruments, the president/provost must hold the deans on task regarding each college's progress toward strategic planning goals. Similarly, the dean should review each department head's progress toward mutually agreed-upon strategic indicators, and the department head should incorporate elements and metrics from the unit's strategic plan into the annual evaluation for each faculty and staff member.

Faculty and staff must also commit to change and to the success of the unit as envisioned by the plan. If the strategic plan was developed through a cooperative and participatory process, everyone should have had input, and, ideally, everyone should feel a sense of ownership of the final plan. Such personal investment and commitment by faculty and staff will ease change, facilitate the implementation process, and enable success.

NOTE

1. See also C. Ahoy's 1998 "Strategic Planning" (Iowa State University, www.fpm.iastate.edu/worldclass/strategic_planning.asp).

REFERENCES

Ahoy, C. (1998). *Basics of Strategic Planning*. Found on Iowa State University's webpage: www.fpm.iastate.edu/worldclass/strategic_planning.asp, and accessed on May 18, 2014.

Paris, K. (2003). *Strategic Planning in the University*. The Office of Quality Improvement, University of Wisconsin-Madison. http://oqi.wisc.edu/resourcelibrary/uploads/resources/ Strategic%20Planning%20in%20the%20University.pdf, accessed on May 25, 2014.

Kansas State University (2013). *College of Agriculture and K-State Research and Extension Strategic Plan*. Found at: www.strategicplan.ag.ksu.edu/p.aspx?tabid=15, and strategicplan. ag.ksu.edu/doc8342.ashx, and accessed on May 31, 2014.

Chapter Twenty-Two

Ten Strategies for Enhancing the Academic Leader's Communication Effectiveness

Jane S. Halonen

Harvard Business School Dean Nitin Nohria once observed that "Communication is the real work of leadership." Leadership in academic settings is particularly complex, suggesting that establishing and maintaining effective communication practices needs to be a high priority for the academic leader. Direct and clear communication generates trust, a commodity that must be in place in the academic setting for an administrator to proceed with confidence. What follows is a summary of the ten most important strategies that contribute to communication effectiveness that I relied upon during my tenure as a dean of a college.

REMEMBER THE ROOM IS FILLED WITH THE SMARTEST KIDS IN THE ROOM

Academic leadership is tricky because those who are being led often don't see themselves as in need of a leader. Faculty can be reluctant and sometimes overtly hostile. I found it useful to adopt a mindset that academic leaders are dealing with individuals who have been profoundly successful in the unique academic pathways that led to their first teaching jobs. For the most part, those faculty members have always been the "smartest kid in the room." A room full of the smartest kids in the room can be daunting. Understanding and respecting that success history can help leaders tolerate the narcissism that is inherent in nearly all successful academics.

MASTER INTERPERSONAL CONNECTION

Every administrator will have substantial experience listening in dyads and groups. A time-tested therapist strategy of paraphrasing establishes that the administrator is actually listening and "gets" the key elements being expressed. I have always marveled at how a well-turned paraphrase (e.g., "You are really distressed about the change in the grant protocol.") assists in making a strong connection before the communication can move on to problem solving. Liberal use of paraphrasing helps to insure that the conversation is collaborative and focused. Paraphrasing also reduces blowback that the leader doesn't listen. This strategy clarifies that there is a difference between listening to a proposition and agreeing with a proposition.

So much of what an administrator does involves untangling messy problems, but at times distressed academics may feel compelled to detail every nuance or every bruised feeling before settling in on an objective or clarifying a request. Although an administrator may have authority to take swift action to solve a problem, sometimes it is more effective to insure action is the desired outcome of the complainant. Particularly when conversations are distressed and overheated, I find it helpful to simply ask, "What specifically is it you think you want me to do to resolve your situation?" The individual may already be able to pinpoint a precise solution that will be satisfying. On occasion, this strategy also can cut through the emotional mine fields. More than once, faculty members have confessed they just wanted to blather about the problem "for my awareness" and did not expect any action. Knowing that such a session has turned into an airing of turbulent feelings can reduce expectations and change how the leader listens and responds.

RESPECT EMOTIONAL TURMOIL

Sadly, good leaders occasionally find that they are in situations that are going to generate pain or frustration for their constituents (e.g., tenure denial). When the leader must deliver turmoil-generating news, it is unrealistic to expect that a faculty member can bounce back immediately within the confines of the conversation in which the upset transpired and move into constructive considerations of the next steps. In my experience, delivering bad news should be followed with options for the faculty member to retreat and regroup. Wherever possible, the faculty member should decide when to return for the constructive conversation, whether five minutes later or two weeks later. In addition, a box of tissues and glass of water near the site of the bad news delivery is essential. The pain of the situation should not be compounded when a faculty member has to fumble for items that will provide comfort.

STAGE A RITUAL OPENING CEREMONY

When I assumed my dean's position, I asked my assistant to arrange an all-college meeting. Her eyes widened. "Are you sure?" she asked. "It's never been done before." So much the better. Convening the academic family signaled an important change in direction and style of operation. It is difficult to foster a sense of "group entatitivity" if those members never have the opportunity to meet face to face. Starting the school year with an all-college meeting produces an efficient way to pass along start-up information, introduce new members, review goals for the year, and generally provide an opportunity for members to consolidate their sense of belonging to the group.

RUN HUMANE MEETINGS

Although I was intrigued with the proposal that all meetings should be conducted standing up, I never tried it. Instead, I opted for good group process, including a print agenda, starting and ending punctually, liberal use of humor, and emphasis on two-way exchange. Meetings that went past an hour could have comfort and digital breaks to provide an outlet for the addicted. Everyone has experienced group meetings in which members divert their attention, sometimes surreptitiously, to stay current with e-mail. Just as in class, I require meetings that are e-mail free. I declared this behavior out of bounds. The main value of refusing to entertain off-task activity was in modeling full attention as a sign of respect and reducing the amount of time spent catching people up from missing details while they were digitally engaged.

CONVENE A STARBUCKS COFFEE HOUR

Coming to "see the dean" or other administrative official can be a very big deal, particularly for faculty who are new to an organization. Consequently, I adopted the practice of posting times when I would linger in the Starbucks in the library on our campus approximately once per month. That informal setting allowed a variety of conversations that could not take place in other circumstances. Sometimes the conversations would be additive as faculty would purposefully drop into unpredictable conversations just for fun. Other times, individuals conducted business that would be challenging or intimidating in a more formal office appointment. For example, faculty senate delegates can "run into you" without formally getting on the calendar to discuss concerns over university operations. However, sometimes the advantage is distinctly personal. I've planned a pregnancy to align with tenure and promotion logistics over a cup of chai tea. Even when little business transpires, the act of setting aside the public hour instills confidence about leader accessibility.

PUBLISH A MONTHLY NEWSLETTER

Blogging or an e-mail newsletter to faculty and staff in the unit is a great way to help constituents stay current on the matters that matter most to the operations. In my own case, I debuted the dean's newsletter, "Crow's Nest," as a monthly e-mail to faculty and staff. (The title reflects an attempt to cohere with the nautical themes that characterized much of my university's penchant to capitalize on living in the Gulf Coast. The vantage point of the crow's nest on a ship should allow the earliest glimpse of whatever threatens on the horizon.)

I found trying to summarize college events too daunting so I relegated that chore to a staff member in a separate but regular notification. That decision freed me to concentrate on providing insight into current administrative challenges or acknowledging faculty accomplishments (e.g., grants, books, or special acts of kindness). The secret to a successful newsletter is maintaining a file where incoming items can be easily accessed as well as regularly reminding faculty to send in items of general interest. Set aside the time to do the job well. Effective proofreading is essential. A standing joke in my office was predicting how soon it would be before someone notified us of a misspelling, typo, or other problem; the record was seventeen seconds. However, in general, each issue of the "Crow's Nest" also tended to elicit favorable comments from faculty about the gratitude of being recognized or of being better informed as a consequence of the newsletter.

BECOME A CULTURE CHAMELEON

In a diverse world, academic leaders will fare best in relationships if they adapt to the culture or expectations of the conversational partner. Although exceptions certainly exist, the majority of Western academics prefer to dispense with small talk and get to the point as efficiently as possible. Some individuals prefer a settling-in before the formal conversation begins that might include inquiring about the family or demonstrating other indications that the leader has retained some meaningful details about the partner. Meeting with new Asian partners typically involves an exchange of business cards in a ritual that involves a slight bow and careful stowing away of the card to demonstrate the preciousness of the exchange. Knowing the cultural background of your conversation partners can help leaders navigate these waters.

MAKE NO PROMISES YOU CAN'T KEEP

Nothing shatters credibility with enduring ill effects more than a broken promise. Particularly in economically hazardous times when a leader has limited resources to address a problem, straight talk about what is possible and what is not will be most appreciated in the long run. Even if the answer is no, the requester can realistically move on to other strategies to resolving problems without undue trust that the leader will magically solve that problem for them. As a side observation, it is easier to serve in a leadership capacity when resources are lean. Saying no to everything requires little explanation and produces an evenhandedness that will fall away when resources come into play.

USE PUBLIC RUBRICS FOR IMPORTANT DECISIONS

When resources are available (e.g., faculty lines, travel funds), the most defensible posture for determining allocation of those resources is through the construction and application of a decision rubric, preferably collaboratively constructed with those who will be affected by any subsequent decisions. Although this process takes much longer than decision by fiat, the payoff is the curtailment of belabored appeals and public whining about the resource distribution. Winners win fairly and squarely, and the posted rubric deliberations make that clear to all stakeholders.

FEARLESS SELF-EVALUATION

Academic leaders at higher levels of administration may not be subjected to the same annual evaluation rigor that befalls a traditional faculty member. That fact is not lost on faculty members. Therefore, many benefits accrue to the decision to initiate and conduct a regular self-evaluation and preferably to make those results public. The survey format can be complex and rubric-driven, or it can be as simple as "What am I doing that is helping you do your job?" and "What could I be doing better?" If you post the results, remember to be explicit in the instructions that you will be posting the results, and remind faculty that civil responses will have the greatest impact. Posting the results can help individuals with strong negative outlying opinions understand that they are in the minority. Leaders who are effective have nothing to fear from an assessment process.

Anne Morrow Lindbergh once observed, "Good communication is as stimulating as black coffee, and just as hard to sleep after." Although the goal of improving communication strategies should not be to render constituents insomniacs en masse, the outcomes of improved communication should produce many benefits for the academic leader and the organization the leader serves. Although perfect communication is not a realistic goal, thoughtful communication strategies can consolidate the academic leader's position and help the unit move confidently forward.

Chapter Twenty-Three

Academic Leadership in a Time of Rapid Change

Diane Halpern

The secret to academic leadership lies in these two words—shared governance. Unfortunately it is such a secret that no one actually knows or can agree on what this phrase means. Here is what it does not mean: It does not mean that all academic decisions are made with equal and joint input from the faculty and administration. Both sides of the institution participate in the important decisions on college campuses, which many of our counterparts in the world of business find very hard to understand. But "participate" covers a wide swath of possibilities and, at times, the dividing line between where the powers of the faculty end and those of the administration begin, and the reverse, has been the scene of bloody academic battles.

A wise administrator will be respectful of the faculty role in governance. Faculty recommend candidates for hiring, promotion, and tenure. Administrators are able to block these decisions, but there had better be a strong reason for bucking faculty recommendations, especially if they are unanimous across departments and schools. Similarly, faculty "own" the curriculum, but ownership in this case can be closer to renting. Ultimately administrators are responsible for paying the bills. And a curriculum that is too costly, or a department that cannot support itself can be fiscally irresponsible. Faculty may have developed a model curriculum, but if few students elect to take the courses, there is a problem that needs a fast solution.

So how does a wise administrator work with faculty in the spirit of shared governance? One way is to get faculty input on all major (and even some minor) decisions on campus and to honestly consider alternative points of view. Sometimes, there is a clear indicator that a difficult decision must be made. Here is a common example. Large German-language departments were the norm on many college campuses a few decades ago. Unfortunately for these departments, the number of German majors sharply declined and few students wanted to study German. Other departments in the university were left to support the faculty in German who had small classes that often did not "make" the minimum class enrollments. In any other business, the difficult decision to eliminate these departments would be clear-cut, but academia is not "any other business." In this example, the decision is clear, but how to get to the endpoint is tricky. Will a reasonable group of faculty look at this problem and decide that it is necessary to disband the department, or will they rally around their colleagues and vote to protect their jobs? Will the faculty who meet to discuss this problem be reasonable? Who gets to define "reasonable?"

Like leaders everywhere, academic administrators have difficult decisions to make. In this example, the tenured faculty in the hypothetical German department (it could be another department, this is just an example) will need to be prepared to take on another position in the university—perhaps they can run the advising center or work as an assistant to the dean, but these transitions require additional training and a willingness on their part to assume new duties at the university that are outside the usual faculty role. In this example, professionals in the advising center and those who actually want to be an assistant to the dean will also be unhappy because they will find their desired career path blocked by the displaced faculty. And, as most readers can guess, the faculty who are reassigned are usually not happy.

For decisions of this magnitude and even for smaller ones, the stakeholders at the university want to have meaningful input and to believe that their views were considered seriously. Decision making will not be quick if you have to confer with various constituents, but it can be more harmonious. Take the time to listen to faculty, students, and staff. It can pay off in better feelings when decisions are made, and you might actually learn something valuable that alters the decision.

If the first principle of successful academic leadership is to confer widely, a close second is fairness. Of course, fairness is always important regardless of context, but it has a special meaning in academia. Most often, administrators will come from academic departments and schools, and different academic entities often feud over resources. As one wise university president told me about the administrators on his campus, individually all of the deans are wonderful people, but put a dollar-fifty on the table and they will fight to the death over the money. When you assume an administrative position, you are now responsible for academic units that you may have (unwisely) dissed in the past. So, even if the School of Business took valuable space from your department or Physics got a larger share of the budget than your home department, it is essential to move forward so that every unit for which you have responsibility believes that you now have their best interest at heart.

You must become a champion for those academic units you failed to support in your previous role as faculty and avoid favoritism for your home department or school.

Loosely tied to fairness is transparency. The best way to demonstrate fairness is to make your decisions openly. Of course, not everyone will believe that you are fair, regardless of what you do, and fairness does not mean that every unit gets the same space or budget (per faculty or per student) as every other, but it does mean that you publicly justify your decisions. When decisions are closed and secretive, most people can imagine a more lopsided outcome than the one you implemented. For example, you may decide that biology needs more space than history, and history needs to take advantage of an unusual opportunity to hire a faculty member with specific expertise. These decisions will not always be viewed as fair by faculty in the other departments, but if you can explain the basis for your decision, in the long run, you will be perceived as "more fair" than if these decisions are made without explanations or under the shroud of secrecy.

Along with fairness and transparency is the critical necessity to communicate your visions and policies consistently to various diverse units. Even though it may seem like a good idea to tell the sciences that your top priority is to make your university "Number 1" in science among peer institutions and to tell your humanities faculty that they are your top priority, this race to the top will soon falter. In general, it is better not to convey "win-lose" strategies. You can be committed to making each department excellent. Of course, decisions about funding, faculty lines, laboratory support, and so on will have to be made, but if they are made with the expressed goal of helping every department achieve excellence, it may be easier for the constituent units to understand decisions, or at least not grouse too much about them.

Academic administrators can help faculty achieve their own goals by finding ways to support scholarship, helping them teach more effectively, and encouraging them to serve on committees that are needed to make universities run. They can find ways to make students, faculty, and staff feel appreciated and thus more committed to the university. There will never be enough funding for everyone's wish list or even need list, but there are other ways to reward excellence. Universities, like all businesses and human endeavors, are at their heart the business of people. Positive relationships, genuine liking, and trust are the foundations for all institutions. When these supports are strong, the institution and its administrators can weather great storms.

Academic administration is not the right job if you need to be liked. There will be lots of hard decisions. You may increase the budget of one department by a substantial amount, provide additional space, give faculty the desired teaching slots, and upgrade their computers, but as soon as you make a decision that is negative, all of the beneficial decisions are forgotten in short time. Faculty never forget the negative decisions. I recall one situation in which a decision was made to postpone the construction of a new building that was designed to house the faculty of one large department. By every indicator, it was a good decision for the university but not for the faculty in the department whose building was postponed. The building was built a few years later, and this department has now been in the beautiful building for over a decade, but the hard feelings about the postponement are never far from the surface. Interestingly, even the new faculty hired after the new building was built seem to carry some of the acrimony toward the administrator who made the decision to postpone the building.

Most importantly, remember that being an academic administrator is a great privilege. It is an ideal job for someone with a vision for how higher education can be an agent for positive change. You can make change happen (okay, you can make it more likely to happen). It is an opportunity to think about what is important in higher education and on your campus. Although there are important differences among institutions in their mission, resources, students, and faculty, all universities are designed, at least in part, to educate. As an administrator, you can make education more effective, more efficient, more diverse, more relevant, and lots more. Are you concerned that too many students are not completing their program? You can take action that will make huge changes in the lives of students who can complete their degree because you cared enough to question the status quo, work for reform, test the effectiveness of the reform, and adjust accordingly.

Higher education is on the cusp of great change. We are moving away from the lecture (with sporadic questioning) model that has been the default since the time of Christ and undoubtedly much longer. Much of what was the sole purview of the university is now available free on the Internet. The wealth of quality materials (ignore the poor ones) is staggering and growing at a rapid rate. Need help with calculus? There are Khan Academy modules with expert teachers to guide you through. Want to learn a foreign language? There is an abundance of software that can be endlessly patient as you conjugate verbs and learn vocabulary. Need to learn microeconomics? There are several MOOCs for that.

The availability of these technology-mediated learning experiences does not threaten the university with extinction. Students need to interact with each other, and faculty need to guide learning activities and provide feedback to students. What these new technologies do is change the university to a more interactive place that can focus on deep learning and complex thinking. And change is hard. There is an old joke that goes something like this: How are a cemetery and university alike? They are both hard to change and in both cases you won't get much help from the inhabitants. Of course, there will be change allies on campus, so be sure to have them on your side as change agents. Not all students are ideal candidates for all types of technology-mediated learning. An open lab for students who need to remediate in math, for example, is likely to fail because many of these students will need more structure to make up for lost time and work diligently in what is likely to be their "least favorite" subject. But, wise administrators can take advantage of what technology does best, what faculty do best, and what different students need. Academic administrators can guide universities through the many changes that are in the near future.

Most people can name a great teacher who changed their life. Great administrators can change many lives.

Chapter Twenty-Four

Leadership and Measurement

Confessions of an Administrator
Without Portfolio

Larry Lyon

"My job is a lot like that of the groundskeeper at a cemetery—lots of people under me, but no one is listening." Bill Clinton is sometimes given credit for this analogy, but I first heard it from another president, William Brody, of Johns Hopkins. It's a good line, evoking knowing laughter from all levels and types of administrators, especially in the shared-governance environment of higher education. It is especially apropos for graduate deans. Graduate deans are often described as being deans "without portfolio," which is a polite way of saying without faculty, budget, or authority.

This unfortunate and unique distinctive of graduate deans has led to a variety of administrative strategies—strategies that are not necessarily unfortunate or unique. If even the presidents of the United States and Johns Hopkins complain about having more responsibility than authority, then some of what graduate deans have learned could most certainly apply to other administrative positions.

From my own experience and observation, graduate school administration strategies include ingratiation, obsequience, and an inordinate focus on the few rules we can enforce (e.g., determining the margin widths of theses). While such strategies may have their place, I would like to advocate another form of influence to offset the lack of authority—the development and promotion of academic metrics.

This is, admittedly, the appropriate time to sigh and roll your eyes at another misguided attempt to bring business practices to higher education, an attempt that is presumed to do much more harm than good. We are all aware

of the criticisms leveled at our most infamous example, the *US News &
World Report* (*USNWR*) rankings. One of the most common complaints is
that "the tail wags the dog" when universities change their activities solely to
improve their *USNWR* metrics. That is a legitimate criticism. However, the
very idea that a small "tail" can influence a large "dog" is worthy of further
consideration. The erstwhile magazine certainly has less authority over U.S.
universities than, say, the U.S. Department of Education. Still, its rankings,
along with the long line of imitators now ranking every university in the
world in just about every way imaginable, may well have changed the behaviors of college students, faculty, and administrators more than the Department of Education. Certainly the publicity given to these rankings is responsible for much of the influence, but I suspect something more basic is at work
here, something that can help administrators with little authority.

MEASUREMENT MATTERS

The more basic "something" is *measurement*. Measurement conveys importance, sharpens focus, and initiates behavior toward desired effects. Measurement makes the invisible visible and opens for debate that which is assumed.
If there is no measurement letting us know whether we are successful in
achieving a certain goal, then it's quite likely that the goal really doesn't
matter very much and that we really aren't reaching it. For many years, my
institution, Baylor University, had little discussion and few measures related
to graduate education because, even if it wasn't clearly stated, undergraduate
and professional education mattered more. It was assumed that graduate
education was satisfactory as it was and in little need of improvement. A
graduate dean, of course, wants graduate education to matter, to be discussed
and improved.

Accordingly, I wanted many of the same enhancements that all graduate
deans want. Enhancements that typically require financial resources and for
which, not coincidentally, multiple measures exist are:

1. more national visibility (as measured by more applicants to our graduate programs);
2. brighter graduate students (higher GRE scores);
3. competitive stipends (compared to those at public research universities);
4. more external support for graduate students (grant dollars for stipends,
   tuition, insurance, and travel);
5. graduate student contributions to their professions and disciplines beyond the classroom (presentations at professional meetings and publications in disciplinary journals);

6. high-quality graduate student teaching in the undergraduate lab or classroom (teaching evaluations);
7. efficient matriculation of graduate students through the university (completion rates and time to degree); and
8. gainful employment of students after graduation (alumni surveys).

Financial resources for these enhancements are often secured through some of the administrative strategies listed earlier (ingratiation and obsequience), and we should all occasionally polish apples, but sustained success is more likely to come through measurement. So, here's the secret to being a successful graduate dean: Simply measure all the things you want (like those on the list above) and show the metrics to your faculty and provost, and they will be so impressed and appreciative that they will provide the resources and behaviors necessary to fulfill your needs. Or maybe not.

Most often, not. In this case, not because anyone objected to my list of enhancements, but because some objected to the measures. It's hard to be against national visibility or bright graduate students, but it's easy to object to the metrics. Critiquing the measures is certainly easier than admitting that the resources need to go elsewhere or that change is hard. Everyone agreed that the list was admirable, but when it came to measuring those characteristics, I was told:

1. The number of applicants is a poor measure because the faculty in our department actively discourage applications from all but the very best students.
2. The GRE is biased and a poor measure of what is needed in our graduate programs.
3. Stipends are not comparable measures because the cost of living is a lot lower in Waco and the tuition waivers are much more valuable at a private school like Baylor.
4. Grants are not a valid indicator of support because they are nonexistent in many disciplines and increasingly difficult to get in others.
5. Presentations and publications make no sense for us because our disciplinary traditions do not require presentations and articles before completing the dissertation.
6. The teaching evaluations are popularity contests that discourage rigorous instruction.
7. Our discipline is exceptionally complex and it takes many years to achieve the mastery associated with a PhD.
8. Gainful employment is hard to measure and our discipline is at a disadvantage because so many (or so few) want jobs in academia.

These quite legitimate objections comprised only a small sample of the critical responses to my graduate school metrics. I was barraged by an almost unlimited number of objections to the various metrics, and most objections were valid. Fortunately, however, a limited number of responses is sufficient to answer an almost unlimited number of objections: The first response is simply admitting that the proposed measure isn't perfect.

THE PERFECT IS THE ENEMY OF THE GOOD

We all agree that perfect measures of student and faculty achievement don't exist, but that doesn't mean we stop giving our students grades or awarding our faculty tenure. We continually debate and improve our student and faculty achievement measures, but we never conclude that, since our measures have flaws, we shouldn't even try. Simply because the perfect doesn't exist doesn't mean that we should not go ahead and use a *good* measure instead.

Yet, many of my colleagues seemed to feel that once a problem with a particular metric was pointed out, that problem was reason enough to halt any further movement toward measurement. And since all measures have problems, it's rather easy to discover shortcomings.

For example, members of my graduate council suggested (perhaps facetiously) that the best way to increase admissions was to waive the application fee. Applications would go up, and then the graduate dean could claim an increase in national visibility. Certainly, applications are not a perfect measure of visibility, but if the application fee remains constant, and the number of applications increases, perhaps at a greater rate than the national increase, isn't that at least an indirect indication of an expanding national presence? Similarly, it was argued that, since the GRE does not consistently predict a student's success in graduate school, we should continue to make our admission decisions based on a gestalt of flexible, unmeasureable, subjective assessments.

Well, maybe, but if data from the National Research Council shows that whatever it is that is measured in the verbal section of the GRE tends to be much higher in humanities programs at Harvard and Yale than at Baylor, or if the quantitative scores are higher at MIT and Cal Tech, is it merely a coincidence? If we include GPAs, research experience, letters of recommendation, personal statements, individual interviews, and the GRE, aren't we more likely to improve our selection process? And if our programs and students get better, isn't it likely that GRE scores will increase, at least a bit? As one last example, humanities programs appropriately observed that grant opportunities were much fewer in their fields than in the STEM fields; thus, grant measures should not apply. However, if we compare grants to English departments nationally with grants to Baylor's English program, can't we learn something from that contrast?

CO-OPTATION CAN BE GOOD

If a measure has problems, and they all do, the logical and politically expedient response is to ask the experts, often our faculty, to provide improvements. For example:

- What do we want our sociology graduates to know?
- How do other philosophy programs rank each other?
- What should the starting salary be for our MBAs?
- How many grant dollars should an electrical engineer bring to the university?

All good questions for measurement, and all questions best answered by those in the respective discipline. Now it is possible, even probable, that faculty will develop measures that favor their own departments, but that's okay. The fact that the measure came from the faculty, that co-optation in the best sense of the term has occurred, is likely to make it a very useful measure. Besides, it's only a start and there are no perfect measures anyway. So, let's begin with measures that our faculty will support. Hopefully, over time, the measures can become more extensive and more useful as we come to accept and even, dare I say it, embrace the idea of measurement.

WHY MEASUREMENT RATHER THAN ASSESSMENT?

If we think for a moment about the measures discussed thus far, we see that they all possess the potential for assessment. In fact, many of the eight measures mentioned in the list above are at least implied assessments. So, why not focus on assessment rather than measurement? After all, that's what the critics of higher education seem to want. Well, you can, but if you think "measurement" is a hard sell to faculty, try "assessment," a hot-button term directly connected with ratings, evaluations, new faculty lines, tenure, and salaries. Most folks employed in higher education are very bright, certainly bright enough to know that whatever we measure now, we are likely to assess later. Talking about measurement may generate a little less resistance than using the "a" word, but only a little.

Measurement, in my opinion, is a good first step because sometimes—not often, but sometimes—measurement is sufficient in itself to produce desired change. Above, I noted that measurement can lend importance to what we measure, sharpen focus on that which is measured, and initiate behavior toward the desired effect of improving the measure. Simply asking faculty to include references to pedagogical strategies and published articles in an annual activity report communicates that the university cares about teaching and research. That communication is likely to produce a greater emphasis on how our students learn and how often our faculty publish. If we don't have the authority to mandate enhanced instruction and research productivity, we might be able to achieve some success through simply measuring those behaviors.

Measurement, then, is a low-risk, low-authority approach to administration. By first engaging our colleagues in developing good measures for certain desired behaviors, and then implementing and focusing on those measures, we increase the likelihood that those behaviors will occur. Of course, moving from measurement to assessment increases that likelihood even more.

WHY MEASUREMENT SO OFTEN LEADS TO ASSESSMENT

Baylor's most recent *USNWR score* is fifty-three. Virtually no one on our campus knows this number—a number that is compiled to represent the overall quality of our undergraduate education efforts. Our *rank* is seventy-five, a measure widely known and discussed at Baylor and elsewhere. I truly believe that if our score fell ten points, but our rank improved by ten places (if all of our closely ranked peers got worse, but we got "less worse" than others), it would be a time of great celebration in Waco because, even though the largely invisible measure of quality declined, the highly visible comparative rank improved. Yet, if the *USNWR* approach has any validity at all, the absolute score should be the more important number since the absolute score supposedly represents the quality of undergraduate education at Baylor. *USNWR* rankings matter more than the *USNWR* scores because the rankings offer easy, relative assessment of an important, widely known, but very complex entity—U.S. colleges and universities. It's the relative assessment that makes the rank so compelling.

Assessment is a measure that is interpreted relative to a goal. The assessment can often tell us the goal, even if the goal is never stated. For example, we could compare Baylor's *USNWR* score against the previous year (up one, yawn) or our *USNWR* rank against other universities (improved by two, yay!); both are assessments, but the latter matters more. This is because our unstated goal appears to be in beating our Big XII colleagues and the rest of the national universities more than it does simply being better than we are now. A clearer example can be drawn from athletics: We might want our cornerbacks to have low forty-yard dash times (internal absolute measure), but what we want even more is for them to help us beat TCU and Texas (external relative assessments) in football. We typically measure in light of a goal (stated or unstated), and that turns our measures into assessments.

If you start with measures, and those measures eventually turn into assessments, then you are a long way down the road toward using measurement to produce desired change. Of course, the idea that we can identify the change that is desirable means that we have some type of goal in mind. How fast do we want our cornerbacks to run? Faster than the TCU wide receivers. We have a goal!

Now we could claim that we simply want our cornerbacks to run as fast as they can and our students to learn as much as they can. In other words, our goals could be internal measures and not based on a relative external comparison. We don't care about the score of the football game as long as each player did his best, and *USNWR* rankings don't matter as long as our students are being well prepared for the next stage in their lives. Those of us in higher education often do make such claims, but few believe us. Internal measures are often noble and sometimes useful, but relative assessments demand our interest and drive our actions.

WHY ASSESSMENT LEADS TO CHANGE

As absolute internal measurements evolve into relative external assessments, their ability to raise the visibility of that which is measured and to focus behavior on improving the measure is magnified—perhaps too much. Many of us already feel unease over the visibility and changes brought by relative external assessments such as those of *USNWR* or big-time college football. Still, this unease should not blind us to the remarkable way in which these kinds of relative, goal-based measures, whether displayed on a website or on a football scoreboard, can lead to change. Our universities have changed in many ways—from simplifying the application process and tying more financial aid to test scores to building new workout facilities and offering higher salaries to coaches—all to improve our assessments on the *USNWR* rating and the Saturday scoreboard. We can, and probably should, bemoan many of the changes, but we should also understand what they tell us about the ability of assessments to induce change.

Assessments lead to change especially when they counter long-held notions supporting present circumstances. No one in higher education cared that much about SAT scores and class size before *USNWR*. We gave some nodding approval that big scores and small classes were better, but we really didn't do much to change things. I doubt that many of us even knew the proportion of classes under twenty in enrollment. But when *USNWR* included measures of SATs and class sizes below twenty, and ranked them, and publicized them, everything changed. Measures began to matter and boasts became harder to make. Before *USNWR*, we could all claim to be one of the best universities in the country, the "Harvard of the South," or Midwest, or wherever. Today, such boasts are less common. In spring football practice, our teams are always greatly improved and everyone is a future all-American. In December, after widely publicized measures on the scoreboard, not nearly so many claims are made.

As long as we can tell ourselves and (especially) others that we are one of the best there is at whatever it is we do, the status quo is worth defending. However, if relative external assessments show us lacking, even if those assessments are based on measures of questionable validity, the status quo gives way to demands for change.

RELATIVE TO WHAT?

I have defined assessment as a measure that is interpreted relative to a goal. Which goal we choose, in relation to which measures, matters a great deal. Going back to my graduate school wish list, in most cases we ended up with goals based on changes over time and comparisons among programs at Baylor. For example, when I began to create and distribute graduate school metrics, one graduate program ranked at the bottom among Baylor programs in the number of applications received each year. The program accurately claimed that theirs was a more specialized, less visible degree than those at the top. For that program, we agreed to simply strive for more applications than the previous year and not compare it with the other Baylor programs. Here's the important part: the program helped design the assessment and the number of applicants for that program has increased almost every year since the annual comparisons began.

After several years of such comparisons, for some measures, for some programs, we were ready to compare not just among ourselves, but nationally. For example, our Master of Accountancy program is quite happy to be compared to other graduate programs nationally on CPA exam results, just as the Baylor Law School is for bar exam results. Our PhD programs in religion, sociology, and information systems now compare well nationally on metrics of publications, grants, and awards. Still, an often necessary first step toward assessment is simply comparing us against ourselves, with a goal of improvement. Then the comparisons can be ratcheted up by steps, beginning with self-comparison, then university-wide comparison, and finally national or even international comparisons.

As we strive to improve our metrics, the strategies—higher stipends, new faculty lines—are likely to cost more than the university is willing to spend. At that point, the low-risk self-comparison may be insufficient and a higher-risk national comparison is needed instead. Nationally, what are stipend levels for graduate students in mathematics? What is the average number of graduate faculty in top philosophy programs? These measures are high risk because they can make faculty uncomfortable if the comparisons show that sufficient resources already exist, and they can make administrators uncomfortable if they show that current resources are insufficient. If our plucky graduate dean demonstrates that faculty are doing less than they should with existing resources or that our administration should be providing more resources, the collective response in either case may be "kill the messenger." Hopefully, our messenger dean moved slowly and strategically, with ingratiation and obsequience, from internal measures to relative assessment, co-opting along the way. If not, then hopefully our dean is tenured and ready to return to his or her first love—the classroom.

CARROTS AND STICKS

Let's suppose and hope that our dean has managed to generate assessments showing a need for improvement and has managed to remain a dean. Sometimes assessments alone are sufficient to induce change, but what happens if the level of dissatisfaction with the status quo is insufficient to induce change? In that case, selected implementation of rewards (carrots) and sanctions (sticks) is required. Of course, graduate deans typically have few carrots and no sticks, so such implementation must be extremely selective. However, even "real" deans, provosts, and presidents will find that almost all of their carrots have already been allocated just to maintain the status quo and that sticks bring about all kinds of public discontent resulting in uncomfortable questions from the governing board. Thus, all administrators might learn from the strategies developed from the desperation of the sans-portfolio graduate deans.

One strategy is awarding virtual carrots—virtual because they don't require resources the way pay raises, new faculty lines, higher stipends, and more research equipment do. I regularly publicize and praise our leading graduate programs for articles published by graduate students, external research grants, Academic Analytics rankings, student satisfaction, and so on. Now, one could rightly question how much an e-mail from the graduate dean or a list in the graduate school newsletter or a mention at Graduate Council can actually enhance desired behavior. Who cares if they get a "warm fuzzy" from a graduate dean? It's not like he's a real dean with real authority. Surprisingly, perhaps, people do care. I know they care because when they do poorly, they quarrel with me about the metrics; when they do well, they pass along the graphs to their fellow faculty, students, and alumni, and most importantly, regardless of where they rank, they will work to improve their program's metrics.

A more powerful strategy, of course, requires real carrots. I suspect that one reason my praise of graduate programs matters to our faculty is that I share that praise with those who do distribute carrots—deans, vice presidents, the provost, and the president. Moreover, I typically seek the assistance of those who do have authority. For example, if I can convince my administrative colleagues who approve new faculty lines to mention to the chair that one of the reasons her department received a new chemist is that chemistry supports so many graduate students through external funding, desired behavior that is encouraged. We should never miss an opportunity to associate a reward with a positive metric.

Although sanctions are delivered at the individual level (e.g., tenure decisions), big program-level sticks are so rare in higher education as to scarcely merit mention. Occasionally, a graduate program may be shut down due to poor performance, but that remains an uncommon event, even during the budget cutbacks that so many universities experienced during the recent Great Recession. We could explore why the stick is not wielded more than it is, but instead, let's simply recognize that receiving a blow from a stick is much less likely than receiving less than one's "fair" share of new carrots. In other words, an administrative strategy of giving most rewards to those programs most improving their assessments does not directly punish any program, but the effect can be positive change for all programs.

RULES, RESOURCES, AND REGULATORS

Let's conclude by revisiting the strategies that were introduced early in this chapter as alternatives to measurements, beginning with what I described as "an inordinate focus on the few rules we can enforce." Rules exist for a reason, and they should be enforced, but they are tools of management rather than leadership. Enforcing rules is necessary to keep things from getting much worse; rules have little to do with improving things much. If everyone uses her own format for her thesis, theses collectively get much worse. However, standardizing margin widths does nothing to actually improve the quality of a thesis. To do that, we first need to develop valid measures of thesis quality (e.g., number that are published, cited, or accessed online) and then seek to improve those measures by strategies that will typically have little to do with page margins. There is a time for management and a focus on the rules; that time is when it's important to reestablish equilibrium, to reinforce the status quo. There's a time for leadership and measurement; that time is when the status quo is insufficient.

Now let's look at the other two related strategies, ingratiation and obsequience. Recall that with my graduate school wish list introduced at the beginning of this chapter, I mentioned that the desired enhancements typically required resources. I then presented a farfetched scenario where administrators and faculty were so impressed by various measures that they supplied the necessary resources. From my experience, ingratiation and obsequience can often prove more effective in garnering resources than measurement can. It's not too farfetched to imagine a provost liking and trusting a dean enough to grant him or her additional resources.

However, it's important to remember that resources are a means rather than an end. Gaining additional resources is extremely important, but resources alone are not enough. During my brief honeymoon period as dean, I received a significant increase in badly needed funding for graduate student stipends. I immediately distributed the funds to my graduate program directors so that they could recruit stronger graduate students—except that they didn't. Stipend levels increased almost 10 percent, but the mean GRE scores were the same as the previous year. Recruiting strategies did not change; neither did the outcomes. And, after the honeymoon boost, the stipend budget was never increased by that much again. Fortunately, however, GRE scores have consistently improved, even in years without a funding increase, due to the strategic use of measurements. When GREs are measured, they matter; when they matter, strategies to recruit higher scoring students are developed; with better recruitment comes better graduate students. Resources matter, too, of course, but when they are linked to measurements of clearly defined goals, they will matter even more.

One last reason to embrace measurement: increased assessment and accountability are imminent. Whether assessments are externally imposed or internally developed is yet to be determined, but it's to our advantage to embrace and drive the accountability movement. Those of us within higher education understand its diversity and complexity and typically critique those metrics that assume we are all the same. However, if all we do is critique, if we do not develop our own alternative assessments, we can imagine the Department of Education, accrediting bodies, state legislators, and foundations and our own boards stepping into the breach. Just as faculty are best suited to develop measures of their departments, administrators should develop measures for their university. And if faculty resist assessing their departments and administrators resist assessing their universities, assessments will still be made, poorly, by external actors. No one escapes regulations, but higher education, if we are proactive, can continue to regulate itself by embracing measurement and assessment.

Assessment is coming. If we get ahead of it and develop our own measures, we can produce more valid assessments and help preserve our remaining autonomy. And, as a bonus, we can become effective leaders even if we are lacking in real authority.

Chapter Twenty-Five

Leading

*An Example from the College of Human
Ecology at Cornell University*

Alan Mathios

One of the most fundamental and important characteristics for the person leading an organization is to have a deeply rooted enthusiasm and passion for its mission. Understanding that mission and creating—for every individual associated with the organization—a line of sight of how their efforts support that mission is a key to high levels of morale, engagement, and the willingness of stakeholders to put in the extra effort that is so often required for excellence.

THE MISSION STATEMENT

The mission statement of the College of Human Ecology at Cornell University is "Improving Lives by Exploring and Shaping Human Connections to Natural, Social and Built Environments." When a college is multidisciplinary, as ours is, it is important to somehow convey this in the mission statement. The multidisciplinary approach implicit in this statement requires a leader to foster collaboration across the fields of design, life and physical sciences, and social sciences. This, in turn, requires a vision that supports and rewards excellence that crosses department and even college lines yet also contributes broadly to the quality of and strength of each of the underlying departments and disciplines. The mission of the college is rooted in the lofty goal of improving people's lives. The exploring and shaping terminology recognizes that pure exploration has its role, though the defining element of the college is that we seek to shape the world through our research, education, and outreach. The word "shape" acknowledges that our influence can be subtle, often difficult to isolate and identify, but important and crucial nonetheless.

Mission statements are very important to academic leadership because they set the direction for that leadership. While settling on the fourteen words that comprise our mission statement might seem to be a minor accomplishment, it is anything but. Unlike most colleges, the name of the college does not convey in a descriptive way the primary units (the Department of Human Development, the Department of Design and Environmental Analysis, the Department of Policy Analysis and Management, the Department of Fiber Science and Apparel Design, and the Division of Nutritional Sciences) that comprise the organization. This is both an advantage and disadvantage. There is an intriguing aspect to the mission's breadth, but it also demands some clarity to help define the scope of our inquiry. The fact that the name of the college does not directly suggest the names of the constituent units themselves leads one to think about the synergies and relationships across the departments that define human ecology.

In today's world, we believe it is important to go beyond disciplinary bounds and to explore the themes that integrate knowledge across disciplines. We have identified eight broad themes that describe what we study when we refer to "human connections to natural, social and built environments"—these include: Lifespan Development, Community and Family Policy, Sustainability, Public Health and Nutrition, Design and Health, Fashion and Technology, Economics and Federal Policy, and Human Neuroscience. In many ways, through these themes we believe that we have created a dynamic, modern version of what human ecology can be. The mission statement and its derivate themes guide my leadership of the college. This conceptual development took time and patience. It suffered from the ebbs and flows of constant debate, but eventually emerged to solidify our sense of ourselves.

It was essential to achieve broad consensus across stakeholders in gaining acceptance for these themes. Putting these very fundamental questions to my advisory council was extremely important—admitting to influential alumni that, at times, we struggle with our identity and the scope of our mission.

A dean always has to look at his or her college in a national as well as a local context. While the college has been developing our focus, the national landscape for colleges of human ecology was reason for concern. Over the last decade or so, several colleges of human ecology programs were either merged with other units or dismantled and the faculty distributed to other units. This fate, of course, can befall other kinds of colleges as well. One possible reason for this national trend among colleges of human ecology is that the organizing principle (multidisciplinary theme–based programs) has outlived its usefulness.

However, my observation was that, in fact, there was a movement afoot away from discipline-based thinking and more of a recognition of the creative innovation that comes from putting faculty together across disciplines to focus on particular themes. Articulating these themes and validating the innovation that comes from this organizational structure is what leadership of a college of human ecology, and perhaps other kinds of colleges as well, involves.

The success has manifested itself in an increasing portfolio of external grants to the faculty of the college, the ability to hire outstanding faculty who excel within their discipline but are focused on multidisciplinary endeavors, the ability to work productively across the numerous colleges at Cornell, the ability to matriculate phenomenal students, and the opportunity to greatly expand philanthropy to the college.

The mission statement should support and guide decisions across many realms. It should markedly influence the types of students who are admitted and the nature of the faculty who are hired, and it should most assuredly influence the facility that houses the college.

Buildings send a message about the work as well as the image of a college. Perhaps because of the role that design plays in the mission of human ecology, I have been consistently and pleasantly impressed with how we are able to tell the human ecology story through the building in which we live our work lives. Having faculty and students working together with our communications team and our facilities team has led to a confluence of ideas that have played out in numerous decisions about how we outfit our common spaces, our studios, our proposed new lecture rooms, and so forth.

We have been fortunate to have been able to construct a new building and renovate our original 1933 home. It could have been an opportunity wasted, had we not, from the outset, raised the storytelling part of the project to utmost importance. In the end, this teamwork approach, which combined faculty, student, and staff expertise, led to the Human Ecology Building being the first, and still only, LEED platinum certified building on the Cornell campus. The building has won numerous awards for its vision, its design, and the way it supports the academic mission.

Students were essential to the process, and it took some courage to provide, primarily to the students, the budget for the fixings, furnishings, and equipment that went into the common spaces of the building. This faith in our students has now become a common approach to facility development in the college, and it is spreading across the entire Cornell campus. Our design students have worked on many projects across the campus, trying to reflect the mission of the unit in its interior spaces.

CREATING A CULTURE OF COMMUNITY

Academic institutions emphasize and value independent thinking. Cornell University, for example, highlights that its faculty "think otherwise." Such organizations face particular challenges in creating a sense of common purpose. There are strategies for creating a strong sense of inclusion and community. Many universities, due to the demographics of our time, are facing significant faculty renewal. The significant growth in the faculty that occurred in the 1970s has now led to a growing number of retirements. The hiring of the next generation of faculty is certainly occurring in the College of Human Ecology, at Cornell University more broadly, and at many, if not most, of our peer institutions.

During my first seven years as dean, for example, the college hired over thirty percent of the current faculty. I anticipate that by the end of my second term as dean, half of the tenure-track faculty members who are in the college will have been hired under my leadership of the college. There are also significant changes at the staff level as well. This generational turnover presents a rare opportunity to set a tone for the community.

Several strategies have been employed to do this, which could be applied in virtually any college. Most of the efforts are led jointly with my human resources team.

First, at least every semester I convene a welcome-to-the-college breakfast for each new faculty member, new post-doc, new research scientist, or new staff member who has joined the college. It allows me to meet every person within a small, intimate setting and present to them the mission of the college, my passion for the mission, and the line of sight that each person has with respect to that mission. Part of the presentation is a look back into the history of the organization—its development from a college of home economics to its current state. Showing respect for the past—especially as this was a common pathway for women to have access to higher education—is an important part of my welcome. Also highlighted during this welcome is our dedication to our outreach and extension mission.

Cornell is both a private and land grant institution, giving it a unique position in the world of higher education. Our mission statement focuses on *shaping* human connections to natural, social, and built environments, rather than just exploring these connections. We take this very seriously. Every person who comes to the college will see that we truly seek to improve lives by translating research into meaningful outcomes for the public. Having faculty, staff, post-docs and others participating together sends a powerful message about the critical nature of each person's role in the organization and its outreach efforts. The academic stature of the college does, of course, rest with the reputation and productivity of the faculty. That productivity, however, is often enabled by the talents of the staff that support the education and research programs. This is made clear in this welcome event.

The second broad strategy of welcoming the faculty to the college is to expose them to the staff that can impact their work life. Our communications team is there to help promote their work and enhance the visibility and impact of their work. Having a get-together where we discuss with the faculty our strategic communications plan has proven very useful. It is now common practice that faculty, without being prompted, independently contact the communications team as they publish research findings that are likely to be of interest to the public. Given the topical and often applied nature of the work that we do, it is almost always the case that there is a "story" to be told about the research generated by the faculty.

The faculty also meet with our alumni-affairs and development group so that they understand the efforts we undertake to obtain gifts and commitments to support their work. They become enthusiastic and willing partners as we bring them to our events to talk with our alumni and friends. Similar meetings with our HR staff, our student support services, and others help to create an environment that builds mutual respect among the faculty and staff. In many academic institutions, the hierarchy between the faculty and the staff can lead to destructive rather than constructive interactions. We have also created informal programs where research is presented to the staff so that they have a better sense of the broad contributions of the faculty.

The focus on new faculty and on orienting them to the culture and mission of the college should not displace the need to communicate with the longer standing faculty. Fortunately, with about one hundred tenure-track faculty members, I am able to continually meet one-on-one with every faculty member on a rotating basis so to have the opportunity to better understand their aspirations, goals, and frustrations and to seek advice on how to best provide resources for their success. Listening to the needs of the faculty—and doing everything possible to facilitate their productivity--is one of the primary responsibilities of the dean.

A FEW GUIDING PRINCIPLES

There are two broad guiding principles that drive the delivery of our mission. *First and foremost is delivering a high-quality educational experience to students by using our expertise in research and outreach to enhance and support the undergraduate curriculum.* The higher education landscape is filled with impressive colleges and universities that provide a diverse set of approaches to educating students. Cornell is in a relatively unique position, being both in the Ivy League and the land grant university system of New York State. The College of Human Ecology is also one of the two colleges that govern the Cornell Cooperative Extension system (along with the College of Agriculture and Life Sciences). This confluence of responsibilities, if used strategically, can greatly influence how we engage with students.

From an accounting perspective, faculty members spend their time on teaching, research, and outreach. A typical faculty member has a 50 percent research appointment and a 50 percent appointment either to teach or to do extension work. For those with 50 percent teaching appointments, the coursework is spread across both graduate and undergraduate courses, along with advising responsibilities to both groups. So from an accounting view of the world, undergraduates account for approximately 15 percent to 25 percent of a faculty member's time. This "minimal" teaching expectation at research institutions has become part of a national debate—one focused on the escalating costs of higher education. However, the accounting perspective is misleading, especially if one finds a creative way to use the faculty efforts in research and outreach to enhance and, in many ways, be a primary source of education for students.

The triple integration of education, research, and outreach is well and alive in the college. The expectation that students engage with the faculty on their research has penetrated deeply into the mindset of our students. Even our freshman students now wonder, not whether they will be in a research lab, but rather which faculty lab they will associate with. Many faculty members have organized their labs so that a significant number of undergraduates work in teams, supervised by either a head undergraduate research assistant, a graduate student, or the faculty themselves.

In these instances, students learn about the content of the research topic, the research methods used to generate new knowledge, the leadership skills necessary to function efficiently and effectively within a team, and the importance of allocating responsibilities across team members in a way that takes advantage of each person's strengths. Each of the college's signature research themes (discussed in the first section) involves significant student engagement. The students work side by side with the faculty in their research labs, in the neuroscience imaging facility, in the design and technology shops, in the human metabolic research lab, and in the various labs that analyze secondary data for policy analysis.

Our efforts in this arena are validated by data collected through surveys. Each year Cornell University surveys all of its undergraduate students and every other year surveys the senior class. One of the key subsets of the survey is a set of questions about the opportunities for students to engage in research with faculty. Students from Human Ecology report the highest level of engagement, with approximately 70–80 percent of the seniors reporting that they have worked with faculty on research for either academic credit or for pay. The university also holds an annual poster session run by the Cornell University Research Board. Whereas human ecology undergraduate students comprise about 8 percent of the Cornell undergraduate population, they typically comprise between 25 and 30 percent of the poster sessions.

The amount of learning evident in the presentations brings me great pride. As dean, I use every opportunity to praise both the students and the faculty—who collectively put in significant work to make this a reality. This is especially time intensive for the faculty—as every student in the lab inevitably needs his or her research mentor to write endless numbers of letters of recommendation and to discuss with the faculty the broader issues that come up with regard to advising and career guidance.

The integration of the undergraduate curriculum with outreach and experiential learning is similarly influential. The college invests in several programs in New York City, has developed international exchange programs with other universities, and sends some of its students to places throughout the world through Cornell Abroad. We have developed a summer-experience program where students are aligned with faculty doing research but also engaging with the Cornell Cooperative Extension system. Students return from the summer with a great appreciation for the role that research plays in directly influencing outcomes for New York State residents. This is a powerful approach to engaged learning—one that often shapes the career aspirations of students and refines which coursework will further shape their knowledge in these newfound interests.

The second guiding principle is *to use our expertise in multidisciplinary team building to develop collaborations across the campus, ones that take advantage of the diversity and strength of the numerous colleges at Cornell.* Given our strength in multidisciplinary thinking around each of our themes, it is natural that we are in a position to foster effective collaborations with our colleagues in other colleges where complementary expertise exists. Rather than provide details on the collaborations that have evolved around each theme, I provide a few illustrative examples of how we have leveraged our focus to create university-wide investment and enthusiasm for these programs.

The Theme of Neuroscience in Human Ecology Helps Lead to the Cornell MRI Facility

The Cornell MRI facility is a new facility that opened in August of 2013 with initial investments from several Cornell colleges, including the College of Human Ecology, the College of Engineering, the College of Veterinary Medicine, and the College of Arts and Sciences. One of the key factors leading to the establishment of the MRI facility was the development of neuroscience as one of the broad themes associated with human ecology. That theme aligned very well with the Department of Human Development in Human Ecology and there was significant interest by faculty elsewhere—especially by an MRI physicist in the engineering college. This faculty member was willing to spearhead an NIH instrument grant to purchase the magnet.

The College of Human Ecology developed the plans for locating the MRI center in its physical plant and for selecting one of its faculty members as co-director of the facility. Faculty from all over the Cornell campus will now have access to a state-of-the-art facility that will enable researchers to blend the natural and social sciences. The use of fMRI methods to better understand human behavior, cognition, youth development, risky decision making, aging and memory, and endless other topics is an exciting area of growth. The establishment of this facility would not have been possible without Human Ecology developing, as part of its strategic planning, the theme of human neuroscience.

The Theme of Family and Community Policy Helps Lead to the Cornell Population Program

Social sciences at Cornell University are situated in almost every one of the seven undergraduate colleges and most of the professional schools. Not only are the social sciences broadly distributed, but, also, each of our social-science disciplines (i.e., economics, sociology, and psychology) have clusters of strength within several colleges. Collaboration requires synergies both within and across these disciplines. The expertise of the faculty in the College of Human Ecology in community and family policy was the driver of the Cornell Population Program. It has four fundamental areas of focus, including (1) families and children, (2) immigration, (3) poverty and inequality, and (4) health behaviors and health disparities. One can easily see the alignment of this program with the signature themes of the college. However, now there is significant involvement in the university broadly, with approximately one hundred faculty associates involved in the program. These faculty members span all of the colleges that have significant social-science expertise.

The center became an NIH-funded demography center, and we now continue to seek long-term support from the NIH to take it to the next level. Similar to the MRI facility, the establishment of the Cornell Population program would not have been possible without the college taking the lead and expanding from its theme-based strengths.

While these are just two examples of how our themes expand into University-level initiatives, there is a similar story with each of our theme areas. Leveraging the strength of the signature themes in the college with the rest of the university has major advantages. First, it positions the faculty to have an advantage in a highly competitive grant world. As the college has developed these multidisciplinary teams, we have seen a commensurate rise in our external funding portfolio. Moreover, these collaborations make for a compelling story for the alumni of the college. While many alumni have allegiances and connections with the particular college they graduated from, they also share a broader "Cornell" experience. When they see that their support for the college is also implicitly supporting other parts of Cornell, it is easier for them to be enthusiastic about the value of their financial gifts.

THE IMPORTANCE OF DEPARTMENTS
AND DEPARTMENT CHAIRS

While I have emphasized the role of a dean as someone who can see synergies across departments and colleges based on the research themes of the college, it is essential that the collaborations spring forth from outstanding departments. The departments are the lifeblood of the college. The faculty are recruited and retained within departments, most of the undergraduate majors are aligned with departments, and national recognition is often achieved department by department.

Success at the college level requires that the primary organizational structure of the academy—the department—have sufficient delegated authority so to avoid micromanagement and sufficient allocated budgets and discretionary funds so that they can be innovative and focus on long-term quality. Every department chair must feel empowered so that he or she feels enabled to make a long-term difference in the life of the unit. Too often, department chair positions are viewed as a rotating obligation rather than an opportunity to shape the future of the unit. Investment in the chairs of departments is a top priority—they should receive significant research support to make up for the time they devote to administration; they should receive compensation that is commensurate with the extensive responsibility they bear, and they should have strong research, teaching, and outreach credentials so that they are credible with the various groups impacted by their decisions. The choice of a faculty member from within the department versus an outside chair is a crucial decision for a dean and depends fundamentally on not only whatever talent exists within a department but also on the life course of the department itself. Departments often achieve a steady state where the productivity in terms of research, education, and outreach are on the anticipated positive trajectory.

Keeping the momentum without a major change in direction is often the desired goal for the foreseeable future of the program. In this case, assuming that the faculty group has a strong candidate for the chair, an internal candidate is likely to be the preferred strategy for selecting the chair. However, should the dean see a need for significant new directions or sense department complacency about the striving for excellence, then an external chair might be appropriate.

Whether an internal or external chair—resources need to flow to the units with relatively little held back at the center.

Directing resources to the departments puts those resources closer to the faculty—the drivers of the academic stature of the college. I cannot emphasize enough the importance of this. Sharing indirect cost recovery with the departments (where many of the administrative costs of grant management are borne) and providing salary recovery on grants back to the departments are just two of the mechanisms used to support the chairs and provide incentive-compatible structures for securing external funds. Having the faculty believe that the dean's office is there to support their work, raise funds for such work, and facilitate the delivery of the research and education that comes from the faculty is crucial.

DEVELOPING THE LEADERSHIP TEAM OF THE COLLEGE

It would be difficult to find any dean who would not immediately talk about the support that he or she needs to obtain from the college leadership team. The team at the College of Human Ecology is truly exceptional, and whatever success the college has had is attributable to the joint and overlapping efforts of this team. For each specific functional area, it is useful to think about the Venn diagram approach to managing a team. Below, I discuss just three of the areas where there is an assistant or associate dean leading the effort. In actuality, there is more complexity as there are numerous other functional areas led by directors or assistant deans (Facilities, Information Technology, Research, Finance, Human Resources, etc.) that have overlapping responsibilities with each other and with the three areas highlighted in figure 25.1.

One of the challenges in leading a team is to get each of the leaders of the functional areas to devote enough of his or her energy, time, and resources to coordinate in a strategic way the overlapping areas of the circles. This is further complicated by the fact that, in addition to these focus areas within the college, there are parallel efforts done at the university level. For example, the Office of Alumni Affairs and Development in the college has significant joint responsibility with the university-level office of the same name.

Typically, the director or associate dean of a functional area within the college will report to the dean of the college and also have a reporting relationship to the university vice president in charge of that area.

It is natural that the overlapping areas of the diagram present some challenges. First, the size of the non-overlapping area within each circle dominates the area of the total. The direct performance metrics tend to be in this space. The staff of the Alumni Affairs and Development Office, for example, is under constant pressure to connect and engage with alumni and, most

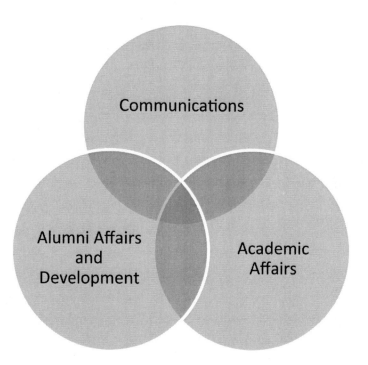

Figure 25.1.

importantly, to reach its fundraising goals. The Admissions, Student, and Career Office within the academic-affairs circle must admit, matriculate, and then support a diverse and talented class of students. Activities that do not linearly and directly feed into these goals can quickly become backburner issues. Moreover, the overlapping areas can create confusion as to who is ultimately responsible for the activities in that space. Lack of clarity on this issue can create frustration for all parties, and one can lose trust in one another. It is the dean's job to develop strategies for addressing these governance relationships in ways that make the work at the intersection to be productive. Especially important to consider is that, while the slivers of overlap may not constitute a large percentage of the area of the circle, the outcomes for each of the units that share some overlap may depend crucially on how effectively that overlap is managed.

THE DEAN AND THE PROVOST

The quality of the working relationship between the dean and the provost can have a significant impact on the college. At Cornell, the deans are considered part of the leadership team of the entire university. The collection of deans and the provost meet on a weekly basis for several hours and discuss virtually every aspect of the university. The deans are asked to participate in committees that develop recommendations on crucial matters facing the university, including budgeting models, financial-aid policies, methods for revenue enhancement, strategies for cost containment, and so on.

While most of the time the goals of the university and the college are well aligned, there are times when these are not congruent. In these cases, it is important to be able to decipher under what circumstances one should support the university, even if the college is potentially impacted negatively. Doing this effectively builds trust with one's fellow deans and with the provost. Given the collaborations across colleges discussed earlier, this trust is essential for effective governance.

It is also important to be willing to "volunteer" significant time to support and participate in provost-level initiatives. During my first term as dean, I co-chaired the committee that authored the self-study for the Cornell decennial accreditation. I now serve as a commissioner for the Middle States Commission on Higher Education, have served on a financial aid task force that evaluated all aspects of Cornell's financial-aid policies, was the dean responsible for working with the Vice President of University Facilities to reorganize the entire facilities division in order to reduce costs and generate efficiencies, served on the Executive Policy Review Group that helps develop and execute all of Cornell's policies, and served on the executive committee examining the need for the new Health Care Center on campus. Those are just a few of the ways in which deans participate in campus governance. Participation in these activities allows a dean to establish a university perspective, preparing them for other leadership roles, either at Cornell or other places.

CONCLUSION

There are several approaches that have helped me manage the expected and unexpected situations that arise on a daily basis. First and foremost is a philosophy of emotional under-reaction to situations and resisting immediate response. Having a calm demeanor when unexpected situations arise puts people at ease and allows them to function more effectively. In fact, one is likely to find that many problems simply go away even with short passages of time. Under-reacting to situations allows one to determine whether a proposed solution is even necessary. It also allows one to make decisions after the instinctual highly emotional state has passed. Making quick pronouncements in a highly emotional state does not typically make for good policy.

The second approach toward managing the college that has worked for me is to be very wary of making assumptions about a human-resource issue prior to having face-to-face discussions with the affected parties. Second-hand information that comes to a dean can be influenced by the path by which the information has flowed. Premature assessment of a situation gets in the way of good listening skills.

A final last thought regards e-mail and electronic communication. To the extent possible, I have found face-to-face communications to be much preferable to an extended discussion through e-mail. Walking to someone's office and having a discussion can often lead to a much more spontaneous and fruitful discussion. In the end, it often saves time, as extended and repeated e-mail exchanges can be quite burdensome. Moreover, in-person discussions allow for frank conversations. When doing business through the exchange of e-mails, it is important to consider that it is possible that the content could be distributed publicly. This can constrain the conversation.

In summary, under-reacting to situations, listening rather than assuming, and using face-to-face interactions rather than e-mail are practices that have helped me lead the college.

Chapter Twenty-Six

"Managing Up" in the Academy

David D. Perlmutter

ABSTRACT

Tenure-line faculty members in higher education are often well trained to conduct their research and spottily trained to teach but ill versed in managing the politics and relationships—that is, the human factor—so crucial for the advancement of their careers. This chapter draws on more than a decade of research and writing about interpersonal relations within academic departments and specifically focuses on the role of, and dyad with, the chair or head of the academic unit. "Managing up" is a vital skill to teach to young faculty. The precepts of how to get along with the chair are detailed within the perspective of the chair's role, motivations, and responsibilities.

After more than a decade of writing about academic careers, I am struck by certain patterns that cut across all of our many disciplines and types of institutions. The foremost is that most problems people encounter as they traverse doctoral programs, tenure tracks, and beyond are people problems. Research and teaching obviously present many challenges, but people— ranging from colleagues to deans to advisees to, of course, the individual sojourner herself—affect progress more than any other factor. In fact, people are the master variable that affects all others: You may be a brilliant doctoral researcher, but a brutal, exploitive adviser may undermine your progress, starve you of resources, and belittle your achievements to the point where your science is for naught. Or you may really care about teaching but find yourself in a department whose chair demands quantity of bodies and seats, where high evaluations are the be-all and end-all of pedagogy. Alternately, you may be the problem: You lack read-the-room skills, fail to play well with others, or generally alienate people trying to help you.

Worse, we confront such people problems with little or no preparation. As I described in my book on promotion and tenure, while most of us do get training to be researchers and teachers, we get little or no training to be *professors* and possibly acquire no understanding of the role and responsibilities of administrators.

The first step in getting along with other people is to comprehend their motivations. Often during my early career, and now through the lenses of the many grad students and tenure trackers I speak to, I have heard some version of, "And then he did this to me for no reason. . . ." Well, there are indeed erratic folks among the professorial and administrative ranks in our trade. But people who act badly, without purpose, and randomly are fortunately rare: In my some twenty-five years in higher education, I have met only a handful of sociopaths whom I would describe as chaotically evil. More likely, good and bad actions are driven by motivations and objectives you just may not fathom.

Of all the people with whom we most need to learn to have a positive relationship, those with some degree of authority over us take precedence. Indeed, there comes a time when every assistant professor, if he or she is to survive in academe, must learn how to "manage up"—that is, learn how to negotiate the intricacies of a relationship with a dean or department head.

That skill seems to come naturally to some new PhDs; for others, like myself, not so much.

A few years into my first teaching job, a student complained to my dean about my classroom conduct. I honestly don't recall now what I was alleged to be doing wrong. The dean sent me a note asking to see me about the matter. I refused, replying that he should simply dismiss the student complaint and "take my side." The dean again requested to see me, explaining that he could not reject a student petition without investigation. After further (and increasingly terse) memo exchanges, there came a confrontation in the hallway. Voices were raised, tempers spiked, and one shocked secretary told me later that she thought a fistfight was about to erupt.

I backed down, grudgingly, described my side of the student dispute and, even though the dean decided in my favor, drove home later in a fury. But sometime that evening it occurred to me that I was angry at my supervisor for doing his job, which was both unfair to him and shortsighted of me, since I had fantasies of one day being in his position.

Shouldn't we all know better? Certainly, for a good deal of our apprenticeship, we are students beholden to advisers, committee members, and—probably somewhat more distantly—administrators. But drawing from observations and from the experiences of friends and colleagues, it seems quite easy to sail through the graduate-student years and not fully grasp what it means to have a "boss."

Many of us approach our academic careers with a certain amount of idealism and even elitism. Isn't the professoriate "different," in that we are granted autonomy in our work and have little in common with those poor cubicle dwellers of the vulgar trades?

The answers to such questions lie in individual experience. Being an assistant professor in a department of French at the University of Pennsylvania, for example, is indeed a different experience from being a sales associate at a midrange paper supply company in Scranton. In no profession, however, are we immune to the need to learn how to navigate the organization so that our achievements will produce the benefits they deserve. Getting along with an academic boss, then, involves a set of basic strategies that probably make sense in any workplace.

IT'S NOT ALL ABOUT YOU: APPRECIATE THE CHAIR'S SITUATION AND GOALS

You work at an institution with many layers of managers who each have their own goals and aspirations. Luckily, your interests often coincide with theirs. At a research institution, if you publish enough, teach competently, and stay out of trouble, you and they both look good. But it is vital to be aware of the benchmarks that are particularly attractive to the leadership of your institution.

To begin, know that, for example, department chairs themselves have a supervisor to whom they directly report, likely a dean, who is much more a "boss" for them than a department chair is for faculty. For one thing, when you are a chair you typically "serve at the pleasure" of the dean—that is, a chair's tenured status as a faculty member does not preclude her being fired from her administrative posting at the dean's displeasure and, as the euphemism goes, "returning to the faculty."

In short, chairs may be powerful, but they are not invulnerable. They likely have a set of acute goals they wish to achieve in the short, medium, and long term—like, say, getting a new academic program approved and installed. They also have continuing interests, like maintaining a collegial atmosphere in the department.

The basis of your relationship with the chair, then, can often be gauged by how much you understand what the chair wants and how much you help her, or at least not impede her. So find out what she wants from you; it is then up to you to what extent you fulfill the role she has planned for you.

CLARIFY MUTUAL EXPECTATIONS

A department chair once described a typical nightmare of anyone in administration. A faculty member made a request for some very expensive equipment that the unit could not afford but that he assured had been promised to him by the previous chair. Promised verbally, that is. And the previous chair was deceased.

A majority of disputes in academia could be resolved if people were in the habit of writing out all mutual expectations in detail. I myself try to send a "recap and clarify" e-mail after any meeting in which I promise to do anything for anyone.

Keep in mind that while you and your chair may certainly be equally "busy," she is almost certainly more distracted and bombarded with many requests, some in mutual conflict. In larger departments, dozens or more staff and faculty, as well as hundreds of others (parents, students, administrators, etc.) may be asking something of the chair. That a chair does not recall the exact details of an agreement with you is not an insult, it just may be an error.

So help your chair help you. Whenever you both agree to something, confirm it in writing and save the correspondence.

BALANCE NOT BEING A PUSHOVER WITH NOT BEING ENDLESSLY PUSHY

No one cares more about your career than you do. Even the most benevolent chair has many concerns about the department and you are but one—perhaps in the scale of things a minor one. This fact can be somewhat shocking to new faculty who perhaps were "stars" in their PhD program and were heavily courted during the hiring process. But the hiring honeymoon can't last forever. So, self-evidently, you will falter on the tenure track if you follow one of two extremes in your relationship with your chair:

a. You are always in her face, complaining, protesting, and radiating an "it's all about me" attitude.
b. You ignore the chair, trusting completely that she knows telepathically what you need and will automatically look out for your best interests.

Both scenarios are scripted for epic fails—for you. Both are ego driven. A middle ground of standing up for your rights and interests without being a pest is far more liable to succeed with a reasonable chair.

PICK YOUR WHINES

Gaining a reputation as a malcontent will not enhance your career. Certainly you may take legitimate grievances to the boss: a leaking office roof, a lazy teaching assistant, a need for more lab money. But it is all too easy, when you are the suffering party, to get tunnel vision about the relative importance of such problems and amnesia about the frequency with which you raise them.

One tip on maintaining a macro-perspective is to keep a diary of your interactions with authority figures. How many times have you made requests and for how much? Were they issues that were truly "dean worthy," or could you have handled the problem yourself?

As important as the frequency of your complaints are the tone and style. Do you present your petitions as reasonable queries or as petulant demands? A simple rule: Never approach a boss with a problem without having investigated two or three practical solutions.

APPRECIATE THE TIME AND TIMING FACTORS

Other dimensions of reasonable attention getting are face time and timing. When I was a department chair, and now that I am a dean, I did and do hold a monthly lunch session with the assistant professors. I find such informal get-togethers, with food as a lubricant, are invaluable to gauging the feelings and thoughts of the tenure trackers. I believe, although I can't know for sure, that they find it useful to have a Q&A, not only with me, but also with their peers. In general, it would be good for you to get some time with your chair at least once a month outside of the interaction when a problem occurs. Good chairs will look forward to such encounters—they sure beat budget meetings!

Besides keeping on the radar of the chair, if you are an adult with normal social skills—something not guaranteed in our profession—you probably know that timing is important in people-to-people interaction. Relevantly, the time to ask Dad for gas money was not just after you had scraped the car against the garage wall. Likewise, after a few months on the job as a tenure tracker you will get a sense of the rhythms of the departmental semester and the mood swings of your chair. In some departments, for example, the best time to bring up a new funding request is very early in the fiscal year when the department has just gotten new funding; in other institutions the optimal time is the end of the fiscal year when departments are scrambling to "zero out" their budgets.

The departmental secretary is a great source of information on such timing considerations, as in, "I wouldn't go in there right now; he just had an unpleasant meeting with the dean. . . ."

So think about the "when" of interacting with the chair. Often that makes a difference between a no and a yes.

HELP OUT EVERY ONCE IN A WHILE

Some years ago I visited the principal of my children's elementary school. The evening before, I had witnessed a contentious parent-teacher-administrator gathering in which there was loud and sometimes caustic debate about some major issues of curriculum, parking, and afterschool care. When I sat down in her office I noted her weary and wary look, as in, "Oh, God, another parent coming to air grievances." Instead I told her that I appreciated her calmness and maturity at the meeting and I thought most of us parents—loud squawkers aside—knew that she was doing her best with limited resources. She was drop-jawed in astonishment and declared that in a decade of K–12 administration she had only a few times gotten such a compliment.

The situation of department chairs today is generally not so extreme. In that role myself, I received enough supportive comments to balance out the complaints and protests. But we all could use some help. So why not do something nice for your chair once in a while?

Actually, volunteering to help out on an occasional department project or two will probably neither make your career nor sink it. However, good chairs will balance out your offering of assistance and might reduce the other work for which they "volunteer" you.

So don't dodge the grunt work. Show up for meetings. Answer your e-mail. Attend your office hours. Every profession, every job, entails activities that are unromantic and seemingly lacking in value for the individual. Academe is full of pointless committee assignments, problem-student advising, and reports that no one will read.

It would be criminal for a supervisor to load up junior faculty members with such tasks to the point that they couldn't focus on their primary goals of research and teaching. On the other hand, no assistant professor should think that personal gratification—teaching only the courses you like, advising only the students who intrigue you, and doing only the committee work directly related to your research—is possible or politically acceptable.

DON'T PLACE ALL YOUR BETS ON ONE CHAIR

Chairs come and go. Sometimes the exit is sudden: They announce they have taken a job elsewhere, they quit in frustration, or they are "returned to the faculty" by the dean. Sometimes their tenure is cyclical; many departments have a three-year rotating chair system.

One young assistant professor was, as he described it, "devastated" that his chair was leaving for another position. He explained that the chair had been his greatest champion in the tenure track and now he worried he might not get tenure as a consequence.

Well, you should never trust that one person alone will guarantee your promotion and tenure. Certainly, a powerful chair may be a key influencer in the final decision, but never spend your six or more years on the tenure track just building the support of any one person; it is more often than not a faculty vote, after all.

The optics and logistics of being the chair's favorite may also not help you. As the biblical book Exodus reminds us, "There arose a new Pharaoh over Egypt, who knew not Joseph." Your tenure bid should be tied to your merits; personal connections can help, but don't rely on the latter at the expense of the former. Build a good relationship with your chair, keeping in mind the other players who will affect your future.

A friend who is a retired university president asserted, "This is the worst time in history to be a department chair." There may be some truth to that. Although there are many joys in helping programs, students, and faculty reach their objectives, chairs today are under unprecedented stress for many reasons, including tighter budgets and tension over changes in the university itself. From the assistant professor's point of view the chair may be in a position of great power, but understand that they have motivations and aspirations that they fret over probably as much as you worry about getting that journal article published.

Get to know the chair and what she wants and has to do to succeed; try to find a way to have her goals merge with yours. Appreciate that helping you is part of her job, but only one part. And don't expect her to be the only determinant of your success.

Chapter Twenty-Seven

Leadership

A View from Veterinary Medicine

Jean Sander

As one of what will hopefully be a tidal wave of female administrators in the formerly male-dominated profession of veterinary medicine, I have often had the pleasure of discussing my journey with younger colleagues who either aspired to administration or who needed to be supported and eventually recruited into that role. What follows is something of a distillation of those conversations. As such, it is inevitably a struggle between being objective and being first person, opinionated, and subjective, but so is the process of mentoring.

I don't think anyone who goes into academia as a career thinks "I want to be a dean when I grow up!" And yet here I am, serving in the role of the "other"—the dean who "doesn't understand what it's like to be a faculty"! I actually had a faculty member say that to me early in my current deanship, and I was rendered almost speechless. How did he think I got here—by clicking my heels three times and repeating, "There's no place like the corner office"? What he did not recognize is that becoming an administrator in higher education is a decision made at one of the forks in the road of what is first a successful faculty career. It is precisely the fact that you have successfully navigated the way from graduate student to professor that first opens the possibility of choosing the administrative path.

A career in higher education administration isn't for everyone, nor should it be. To be successful as a dean or president, the first, and perhaps most fundamental, change you must make in your "worldview" as a faculty member is developing the ability to step outside of your own area of expertise to focus on the greater good of the whole. As faculty, we are rewarded for doing just the opposite. Faculty are trained in and expected to focus on the area they know best and to delve deeply enough to mine new knowledge from that depth. While the ability to collaborate is encouraged, it is for the purpose of advancing of the faculty member's personal academic success and the ability to use other disciplines to dig deeper into one's own. Conversely, the skills and abilities required to be a good administrator lie in appreciating the breadth of the college or university's mission and the overall success of the entire faculty. So before you consider embarking on an administrative position in your educational institution, take stock of what matters most to you and what you want your professional legacy to be; do you want to personally discover the new mousetrap or help the group rid the world of mice?

My academic journey has included a great deal of evolution, but like many who have made the choice for administration, I can identify a "tipping point." Much of my career simply "happened *to* me " until I went to a month-long institute for women in higher education. During that time I heard of the variety of areas that administrators are responsible for. At the end of those four weeks, there were some who had learned that administration in higher education was not for them, whereas I was encouraged and excited to know that the skills and desires I possessed were a good fit for leadership. From that time until the present, I laid out a course to embrace my strengths, accept my limitations, and alter my academic career in a direction where I might have the chance to influence the profession that I love in a way that I feel will preserve what is good, modify what needs to change, and be a part of creating what it might be. As with all things, research and knowledge lead the way in making career decisions, and I encourage everyone to explore and discuss this potential career path with as wide a group as possible.

While serving in an administrative role can be very rewarding, it is not an easy road. Because of the nature of academia, and the fact that faculty are expected to focus on only their area, it is a common occurrence for any individual decision made by administration to be well received by some and to anger others. To be able to survive and continue leading a college forward requires the person in charge to be centered in his or her vision and have the strength of character to know that the disgruntled comments are not personal, but rather expressions of disagreement with how any one particular administrative decision might not benefit that individual's professional goals. What detractors call a "thick skin" is actually a well-developed appreciation of that principle.

My role as dean is to facilitate the success of each person who works here, thereby promoting the success of the whole. I also believe that complacency and trying to keep the status quo make success difficult, if not impossible. Moving forward means change, but it goes against human nature to embrace change. I can see a few reasons for that; we all want to ensure our career survival, so change may be perceived as threatening; or there may be a fear that others will end up receiving the benefits we currently enjoy, at one's own expense. For whatever reason, the unknown is scary and takes a lot of effort.

As an academic administrator, you will be looked to for a sense of boldness that will support the faculty and staff as they enter uncharted waters. You will be called on to model the fact that a fear of failure can increase your attention to details, but that when it becomes pathology, it can paralyze your actions. As the chief manager of change in your organization, you must even become adept at knowing how to fail, which is also an important characteristic for a successful administrator.

I learned this lesson very early on when I went skiing for the first time. I was already an adult so decided it would be wise to take a lesson before hitting the slopes. The first thing they taught me was how to fall down; in other words, how to fail. And I can assure you that that skill was a necessary part of my progress. Had I not learned how to fall safely I would have likely never gone up the mountain, would still be on the bunny slope, and would have missed the thrill of success. The same holds true in all aspects of life, but it will be your job to remind your organization of that process.

So how do I as a dean make change safer? I do that by allowing mistakes as a normal part of the process. My approach is different from that of many. I have embraced my mistakes, as they have been my greatest teachers, and I have openly shared my mistakes with others so they see that it's really okay. . . . I've made them, too! If I want others to take ownership of creating a better future, I need to not only empower them to do so but also provide a safe environment for them to try and fail. My experience with this approach has been to see many young faculty members step up and take the lead on new initiatives, bringing a fresh new perspective and providing them with leadership opportunities that will help them as they grow into their roles.

So what are the skills and abilities that I feel have helped me along the way? One characteristic I have found to be essential in my success is to be "real" and let folks get to know who you are. In an earlier administrative position, I saw so many things that needed to be done differently that I set out to "make the wrong right" and was shocked when the great ideas I presented were not deemed to be of the exceptional brilliance I thought they were (just joking). I received little to no support for any of the ideas I pitched to the faculty, which progressed to a state that no matter what I did, it was not going to be accepted.

In retrospect, I came to see that the folks who were my greatest resistors had no knowledge of me before I suddenly appeared to tell them how to do things better. Also, I failed to include them in the discussions that led up to the proposed changes. I think it is fair to say that the unknown will generally always be suspect, and when it is presented by an unknown person, the skepticism kicks in, and even great ideas die a slow death. Valuing diversity, collaboration and wide input, coupled with the patience needed to let those processes work, is also a vital skill for an academic administrator.

While I am capable in my own role and I know it, I have learned to always demonstrate my belief that any person with whom I work, whether they hold positions superior or inferior to mine, are not any more or less important than I am in my role as dean. We all have roles that are important to the success of the whole and, therefore, the level of respect given to excellent work and positive contribution should be the same from the janitor to the regents. How this visibly manifests itself is that when I see something that needs to be done, be it a spill to be wiped up or a chair that needs fixing, if I am able to, I stop then and there and take care of it. I believe the message that nothing contributing to the mission is so insignificant that it is not worth doing is best sent by showing folks that I do value what others do to keep the place up and running. The strength of our individual roles is that diversity—in people, abilities, knowledge, and areas of responsibility—complements each one. I do not expect others to be good at the same things I am, nor do I hold myself to an unrealistic standard of knowing more than everyone about everything. I fully engage my leadership team in developing plans and making decisions, as each person brings a different perspective, and only when all angles are considered are the best decisions made.

As an aside, that valuation of diversity was very different from the several deans who served before me, and I believe my style unbalanced folks somewhat. I'm sure there were those who saw my engaging them in decisions that affected the college as a demonstration of my inability to lead. For me, both wide engagement and diversity in all things were essential for the development of ownership of the outcome. With that said, I had to always be aware that the final decision (and any fallout that resulted) was mine to own.

Academic administrators who "lead" without diversity and engagement often rocket their organizations down the wrong path. If the folks around you are not invested in the outcome or are not empowered or allowed to participate in creating a better future, they may not be willing to tell you when you are about to make a mistake. With each new hire I've made, I've advised my new team member that they will not be helpful if they simply agree with everything I say or propose. A "yes man" won't keep you from stepping off the cliff if you seem to appear determined to do it. Administrators need to remember that they are viewed as "the boss," and therefore others will believe that you must surely know that stepping off that cliff is the right thing to do! A further essential skill for academic administrators is to develop the ego strength to give those around you permission and encouragement to tell you that you are about to make a big mistake.

Each person brings inherent personality characteristics that must be assessed (because they will work both for you and against you) and developed into strong, positive themes of your personal style of leadership. For example, I have always been very direct in approaching issues. Perhaps my strongest belief, which I carry throughout my administrative activity, is that being clear and honest in one's conversations with others helps them to clearly understand your expectations. I don't expect people to be able to read my mind, as I am pretty bad at doing that with others. In addition, I expect others to be willing to say what needs to be said, as I do. In short, I want folks to be willing to have the difficult conversations *with* the people who need to hear them. We all know of situations where a person with a grievance will tell everyone *except* the person they need to talk to. Somehow we simply expect others to know when we are unhappy with how things are and believe the ill-doer is somehow doing it to them for personal reasons. Given that scenario, it's easy to see why folks take it personally and avoid the interaction. But the reality may be very different if the difficult conversations actually take place.

However, my "direct to the point" style of communication has been problematic with those who avoid direct confrontation, as well as with people who feel it necessary and important to spend a certain period of time with small talk before entering into the topic of the conversation. I've had to work at controlling my inherent style to allow those who come to me to discuss something the chance to get to the point on their own terms.

By way of example, a peer administrator at one institution, who very much enjoyed having the floor, came to my office one day to discuss a problem that affected both of us. Very early in the conversation I became aware of where this was going and what he wanted to discuss with me. I tried a couple of times to short circuit the conversation so we could spend the bulk of the meeting actually working on the issue. After trying a couple of times to jump ahead, I realized that unless I allowed this colleague to share the story in his own way at his own pace we were never going to get to the point. So I leaned back and listened, and listened, and listened until we were able to finally address the problem. Had I continued to try to move it along, we might still be in that office trying to get through the conversation!

I carry this same philosophy up the hierarchy to those I work for. While it is essential to be open and honest about what you want and need in workplace interactions and culture, you must also be willing to have these honest conversations with those whom you report to. Until you are able and willing to do that, you will never hold a position where you can do your best work and should certainly not choose an administrative role.

In a former administrative role, I was the only female on the leadership team. I found that time and again the ideas I brought to the table were overlooked, while similar (or sometimes identical) ideas when presented by my male colleagues were deemed worthy of consideration, and that questions I asked or input I provided were never acknowledged. Over time, this made me feel that the expertise I brought to the table was unimportant and that I was being dismissed. Realizing this was not a sustainable situation for me professionally I went to my superior and shared my concerns. I was very frank in saying that I wanted to be answered when my questions were asked and to have my input accepted on its value alone. My boss was surprised and unaware of how I perceived his behaviors and actions and appreciated the opportunity to do differently. Had I not been willing to "lead up," he would have gone on with the same behaviors, and I would have eventually left the position out of frustration at my inability to make a difference.

Having identified your positive commitments and methods for making them work for positive change, you will also want to share those principles with those who work for you. I make sure that directness and having difficult but necessary conversations is encouraged throughout my organization. When a supervisor doesn't hold his or her people accountable for bad behavior, the supervisor is thereby rewarding the ones who are not doing as they should by requiring others to carry their weight. That sort of leadership, often excused because confrontation is difficult and reprimanding folks is "not nice," can only lead to an overall decline in productivity and performance. Avoiding discipline does nothing to reward deserving members and in fact sends a strong message that their efforts are neither recognized nor valued. Each person, regardless of his or her role, must be treated fairly and justly.

In summary, although directly confronting issues is a personal commitment, it is also a *sine qua non* for a successful academic administrator. When considering this career path, it is worth having a brutally honest conversation with yourself as to your ability to be consistently truthful with others for the benefit of the institution and the mission.

In contemplating your personality traits and philosophic commitments before embarking on an administrative career, you will uncover (if you are honest) some weaknesses that may not be easily overcome. To be a successful leader you must be willing to take a hard look at yourself and figure out what your abilities are and where you need to rely on others for those skills you don't possess. Once you've discovered those areas where you do not excel, you need to find others who do possess those abilities. Then these others must be empowered and instructed on how to fill in the gaps that your abilities leave to allow you to be successful as the face of the college. I have no trouble accepting that my assistants are better at some things than I am, and I always let them know how important their actions are in keeping me informed and competent. You must develop the ability to allow others to work with you—not as a negative but as an extension of your self-awareness and confident leadership. Get good at delegating. It's hard at first because we know how we want things done, but the truth is that there are many ways to accomplish the same result. When the outcome isn't successful, help them help you better. Taking the time to develop a "good right hand" or two is efficient and can allow you to realize greater success.

Developing good "right hands" goes beyond the avoidance of mistakes. For every administrator, there are simply not enough hours in the day to complete everything you need to do. Academic administrators need to be masters at multitasking, as they are often a central point for multiple functions of the organization. There are days when I go from meeting to meeting without a break and need to be able to transition my thoughts to different topics on a dime. You are also the face of your institution and are expected to be involved in things going on in your college, within the university as a whole, in the community, and possibly (as in my case) in a profession. I'm showing my age, but I've often likened my job to the plate spinner on the old *Ed Sullivan Show*. You run from pole to pole, giving it a quick spin to keep the spinning plate aloft. If you slow down, your plates will all fall and break. That's not a good way to be successful.

Academic administrators, therefore, also need to have lots of energy because of the expectation that you will be involved in everything that is going on. As I just mentioned, being present is essential as it sends the message that you are interested and care about whatever it is you are attending. When you skip an event, you run the risk of having folks fill in your absence with the incorrect perception that you don't care about their particular activity. The perception, however inaccurate it may be, can become how you are viewed. This is not a nine to five job, and you need to make sure you have the endurance to not only stay in the game but to do it with grace. Being in good shape and taking care of your health is essential. Eat and sleep well so you can keep up with all you are expected to do. Establishing a good work/life balance is critical to your sustainability.

"God grant me the serenity to accept the things I cannot change." I went to the undergraduate college that the author of the Serenity Prayer, Reinhold Niebuhr, attended, and this bit of philosophy has been with me ever since. As an administrator in academia, you shouldn't allow yourself to become totally invested in outcomes. No matter what direction you take or what changes you see that could be made to improve things, you will not always be totally empowered to make those changes. So focus on doing the parts you are able to influence to the best of your ability, while reserving the strength to accept whatever final outcome emerges. To do otherwise will cause disappointment and frustration that can grow into resentment, and once resentment has entered the picture, your ability to connect positively with those around you will be lost. You will need to be flexible, nimble, and creative because as things change you need to change with them. All you are able to influence is the process. For example, you may be developing collaboration with another college to discuss how together you might proceed to a given outcome when the other school gets cold feet and backs out. This is an opportunity to change what you can—find another college that can be an adequate match and take all you've done up to this point to the new opportunity. I've been amazed at how often better opportunities stem from initial disappointments if you are just willing to see what might be.

As an academic leader, you will be looked to as an advocate for new possibilities and positive change. In that role, having a "can do" attitude will go a lot farther and successfully draw in more productive and effective partners than talking about budget shortfalls and the decline of society. There is nothing as annoying as listening to how many ways we *cannot* do something or how we are not empowered to do what we want because of the many barriers. I see barriers as opportunities and have used situations like this as incentive to change policy and culture where it is needed. There are always ways to make things better, and just because a process is in place does not mean that it is the best process for success. As a leader in higher education, it is your responsibility to address these things when you see them and to support positive change and growth in the institution, even when those programs are not within your sphere of authority.

Finally, it is essential that you recognize the tremendous responsibility that you take on as an administrator of the academy. In a very real sense, you are declaring your personal responsibility for preserving and advancing the system that allowed you to succeed. From the time you commit to an academic career until your retirement and beyond, you must stay up on the issues affecting higher education, your profession or your academic discipline, and society as a whole. Higher education is at a crossroads today as we are being challenged to reduce costs despite the research that shows that employment benefits are significantly enhanced by advanced degrees. We have not done a good job at telling the story and showing our benefits. We assumed others would know, since it was so clear to us. In addition, colleges and universities have struggled to entice bright young minds to enter into academia, as it is not as lucrative as many industry positions, and the lifestyle can be grueling at times.

Beyond contemplating your skills, abilities, personality, and knowledge, your final question before embarking on an academic leadership career is solely personal. Do you want to take responsibility for the future of higher education, for the success of students, faculty, and staff as a whole, regardless of their fears and concerns? Will this career path bring you the challenge, excitement, frustration, and joy that your academic discipline once provided? If so, welcome—you will find true colleagues here.

V

Chairs and Past Chairs

Chapter Twenty-Eight

Being a Department Chair

Fifteen Tips for Success

Henry L. Roediger III

Academia is a strange business. Like all businesses, it needs leaders. In the world of for-profit business, leadership is a huge topic. The same is true in most organizations, whether military or sports or whatever. Yet, unlike other organizations, people in the upper administration in universities are hardly ever really trained for their role. Unlike in business or the military, where courses in leadership are expected (even mandatory), hardly anyone in the upper administration of universities has explicitly learned about leadership and other topics unless they chose to read up on it themselves. Graduate programs in chemistry, engineering, history, or English would never have a course in leadership, and the same is true in most fields (there might be such a course in psychology or in business programs). Yet academics from all fields are needed to go on to leadership roles in universities. How does this happen?

The first step is usually by someone being selected by his or her department and by the relevant dean as a department chair, the first rung on the administrative ladder. Probably that person has served well on committees, has said wise things at faculty meetings, and is perceived as reasonable and fair. However, some chairs are selected without these qualities, either because the department and dean made a mistake or because the department or dean was desperate (no one in the department was really interested and qualified). It is a curious fact of life that many members of a department immediately hold anyone in suspicion who seems eager (or even willing) to be its chair.

That leads to the interesting question of why people want to be department chairs. When people would ask me, I had a stock phrase: "Ever since I was a child, I have had a dream of having a job in lower middle management." That is, of course, the business-word equivalent of a department chair in academia, except that in business most people are hungry for advancement, to go to upper management. That seems much less so in academia. One friend told me "I feel as if I am stepping down from the faculty to be department chair. It's not a step up. I would rather be doing my research and teaching."

Finding the right chair is often a slow dance of a somewhat willing candidate (someone who does not immediately say no) having her or his arm twisted slightly by the department and the dean. Somehow, every academic department in every college or university must find a chair, and it is not always an easy process. But let's assume the process has moved along, and now you, dear reader, find yourself as chair.

Being chair of a department is hard work. Like being a journal editor or like being a parent, a person not in the situation can vaguely appreciate that it is hard, but you can't really know how hard and why until you have experienced it for yourself. I have been a chair once, for eight years. I was an "external hire," meaning I came into a new department from the outside. I had never previously served as chair. At the time I took the job, I had observed seven chairs of departments at three universities. I thought I knew a few things via observational learning, and I did, but the relevant word in this sentence is *few*. Many of the tasks that a chair performs are hidden from view to members of the department. One important step I took immediately was to ask a trusted colleague whom I had known for a long time (Dave Balota) to be my associate chair. He could tell me about the folkways and mores of the department and university because he had years of experience. He kept me from making many blunders.

My dean (Ed Macias, a chemist) was helpful and wonderfully supportive when I came to Washington University, but he taught me one important lesson early on. I was having some particularly vexing problem (now blissfully forgotten) in my second year as chair. I went to Dean Macias, the man who hired me, for advice. He listened to my problem and, in the course of giving advice, he said, "Remember, the hardest job in the university is being department chair. You frequently have to say no, and the people you are saying no to are your colleagues, your friends, and the people you live with and see every day. I say no a lot as dean, but I don't live with the people every day the way a chair does." I told him he didn't mention this feature of the job when he was hiring me.

Departments come in all shapes and sizes, just as universities do. One important feature is whether you are in a highly democratic department (some have written rules, bylaws, lots of committees, and vote on everything). Some departments have meetings every week. In this situation, the chair is often more a mediator than an inspirational leader, due to the situational constraints. Other departments, often ones where the leader is called a "head" rather than a chair, expect the head to lead without as much discussion from the department members (who like to go about their own work and not be bogged down in debates). My own department called the leader a "chair," but the system was more like a head system. The custom in my department before I arrived (and still today) was for the whole department to meet infrequently, and everyone seems to like it that way. Department meetings often produce more heat than light.

Below are my fifteen tips for department chairs. Some come from my time being chair, some come from friends, and some come from my role in working with other chairs as an associate dean for some years. Of course, as just noted, because psychology departments come in all shapes and sizes, some tips will not apply in all cases.

1. *Have a vision.* One of the first jobs of the chair is to create a vision for what he or she wants to accomplish and a realistic plan to move ahead. That plan should include how to bring people along with you, not to dictate to them. I came into a department of fifteen members with a brand new building (half empty when I was hired), and the vision of the whole department was to move ahead with hiring and building. When I left the chair's office, we had thirty faculty members and had filled the building. When money is flowing and you have a chance to build, you can enjoy being chair. Of course, even under these conditions, it's not all sunshine and roses, and hiring can be quite stressful as well as rewarding. For every person you hire, you interview maybe four people, and I still remember several candidates we wanted who eluded us.

Of course, the vision for the department depends upon the type of department you are in and what resources are available. Your vision might be to improve your undergraduate program, your research profile, your graduate program (or some combination). Discuss your vision with the faculty and get their input.

2. *Start slowly: Learn your faculty and your department.* This is especially good advice—even mandatory advice—for a chair coming in from a different university, but it is good advice for "inside" chairs, too. For the latter, you have been in the department, but not as its leader. You need to understand various sides of any issue before you launch into changing it. Leaping too fast, before you know the landscape, can be a recipe for disaster. Talk to people. Listen.

3. *Be upbeat.* The members of the department look to you to set the tone, even if it is a more or less unconscious process. If you want morale to be high, you need to set an example. Even if you are having problems (or maybe even especially if you are), don't whine and complain. If a chair portrays continual gloom and misery in being chair, the department will pick this up. Emphasize the positive when you can; keep your mouth shut most of the time

when you can't. Keep in mind you want to get someone good to be chair after you are done. If you make the job sound totally unappealing, that will be a tough sell. Don't overdo positivity when it is unwarranted, of course, but if it is possible to portray a glass as half full, do it.

4. *Be organized.* This one sounds like a no-brainer, but you would be surprised. If your personal style has been to be kind of scattered and to let others remind you of duties and deadlines, you need to change. You need to control your own schedule and make the most of your time. You cannot afford to let matters slip when other people's fortunes and careers are riding on your performance.

5. *Build a calendar of events.* The academic year has a rhythm. The first year as chair everything is new, but after that you face the same tasks and the same deadlines every year. Get prepared. Put them on your calendar and put in reminders for the weeks leading up to them. In my university's system, we need to send out letters for tenure and promotion in the summer to have them in by the fall; we need to prepare budget documents in the fall for a meeting with the dean and the dean's budget officer in December; we need to evaluate performance of junior professors in February so we can get a letter to them by mid-March. And so on. The calendar of events (which the prior chair can help you with) is critical to good organization.

6. *Develop an effective staff and treat them well.* Nearly every department in which I have served has had a few effective staff members who kept the place on track. Depending on the size of the department, the chair may have an assistant, a budget officer for personnel, a grants person, and assistants for other purposes (undergraduate studies, graduate studies, the clinical program). Your assistant is critical. The cooperation and attitude of the staff and how they interact with you and faculty helps to determine how well the department runs. Consult the staff, respect them and value them, from the maintenance crew on up. They often know more about what is going on in the department than the faculty.

7. *Get along with the dean.* The former chair of a major department recently told me that his biggest surprise in becoming chair was how important his relationship with his dean was. In hindsight, he said, this should have been obvious—but prospectively he had overlooked it. In most university systems, department chairs can get little done without the support of the dean. You need to work on that relationship, even if (or maybe especially if) you find it painful. If you get in a big fight with the dean (or lose her trust), your department will suffer and you will have more sleepless nights than would be good for your health. Remember, in most systems, the chair serves at the pleasure of the dean, and the dean has the right to replace the chair.

8. *Cultivate relationships with other chairs.* Yes, in a way they are your rivals. It is your job (and their job) to get more than your (their) fair share of the budget. But you need allies and confidantes. I was fortunate, in coming in

as an outside chair, that several current chairs in other departments took me under their wings and instructed me on various items I should know.

9. *Learn the critical phrase: I'll get back to you on that.* A faculty member (Y) comes flying into your office in an uproar. "You won't believe what X has done now. You have to do something." The faculty member and X may have a long history of this kind of thing. First, calm Y down. Second, say you will investigate and learn about the situation and get back to X. Say you are busy and it might take a couple of days. Often Y will calm down, and it will blow over, but of course you do need to investigate (with X and with neutral parties, preferably those who witnessed the event in question). Then, of course, do get back to Y with your thoughts on the matter. Maybe some corrective action does need to be taken. However, many academic flaps can be ameliorated with the passing of time and some discussion. (Remember Sayre's Third Law of Politics: "Academic politics are so bitter because the stakes are so small.")

The point is: never act on an important issue after hearing only one side of a story. There are always two sides. This rule is frequently violated, in my experience as an associate dean in mediating disputes.

Just because someone wants you to take some immediate action does not mean you need to do it. Be deliberate—but do get the issue resolved within a short timeframe whenever possible. Saying "I'll get back to you" means you should.

10. *Walk around.* Don't just sit in your office, waiting for news and issues to come to you. Wander around the department several times a week. Stop and chat here and there. Talk to students and staff. Find out what's going on. Attend some of the area brown bag lunches and talks in your department, even if they are outside your academic area of interest. Try to keep up with what is happening in the various areas of the field that are represented in your department, too. Take an interest.

11. *Set an example.* Let's say you need to encourage your faculty in certain behaviors—attending colloquia outside their areas, teaching enthusiastically, being around the department and not hiding at home, spending time with students, and so on. Well, make it a point (as much as you can) to follow these same rules. Don't say "I'm too busy to teach and attend colloquia." Maybe your teaching will be light, but don't make a habit of not following the practices you expect of others. Everyone is busy.

12. *Say no nicely.* You wind up having to say no a lot, because people ask for favors ("But it's me! I'm different."), or they ask for money for some special (or not so special) purpose. And so on. And often it is the same few faculty who make repeated requests. (A rough estimate among chairs is that 10 percent of the faculty consume 80 percent of your time.) Of course, you want to do what you can to support good ideas and move the faculty members, their careers, and your department forward, but your budget will not

permit you to do everything. And policies of fairness and equity should prevent you from cutting special deals for some faculty over equally worthy faculty. Still, even when I had to say no, I tried to do it in a way that was not dismissive of faculty members' concerns. I found that often they had ideas I wished I could support if we had the funds.

13. *Repair relationships.* It is very hard to be chair without annoying people. Some decisions you make will favor one party lobbying for something over another party. The slighted party may feel angry and hurt that you did not support his or her side. There is really nothing you can do about this situation beforehand or during the moment—reasonable people simply disagree (and not everyone is reasonable). However, after a few days, you should try to repair your relationship with the slighted party, if you can. I would typically wait a few days (tempers cool) and then ask to meet with the faculty member in his or her office to talk about the situation, to say that I value the person's opinion but that I simply disagree in this instance. You may not always succeed in repairing a relationship, but just the effort may help to bring the two of you closer over time.

14. *Remember George Burns's advice.* Burns was an American comedian who lived to be one hundred and was noted for many things, including the following aphorism: "The secret of success is sincerity. Once you can fake that you've got it made." When you are chair, some situations you face are just too boring or depressing for words. You have the same pathetic meeting with the same people over the same issues that will never be settled, in your lifetime, to the satisfaction of everyone involved. You can attend the meeting and sit with your arms folded and your bored, frowny face on, or you can just embrace the moment and pitch into the hopeless situation. Why not? Try to enjoy it. This advice is even more critical for the upper administration than for chairs. Think of all those fundraising dinners.

15. *Know when to say "time's up" for being chair.* This last tip is critical; don't overstay your welcome. Departments differ in their practices on terms for chairs. The three-year rotation is popular in some places, but for me that seems too short. At about the time you know what you are doing you are finished. For someone who maintains his or her enthusiasm, six years or more may work. But if you feel your attention and enthusiasm fading, it's time to move on and let someone else take over.

CONCLUSION

Being a department chair can be extremely rewarding. Most former chairs tell me they are glad they did it, although one does occasionally hear "I learned some things about my colleagues that I wish I didn't know." (Another tip is keeping your mouth shut and not spreading gossip.) Yet some people like being chair so much they seek further experience in administration, going on to be dean, provost, and president. I applaud these decisions because we need strong leaders in academia. Other people learn while being chair (and in my case in being an associate dean) that they really want to stay with their profession, with the reason they went into academia in the first place—research and teaching in their field. Still, I was glad for my experience as a department chair and enjoyed it most of the time. Good luck with your experience.

NOTE

This chapter is adapted from a column that first appeared in the *APS Observer*. Dave Balota and John Wixted provided sage comments on an earlier draft of this column.

Chapter Twenty-Nine

Chairing Stories

Heidi Bostic

Among the many roles of a department chair, perhaps none are more important than those of listener and storyteller. The job requires attentiveness to the compelling stories told by colleagues and students. It also requires the ability to shape these disparate stories into a unified narrative that supports the institution's overall goals. Given our frontline contact with students, faculty, and staff, the stories that department chairs hear, repeat, and create play a vital role in setting the tone, fostering an atmosphere, and implementing the mission. Chairing stories entail caring for others and crafting a vision.

How do we acquire such narrative skills? It is often claimed that our academic training did not prepare us to serve as administrators. Of course in some sense this is true. But we sell our education short when we do not recognize in it many tools for successful chairing. We read and research. We question and investigate. Then we experiment to see whether our understanding is correct. We remain open to changing our minds when fresh evidence emerges. We share and collaborate with colleagues. We guide students toward new discoveries and help them mature as thinkers. It may sound like "spin," but in fact it's doing what we've been trained to do as teacher-scholars: interpret and narrate.

NAMING THE MACGUFFINS

Let me illustrate this narrative charge through a couple of stories. The first one entails understanding the symbolic weight borne by an object or incident from another's perspective. I call it naming the MacGuffins. Fans of Alfred Hitchcock know what I'm talking about: a MacGuffin is an apparently unimportant object that forms the goal of someone's quest.

A senior faculty member wanted a junior member in the same research area to inherit a piece of office equipment that had been purchased under the auspices of a now-restructured academic program. When the equipment was purchased, the senior member had budgetary authority in that program and actually selected the piece. The idea that the junior member would inherit it took on seemingly exaggerated importance in the eyes of the senior colleague. This equipment was the MacGuffin. I had to explain what was going on to the staff member charged with ensuring that the inherited equipment was moved into the junior person's office, and who was bewildered by all the fuss: in the wake of the program's restructuring and the senior member's loss of budgetary authority, this equipment had taken on great symbolic weight. In the senior colleague's story, the equipment embodied the proud vestiges of that program. I adopted two strategies: first, I encouraged the senior faculty member to take a wider perspective ("equipment is just equipment"); second, I enabled the staff member to be the "hero" of the story, the one who stepped forward eagerly to agree that this equipment would fit the junior colleague's workspace. Note that I did *not* "name the MacGuffin" directly to the senior colleague. Rather, I tried to ask questions and to make observations that would (hopefully) lead that colleague to consider the office equipment—and, hence, the program restructuring—within a broader framework.

On a similar but more serious note, some colleagues seem mired in past wrongs. Their plight reminds me of a 2013 cartoon from the *New Yorker* magazine that depicts a man bent over some documents at his desk, speaking the following words into the telephone: "Oh, not much. Just sitting here sifting through an old scrapbook of past injustices and imagined slights." We need to remember that some narratives can erect barriers, leading to an "us versus them" mindset. Our job is to help people reframe the past.

SEEING ALL SIDES

The nuance, complexity, and power of stories emerge clearly when you think about how often you have heard the same incident recounted from different points of view. Each retelling may yield a markedly different tale. A case in point is my second story. Let's call this one "Seeing All Sides." A student describes her dealings with a professor who, she thinks, has treated her unfairly by giving her an "F" in a class. The professor, on the other hand, recounts how he labored to offer this student extra help, but notes that in the end her weak foundation in the subject led her to fail. The student's academic advisor, from another unit in the university, tells you that this student has faced several personal challenges, including early graduation from high school, a lack of social adaptability, and the recent death of her grandmother. Each narrator tells a story that she or he considers the unambiguous truth.

You are left to sort it out. What matters above all is truly hearing and valuing all of the stories—that is, trying to see all sides. After that, the focus is not simply which version of the story you deem most credible, or whether you can plausibly synthesize the stories, but which action steps follow from your interpretation. Should the grade be changed? Should the student repeat the course? How should you respond to each of the three narrators? You must interpret and act even though you, as a finite human being, necessarily lack complete information. A tolerance for ambiguity is crucial.

Stories are always with us in part because there are always differing perspectives and aims in human life. Tension is what drives transformation and, thus, the plots of our lives. Realizing this allows us to accept a certain amount of conflict as inevitable.

ANYTHING GOES?

Let me emphasize that I am *not* advocating an anything-goes approach to the world and to others. We do not live in a realm of pure discursive construction. And I am not claiming that stories alone can solve every ill. Telling a new story will not magically increase the budget or reform the recalcitrant colleague. However, stories do guide our response to these situations. In times of tight resources, narratives are what we can offer: hope, encouragement, and recognition. And if we remember that all human dealings entail interpretation, we are freed from being locked into a certain mindset or response. We can maintain not only a sense of perspective but also the optimism needed to be a positive force for change.

A major challenge in interpreting and developing narratives is simply finding the mental space and time to devote to the task. Some days, I relate to characters in Kurt Vonnegut's dystopian short story "Harrison Bergeron." Just as they're forming a thought, these characters—who are required to wear government-issued headsets—hear a crashing cacophony in their ears that shatters their concentration. We simply must make story shaping a priority, and carve out spaces—both individually and communally—for undertaking it.

CELEBRATING ACHIEVEMENT

Among the most important stories we can tell are those about the successes of our colleagues. We must publicize excellent teaching, awards, grants, major publications, and exemplary service. As chair, your fundamental job is to share those stories with all constituents. Even more, you must play an active role in nominating high achievers for fellowships, honors, and prizes. This, too, is part of caring for others: publicly recognizing their accomplishments. And it's also crucial to celebrate achievement within the unit. In my department, there is a tradition of distributing a list of faculty publications and presentations once a year at a departmental meeting. A staff member then forwards this list to our campus newsletter. More personally, tell one faculty member something positive about another, especially if the two don't particularly like each other: "She's done such a wonderful job mentoring undergraduate researchers these past five years." There is a second-person kind of celebrating (congratulating an individual) and a third-person kind (distributing the press releases). Both are important.

Although it is easy to celebrate significant accomplishments, a much more delicate task is to guide faculty members in gauging the level of importance of various achievements. We shouldn't settle for too little. Someone who hasn't been very active in research may crow about a recent publication, and this person's pride may be real, but you as chair must take an objective look. If this is a publication without peer review, you congratulate the faculty member, then (perhaps some days or weeks later) encourage him or her to aim higher next time. This kind of example also takes other forms, such as when folks forward to you every flowery e-mail they receive from a former student, or brag that a senior scholar elsewhere has agreed to look at one of their manuscripts, or list serving as an external tenure reviewer as an "honor" (rather than as ordinary professional service) on their yearly evaluation form. To me, such incidents indicate that the story needs a tweak.

Remember that our stories establish expectations. They help to craft our shared vision. On the one hand, celebrate significant achievements. On the other hand, follow the advice of the wise football coach: when you get into the end zone, act like you've been there before. Communicate that yours is simply the kind of department, college, and university in which faculty members do X (win large grants for research projects, publish books and articles in top-tier venues, attract donor support for student scholarships, and/or serve the community in discipline-specific ways). Finding the right balance between celebrating achievement and norming behavior takes ongoing narrative effort.

CREATING LINKS

Crafting a vision means creating links between local and larger narratives. I once requested university funding to enlarge and remodel the office of our instructional technology staff member. I provided numbers (3,500 students served each semester; current versus potential square footage) and other data (the staff member's job responsibilities). But I also told a succinct story using vivid language. My story painted a mental picture of Chris struggling to meet instructional needs in a cramped cave, jam-packed with equipment. It worked. Funds were allocated and the office was enlarged. Subsequent conversations with decision makers suggested that the narrative brought the numbers to life, linking the project to university priorities.

Faculty and staff members want to see how their individual accomplishments can help the department, the college, and the university achieve broader goals. People want to be part of a larger story. Then, someone is not merely toiling away alone in the classroom, but feels like he is truly contributing to the institution's mission to excel in undergraduate education. A colleague who places an article in a top journal can see that she is helping the university meet its research goals. This is the vision-shaping part of narrative: stand-alone stories connect compellingly to broader narratives. Individual and departmental achievements become steps along the way toward fulfilling the university's mission.

STORIES IN PERSPECTIVE: EMPATHY AND HUMILITY

Underlying everything I have suggested thus far are the twin values of empathy and humility. One of the most important empathic lessons for a chair is to take your ego out of the equation. If you need lots of external affirmation, seek it elsewhere, outside of your department. Don't let the institution be your sole, or even primary, source of self-worth. A well-kept secret in chairing is that the work can enrich one's self-awareness and development. Chairing can help you recognize your own strengths and weaknesses. Closely related is the principle of generous interpretation. There is a fundamental humility in recognizing that there can always be another interpretation. No one perspective is inherently superior to another. We must not become too attached to our stories. We must always remain open to revision and reinterpretation as we listen to others' tales.

We can help colleagues develop their empathy and humility by contextualizing their individual requests within a larger framework. Just because someone has an advanced degree, can teach and publish, doesn't necessarily mean that that person is skilled in appreciating others' perspectives. The competitive and even combative atmosphere of graduate school can crush empathy. We are trained to be critical. I've found that it takes patience and perseverance to help others cultivate what may be the forgotten characteristics of empathy and humility. But it's worth the effort. In doing so, we distribute the leadership: we equip others to take on responsibility.

INTEGRITY AND THE NARRATIVE ARC

A department chair must possess integrity. This term has two meanings: integration and trustworthiness. By integration, I mean that we must strive to live an integrated life. Given the multiple demands we face as university administrators, the only way to thrive is by finding some kind of harmony and unity—one predominant narrative arc—among these demands. We've lately been reminded that the word "university" itself implies a unified purpose. As for trustworthiness, so that others may feel comfortable sharing their stories with me, I must always keep the confidences with which I am entrusted. If you occupy a leadership position in a university, you already know that many of the stories we hear are ones we would prefer not to. There are complaints directly related to the workplace but also the personal tales of grief, illness, or family discord. Serving as a repository of stories that can never be repeated is a burden that leaders must learn to bear lightly so as not to be weighed down.

CONCLUSION

Regarding others' stories *as* stories can transform how we deal with them. Rather than groaning at the thought of another difficult situation to sort out, we can embrace the opportunity to untangle an interpretation that may need to be revised. Similarly, we learn to see our own position in terms of stories that are susceptible to being told differently in light of new information. Sometimes the most self-evident appearances prove to derive from nothing more than tales badly told. You can learn a lot about yourself and your colleagues by paying close attention to the kinds of narratives we all recount. And you can help to shape the present and future of your department through taking care with your chairing stories.

Lest this all sound too cut-and-dried, let's acknowledge that stories, like lives, are full of ambiguity. We must develop a tolerance for ambiguity and an ability to make decisions even in the absence of complete information. In fact, there is no such thing as complete information, just tales told from a certain perspective to someone else for some purpose. Stories teach us and others who we are and what we care about. As chair, you are sometimes a protagonist and most often a minor character. You are never an omniscient narrator, but are frequently called upon to narrate. And you are always a listener and a storyteller.

Chapter Thirty

The Science Chair as Scientific Leader

C. J. Brainerd

And now for something completely different—a story of administrative leadership that is about scholarly models rather than the personal challenges of academic administration or the pet peeves of chairs, though we shall come to some of those near the end. This is the tale of what was once, at the time I was a graduate student, the aspirational model for chairs of science departments and programs of instruction in the natural and social sciences.

My view is that the main challenge of a chair in the sciences is not administrative—it is providing educational leadership, and that means training natural and social scientists to be absolutely the best scientists they can be. And that means focusing on education, not on pushing papers or on making political contacts. Those things matter, too, but they are secondary.

I was steeped in that model in the heartland of experimental psychology, the American Midwest. The model came largely out of the thinking of Kenneth Spence, a world-renowned experimental psychologist and chair of psychology at the University of Iowa.

So, what were the key elements of the Iowa model? One trumped all the rest. With the help of a philosopher of science, Gustav Bergmann, and one of the early leading lights of social psychology, Kurt Lewin, Spence developed a training program of great intellectual force, for the simple reason that its core principle—the axis around which everything revolved—was substantive scientific theory. Actually, it would be more accurate to say: substantive theory as the engine of empirical research. That is, theory was not something about which one speculated and wrote reflective tracts, but rather, it was the workhorse pulling the research wagon. The idea was that the path to advancing scientific understanding in any discipline was through the mechanism of theory-driven research.

In practice, doing theory-driven research meant a trio of obvious things. First, it is necessary to regard scientific data not as interesting things in themselves but, rather, as a means to the end of conceptual understanding; as being of greater or lesser significance according to how well they make contact with deep theoretical principles rather than magazine readers (then) or the blogosphere (now). The emphasis was not, as it often is today, just on empirical findings, but on what the findings mean. Second, it is essential to have theoretical principles in the first place—better yet, competing ones—in order to conduct the most instructive research.

Third, for research to truly advance scientific understanding, the connection between theory and design must be intimate. Designs should be hypothesis driven in the sense of delivering critical tests of theoretical principles. This means that theory is not something that authors write in discussion sections of research reports as an afterthought, but rather, it is the centerpiece from the first sentence. Theoretical principles must be clearly stated and critical tests of them must be derived before there is any thought of gathering data. In other words, let's-run-a-study-and-see-if-anything-interesting-happens was quite out of the question. Of course, this third feature of theory-driven research was the most difficult of all in practice because one cannot simply "do research." One has to think (and think and think) before doing any actual experimentation. The difficulty of this—indeed, the severe decompensation that the mere prospect of it can induce in students—will be well known to any reader who has had occasion to say to a thesis advisee: "What's your hypothesis?" or worse, "Didn't you skip the thinking part?" or worst of all, "There is no escaping the thinking part."

Nevertheless, clear statements of theoretical principles and the derivation of critical tests of principles were the crux of the Iowa model of research. Just how central they were is encapsulated in a story that Stanford psychologist Alberta Bandura often tells about his days as a graduate student there, in the late 1940s. According to the story, there was a yearly spring ritual for graduate students, which consisted of boarding a train for the Midwestern Psychological Association meetings in Chicago. The objective while there was to discuss and argue about theoretical principles in one's area of research and to discuss and argue about what the critical tests of those principles might be. This was done with a view toward arriving at some sort of consensus as to what the critical tests were before the return train left for Iowa City. Then, everyone returned, built the necessary apparatus, and conducted the critical tests, with the firm intention of boarding the Chicago train next year to present the results of those tests.

To state the obvious, strong theory-driven research is not an easy business to be in, especially the part about constantly thinking about ideas and how to implement them. First-rate graduate training is necessary to achieve that result, but it was training of a particularly broad sort that was a hallmark of the Iowa model. When most of us think about graduate training in the sciences, what comes to mind are courses and seminars in the usual content areas plus data analysis, along with working in faculty labs in order to develop research projects. However, three other forms of training are essential for theory-driven research to thrive: history of science, philosophy of science, and cutting-edge mathematical modeling techniques. History familiarizes us with the main currents of theoretical development over generations, with their strengths, with where they fell short, and helps to ensure that we make progress rather than repeat the past. Philosophy of science teaches us the elements of good researching—what will ultimately advance understanding—in ways that inoculate us against the siren songs of attractive but wrong-headed alternatives. Mathematical models supply the most incisive critical tests and sometimes the only critical tests. It is often the case—this is true in my own area of research, memory—that competing theoretical principles, even ones that make starkly different psychological assumptions, do not differ in their simple directional predictions (e.g., hypothesis A predicting that word frequency will improve recall while hypothesis B predicts that it will impair recall). Instead, principles often predict the same directional differences while attributing them to different underlying processes (e.g., conceptual understanding versus rehearsal). Testing these more subtle expectations requires that the underlying processes be measured, which can be done if principles are implemented in appropriate mathematical models.

To readers who are or have been chairs, an especially pleasing aspect of the Iowa model is its ameliorating influence on one of our pet peeves: tribalism. To those readers, it no doubt seems that when attempting to secure faculty agreement on the hiring of new professors or the admission of new graduate students, the constant refrains are, "Hire another one of me," and "Admit another one who will turn out like me." In the Iowa model, the best-person rule was supposed to operate, which meant professors and students who were most likely to do excellent theory-driven research (whether it happened to be on clinical or developmental or social or perceptual phenomena).

Coming at last to administrative leadership in the more traditional sense, what was the role of the chair in all of this? As I see it, there were four key types of leadership.

The first is as the person who possessed a clear vision, in this case of a model of instruction and research that was theory-driven. There is no model without someone who has the vision. Of course, that vision was not a sudden brainstorm.

The second type of leadership is ambassadorial; as the person who persuades others to support the vision—either actively by supplying resources or passively by not mudding pools or setting backfires. In universities that means two things—persuading higher administration, the deans and provosts who control resources, that the vision is good for their institutions and persuading colleagues, the faculty who will implement the vision, that it is good for their careers. It is in this role that scientists so often fail, as it requires levels of persuasiveness, sociability, and adroit sensitivity to the needs of others that are utterly foreign to their nature. Here, Spence was a rare specimen, a master scientist who was also a master of social persuasion—some said he was a natural politician, others that he was a natural salesman, and others that he was a dream merchant.

The third type of leadership is that of administrative management in the narrow sense; as the person who does the spade work that is necessary to get the model off the ground in the first place (hiring the right faculty, putting the facilities in place, developing the programs of instruction), followed by the maintenance work of constant monitoring to keep the engine running smoothly (maintaining the flow of resources, hiring replacement faculty, developing new facilities for emerging research areas, fine-tuning the programs of instruction, etc.). Spence was a master of that, too.

The fourth type of leadership is as a scientific exemplar of the vision—as a role model, in other words. Deeds speak louder than words, and even if one possesses the right model and is eloquent about its worth, buy-in is apt to be scarce if it is not exemplified in one's own research. Mutterings of hypocrisy may even be heard. Here, Spence's personal research program was an unmistakable example of theory-driven work.

In closing, let me mention the other reason why I chose this particular illustration of leadership. The first, which was noted earlier, is that it is an unusual example in which leadership is fueled by a dispassionate scholarly model of a discipline. The other reason is that it is a decidedly optimistic example of the personal possibilities of academic leadership inasmuch as it shows how extensively a discipline can be influenced by a single administrative leader. Let me stress, before moving any further in that direction, that influence grew out of the rightness of the scholarly model: everything we know from the history and philosophy of science inclines toward the conclusion that deriving hypotheses from theoretical principles and conducting critical tests trumps all other forms of research. With that proviso, however, it was Spence's leadership that made things happen, and remember just how big those things were. For a generation, the Iowa model was *the* model that others aspired to.

Chapter Thirty-One

Confronting Trade-Offs in Academic Settings

Frank C. Keil

I write this chapter as someone who has occupied low- and midlevel leadership roles in two universities. I have served as a head of a residential college community at Yale of roughly 450 students with a substantial custodial, dining, and administrative staff. I have also served as chair of the twelve heads of all such residential colleges at Yale. And I have also served as chair of a midsize academic department at Yale (twenty-five ladder faculty, several lecturers, a dozen office support staff, and a large population of undergraduate and graduate students). Finally, at my prior university, Cornell, I served as head of an interdisciplinary program in the cognitive sciences. Through these varied administrative positions over the past thirty years, I have acquired a reluctance to impart specific gems of advice on academic leadership, given that the right courses of action to take can vary enormously as a function of situations. Nonetheless, there may be some value in describing certain trade-offs that frequently recur in academic settings and why it is important to be aware of them. Put differently, it may be helpful to have a clearer vision of the critical dimensions that often underlie decisions in academic settings. I will therefore briefly discuss four such dimensions and the trade-offs they impose.

IDEALISM VERSUS PRAGMATISM

Universities are communities that pride themselves on their honoring of ideals: free speech, encouraging all areas of scholarly inquiry, equal opportunities and privileges for all members or potential members of the academic community, and environmental sensitivity, among many others. But, in reality, no institution, no matter how wealthy or principled, can follow these ideals to their limits. Certainly, idealism and principles may be more important in universities than in many other organizations, but they can rarely be embraced categorically. All elite universities do make some accommodation in admissions for children of the extremely wealthy, despite stating and believing that admission should be based solely on merit. Such practices are often justified by the pragmatic argument that the resources that come with admission of a few wealthy students are of such substantial benefit to the university as a whole, including some of its most disadvantaged members, that they make good sense; but these practices also clearly illustrate the limits to an ideal. These practices may, in their best forms, still demand impressive merit credentials from such applicants and make only modest accommodations, thereby continuously keeping the ideal in mind.

Similarly, universities argue that they adhere to higher principles in the ways they invest their endowments, avoiding companies that engage in unethical or unseemly behaviors. But, in the limit, if all companies with checkered records were excluded from investments, a university might suffer in terms of endowment performance. When universities do decide to make their investments "fossil free," such decisions are not made in an idealistic bubble. The practical consequences of divesting are carefully considered, and only if the financial hit is minimal or modest is divestment undertaken.

Free speech policies are rarely able to adhere completely to the ideal that all points of view are welcome in the academy. There are widely agreed upon cases of "hate speech," where conflict with another ideal, that of not inflicting harm, can pose difficult challenges on strictly idealistic grounds; but often the cases are more fuzzy and are influenced by pragmatic factors. I was once asked by some students to bring in a speaker who would advocate the merits of polygamy. In consulting with other students, colleagues, and more senior administrators, I was never strictly forbidden to bring the polygamist in, but it soon became clear that the event would be a media circus with many groups actively demonstrating against the speaker, whose scholarly credentials were nonexistent, and that some students would be personally offended. In the end, it just didn't seem worth pleasing a small group of strong advocates, given these other factors. At the same time, there was great enthusiasm when we brought in equally unscholarly proponents of more popular causes or trendy media celebrities with no causes at all. One has to weigh the intellectual and moral value of a speaker against many pragmatic issues and cannot simple apply a fixed policy.

Across all these cases, the same general idea recurs: one should always be mindful of the relevant ideals, but one has to consider them in context and cannot devise prescriptive rules to be robotically followed.

COMMITTEES AS INDEPENDENT AGENTS VERSUS ADMINISTRATIVE SMOKE SCREENS

Committees are essential to the functioning of a university that embraces faculty governance, yet committees usually do not have complete autonomy and independence such that the faculty truly "run this place," When senior administrators charge a committee, it is rare that they have no expectations about likely outcomes, and indeed the charge is often crafted in such a way as to bias the committee toward a particular outcome. In addition, it is not uncommon for an administrator to request, not a specific recommendation, but a set of choices, such as a set of final candidates in a search for a senior appointment or a set of options for a new policy, such as allocation of faculty slots to departments. Even then, administrators often reserve, and sometimes exercise, the right to ignore all the choices or options and come up with a completely novel decision. The staffing of committees is another way that administrators strongly influence the committee's actions. The chair is frequently someone closely aligned with the administrator's point of view, and the other members are often selected so that a clear majority is similarly inclined. In addition, support staff on a committee, who often come from the requesting administrator's office, can play a critical role in how reports are framed and in updating the administrator on any developments that might need a subtle intervention, such as a brief chat with the committee chair.

The trade-off here is between empowering the faculty and harnessing their talents, on the one hand, and trying to develop a coherent forward-moving master plan on the other. The two extremes are cases where a decision is completely preordained and a committee is merely a smokescreen designed to provide a veneer of consensus and faculty buy-in or where faculty committees are completely rogue agents that heedlessly make recommendations with no sense of broader priorities or are oblivious to highly sensitive information that make their recommendations unfeasible. When administrators come too close to a smokescreen model, they run the risk of alienating their faculty and causing an ever-increasing reluctance to get the most active and engaged faculty to be willing to serve on committees. When they come too close to the ideal of total committee autonomy, they run the risk of getting impossible-to-use recommendations.

The most effective committees are ones in which the members have some sense in advance of the constraints under which they are operating so that they are not blindsided by what seems to be an autocratic administrator. To claim that the committee has complete autonomy, when in fact a particular outcome is predestined, is to undermine the effectiveness of all future committees. When charging a committee, I try to make clear to all members the real agenda that is at play and how their input will be helpful and productive. Some confidential information may have to be shared with just the chair of the committee, but always with a goal ensuring that committee members know as much as possible about what is really at stake and why. In my cases of chairing and serving on committees, I have felt most useful, and not "used," when I was told up front about such things as the range of possible decisions, certain options that were off the table, and the extent to which the charging administrator had preconceived biases. Similarly, it is encouraging to know where independent ideas and real innovation would be warmly welcomed.

I once chaired a committee charged with evaluating and making recommendations about an undergraduate teacher-preparation program. It was incredibly helpful for morale and committee productivity to know in advance what kinds of recommendations would be considered unrealistic for financial and staffing reasons, which groups had strongly divergent views about the future of the program, that student input would be taken seriously, and in what realms innovative suggestions would be welcomed. This is in strong contrast to other committees, where little information was made available up front, and where, despite a vague and rousing charge, it soon became clear that the decision was already made and that our role was merely to make it look like broad faculty involvement had occurred. A more subtle variant that occurs quite often is when the administration has in essence made a decision but forms a faculty committee to make sure that there will not be a firestorm of opposition. A gifted administrator should be willing to use the committee's input to modify a decision or at least realize a need to try to persuade the faculty of the merit of the proposal by fully addressing their concerns.

AXE-MURDERER VERSUS KUMBAYA HIRING PRACTICES

Every so often, a senior faculty candidate emerges in a search who is a truly extraordinary scholar but a notoriously impossible human being. Excluding cases of criminal behavior or behavior with extreme "moral turpitude," there are still outstanding scholars who are known to be terrible citizens, disparaging of all colleagues, ravenous for resources, paranoid about threats, and brutal to subordinates. Any department with aspirations for being one of the top departments in its field wants to attract the best possible scholars; but to embrace scholarship at all costs can have disastrous consequences. At the other extreme, an excessive focus on ideal human beings who will "fit in" with the existing group and who are passionately service oriented, modest, caring, and warm can doom a department to an undistinguished future. Striking a balance can impose a major challenge and can involve diverse strategies. One strategy is to tolerate one, and only one, horrific person if his or her scholarship is truly unparalleled. If the department is full of other great scholars who are also strong citizens and mentors, one problematic person can usually be incorporated and sometimes even, surprisingly, socialized. There are still risks, but they pale in comparison with having two such individuals. A second strategy is to broaden the scope of the search. If it initially focused on one subarea of a field and the only exceptional scholar was also an impossible person, rather than settle for a distinctly less impressive scholar in the same area, the department should be willing to broaden its search target to include another person of equal scholarly eminence but who is a less destructive.

There are dangers to the other extreme as well. Departments that focus primarily on personality not only risk reputational oblivion, they may also drift toward an uninspiring homogeneity of personality types. Even if there is full ethnic diversity, a department that has nothing but mellow, nonconfrontational, anything-but-edgy members may be a very dull place indeed. One doesn't need every colleague to be a close friend or have them all in a quasi-incestuous social circle singing "Kumbaya" around the campfire. In addition, people can be flat wrong in assessing personality and might find that their ideal colleague is merely dissembling and is deeply problematic. This uncertainty has led some departments to proclaim the "axe murderer" model. As long as a candidate is not literally an actively wanted criminal, personality and past deeds should be completely ignored, and only scholarship should matter. Few departments, however, actually adopt the axe-murderer model completely as they know all too well how a few difficult people can wreak havoc on a midsize department.

The most successful search strategy may be one where one will not compromise on scholarly quality but is willing to wait, sometimes for years, or willing to broaden the search target to achieve excellence without massive personality costs. It also involves doing a great deal of homework about potential candidates, especially at the senior level, where the unshakable commitment can last for many decades. This involves asking why a person is interested in moving, how the person has functioned in past departments, how the individual has mentored, how well the person has given others credit where deserved, and how the person deals with the lowest level staff when no one is watching. All these questions are fraught with the potential for misinterpretation and excessive intrusion on privacy, but surprisingly convergent portraits can be gathered with enough hard work. Sometimes supposedly difficult people are really just in a very bad environment for them, and sometimes supposedly wonderful people have been carefully managed at great expense. The details matter enormously as does an assessment of one's own department and its ability to absorb a person with a challenging personality.

248 Frank C. Keil

SECLUDED SILOS VERSUS MEDIOCRE MUSH

Departments, programs, and even universities as a whole, are often enjoined to "build on strength." Find areas of excellence and use them as magnets to attract other stars. This seems like an obvious strategy, but in the extreme, it can lead to walled-off silos that defeat the purpose of the university as an interactive community of scholars. This is true at the university level, but especially at the departmental level, and it also poses another challenging trade-off. To be sure, recruiting can often be greatly facilitated by having colleagues already present who have the same interests, an effect that can be amplified by creating a greater pool of high-quality graduate students who share facilities and area activities. This is a tried-and-true method used in many universities. It is meant to combat a feared mediocre mush that can occur when a department seeks to have "one of everything" and not be especially strong in anything. But it can create a substantial cost, namely, that if a department adopts too much of a "like begets like" model, it runs the risk of reducing needed diversity of scholarly interests, and even more importantly, it can lead to a set of silos that barely communicate with each other, even within the same department.

The silo effect can happen in virtually any department in the university as well as in cross-disciplinary programs, such as a cognitive-science program that adopts one narrow perspective or pulls largely from one department. At the departmental level, it can result in sharply distinct areas with almost no communication or collaborations between them. This can result in gradual drifting apart of cultures, training philosophies, and research methodologies and eventually result in heated disagreements about allocation of future faculty lines as well as to deadlocks over job candidates. All this is bad enough in a large department of fifty or more faculty, but it can be especially harmful to smaller departments of thirty faculty members or fewer that might have three to five "areas" that form secluded silos. Even if each area is fairly strong due to its build-on-strength model, the department as a whole suffers because the silos thwart efforts for cross-collaborations and can impair graduate student training and recruitment. In addition, as the field as a whole changes over time, a siloed department may be much less nimble in its ability to adapt to new cross-cutting themes that don't neatly fit into any single silo.

The other extreme is to never have a critical mass in anything. Smaller departments can't pretend to have great concentrations of scholars in all the subareas of their field, and if they try to be good at everything, they can end up having marginal presences in every subarea. Such departments have no distinctive imprint on their larger communities and have ever-increasing difficulties recruiting outstanding scholars and students.

One strategy for addressing concerns about both extremes is to look for new faculty that, even as they build on a strength, have a demonstrated ability to collaborate with at least one group outside their primary area. If one takes that mindset, many outstanding candidates in one area can be found who naturally have links to other areas. This strategy can be further amplified by trying to hold as many completely open area searches as possible, rather than constraining them narrowly to one clear silo. Open searches can often uncover surprising and quite unanticipated "bridges" between two areas that greatly enhance the department by opening up whole new avenues of increasing collaboration without diluting the quality of any. Open searches also enable departments to be more accepting of new trends in their field. Finally, departments can strongly encourage graduate students to engage in at least a small project with a faculty member in an area outside that of their major advisor. This not only gives the student stronger letters when looking for jobs and makes them appealing to search committees, but it also very often brings faculty together into new collaborations.

In short, departments, interdisciplinary programs, and even broad divisions of a university can build on strengths to increase their visibility and to attract outstanding new members but can avoid the problems of silos if they also adopt strategies that enable and encourage collaborations. They need not be strong in every area, but they should have enough areas of strength to enable innovative interactions across those areas and the ability to evolve toward new ideas that don't fit neatly into any of the traditional subareas that they already have.

CONCLUSION

These trade-offs hardly exhaust those that challenge people in leadership roles in academic settings. Others can include transparency versus privacy, quality versus quantity of scholarly contributions, and merit versus equality, among many others. Across all such trade-offs, however, a few common themes do emerge. First, it rarely works to have some fixed rule for how to address each trade-off instance. Context matters greatly, and one needs a process or framework more than a simple prescriptive rule. Second, if it all possible, one should be continuously mindful of both extremes and why they have both costs and benefits, asking how any local decision reduces costs and enhances benefits at both ends. Third, it can be extremely helpful to compare notes with others in similar leadership positions. One certainly doesn't want to merely clone what other great programs are doing, but comparisons can be very illuminating. Finally, things are continuously evolving in a successful forward-looking academic setting, and one needs to be constantly adapting when appropriate. Whichever trade-off strategy worked a decade earlier may no longer be effective in the same institution today.

Chapter Thirty-Two

Strategic Planning

View from the Department Level

Lise Youngblade

I see strategic planning as a map. Maps are helpful when you know your destination but need to ascertain the route. They become completely essential, maybe even life saving, when you are in uncharted terrain. Maps lead you to a destination, but a good map also shows alternate routes to get there and identifies areas of danger to stay away from. Perhaps most importantly, utilizing a map to reach a destination forces forethought and planning, analysis of the route, and assessment of the resources needed to reach the destination.

The theme our group is considering is strategic plans, and staying the course, especially in times of limited resource. My charge is to consider this from the perspective of a department head. I believe this to be quite an interesting vantage point because, on the administrative ladder, this is the first time that many of us actually confront the realities of the strategic planning process as a critical activity that has tangible implications for people and activities in a unit and has significant consequences for which *you as department head* are inherently responsible. Departments are often the places where the rubber hits the road, and serving as head provides a context of responsibility that is both exhilarating and humbling.

I am the department head of Human Development and Family Studies (HDFS) at Colorado State University. This is a large and highly productive department, and, in fact, we hold the fifth largest major on campus. We currently have seventeen tenured/tenure-track faculty, three full-time special appointment teaching and research faculty, numerous adjunct instructors, eight hundred resident undergraduate majors and another 130 students majoring in our online degree program, thirteen PhD students, and another thirty or so master's students. We house the Early Childhood Center, a large lab school, as well as the Center for Family and Couple Therapy, a clinic serving our Marriage and Family Therapy program. We have an active research agenda, with annual research expenditures that have risen every year that have exceeded $1 million per year for the past three years and are represented by a tenfold increase from a decade ago. As a commitment to our land grant mission, we have a vibrant Extension connection to the citizens of our state and nation. Our field is multidisciplinary, spanning family sociology and developmental psychology, and approaches research and learning from basic and translational lenses, in context, and across the lifespan. My department is complex, diverse, and at any given moment, there are a multitude of competing demands. Clearly, without a map, we would be lost. With a clearly delineated strategic plan, we have not only survived the recent economic downturn, but also experienced steady and significant growth over the past several years. This is evidenced by new positions, new programs, an expanded budget, and a significant increase in assignable space, and this is despite three years of base budget cuts to the university that occurred during the several years of the recession and that affected nearly every unit on campus, ours included.

I believe that we have been successful, and remain poised for future distinction, owing to several factors. I am going to outline them below, but I will also state that (a) these are not exhaustive but rather are several key tenets that have worked for us; (b) they are inherently interconnected; (c) after the first point, they are not in a hierarchical or sequential order; and (d) all of what I am discussing worked because we have a tremendous faculty in which all are engaged and committed to working together to meet the commonly agreed-upon goals. For each of the topics below, I will provide examples from our department's experience, as a way of highlighting the point.

(1) *Setting the vision.* In my opinion, this is quintessentially and inarguably the first and most critical step in the process, and it becomes the foundation for the rest. A department simply cannot effectively get from point *A* to point *B* if all of the people involved don't know where they are going and what they are aiming to achieve. I also believe, firmly, that it is the only part of the strategic process that needs to stay immutable—within (although arguably beyond) the timeframe of one's plan. In other words, the destination is fixed—and although the desired route might be mapped, it is also reasonable to expect that there are deviations and alternative, maybe even better, routes that may emerge over time or under changing circumstances. I believe this is especially true in times of limited resources—when the vision becomes the litmus test for what decisions are made, but the means for meeting the goal may not be what was originally envisioned anymore, owing to a changed landscape.

Our department embarked on a systematic journey in strategic planning in 2006 when we came together and began to articulate our vision for increasing the reputation of the department internally as well as externally. This included a deliberate intent to position ourselves as a top-performing department at the university through the successful growth of our undergraduate and graduate programs, research portfolio, and outreach activities. We also were highly cognizant of the external landscape, and especially our aspirational peers—with the explicit goal of working toward being recognized as one of the top HDFS programs in the country. Quite simply, our vision has been and continues to be excellence in teaching, research, and outreach. Our plans for steps that move us toward that goal, or addressing challenges that have the potential to move us away from that goal (like budget cuts), always begin with a discussion of how what we are considering meets our vision for excellence.

Of course, vision by itself is necessary but not sufficient for progress. Progress is also determined by the translation of vision into specific goals and actionable objectives that achieve defined and desired outcomes. Toward this end, strategic plans follow more or less a similar format: a description of vision, mission statement, goals, and objectives over a period of time and how specific individuals (or groups of individuals) within the unit will achieve outlined objectives within the specified timeframe. Our plan is no different, and addresses the key mission areas of the land grant university (teaching, research, and service/outreach). It had to be aligned with the strategic plan of the university and of the college. It was developed by committee, with every faculty member serving on a core part of the plan and with all parts of the plan agreed to by full faculty consensus. What is different for me in this plan, compared to others, is that I have been involved in the following: (a) it is actively used, not just polished every few years and then sits on a shelf; (b) it was developed with the full inclusion of the faculty and key staff and administrative professional in the unit; and (c) although it is clearly aspirational, it is also deliberately evaluative with measurable outcomes.

(2) *Understanding context.* I am trained in a discipline in which there are few across-the-board truisms, and most of what we know is qualified by context (e.g., by age, by gender, by social or economic context, by history, and so forth). Context is critical in strategic planning as well. There are any number of important contextual issues that departments must consider including, for example, the political landscape that the university faces, the strategic aims of the college and the university, the population of students and their interests, financial constraints and opportunities, and the talent pool of the faculty. In our strategic planning efforts, one of the biggest contextual factors has been our institution's support of entrepreneurship.

Although unit base funding had remained stable for many years, but in fact was cut over several recent years, our university supports revenue models that allow significant retention of entrepreneurial dollars *at the department level*. This is evidenced by salary savings, fee-for-service outreach, indirect cost returns on grants, and continuing-education dollars. Given dwindling state support for higher education, as well as historic base funding models, these mechanisms become essential for the success of the department—especially in units that want to grow. Accordingly, our strategic planning process has included a core focus on entrepreneurship from its inception but specifically because it strategically capitalizes on the context of our institution and brings resources back to the department that we can deploy in pursuit of our goals.

As a result, our department's activities and financial infrastructure have shifted dramatically over the past eight years. Our overall budget has quadrupled, with base funding shifting from 71 percent of the overall budget in 2006 to 33 percent in 2013. This includes a 9 percent summative cut to base funding, but on the revenue side, in accordance with our strategic plan, we have grown in strategic areas related to research, graduate student funding, support of our lab school and clinics, and online education. Moreover, with a more diverse portfolio, we were able to backfill cuts to our base funding through these different revenue streams. One of our values is to be nimble, and our efforts in utilizing *proactively* the core contextual feature of our university related to entrepreneurship, has allowed us to be so.

(3) *Timing is everything.* Sometimes timing is simply fortuitous, as it was for us. I began my post as department head at CSU in 2006. Our first activities together involved setting the vision and developing our strategic plan. Timing worked in our favor for multiple reasons. Most obviously, the economy was relatively solid then and there were resources available for growth at our university. We had a dean who was actively engaged in growing the college and highly supportive of our efforts to build our department. This allowed us to attract base funding early in the planning process for several new hires, as well as successfully become approved for a PhD program. These initial successes had some very tangible results, not the least of which was boosting morale and engendering faculty commitment to continuing with our plan.

In hindsight, I believe this morale boost from a few initial successes was a watershed moment in our efforts. Strategic plans often start with a motivation for growth or change. It sounds great in a plan to say "if we do X, then we can expect Y." But the reality is that change is hard. Often the action items that are necessary to achieve significant goals require personal investment, personal growth, and sometimes a rather harsh look in the mirror about one's place in the organization. This has the possibility to really fracture a unit, and I believe two important lessons came out of this process. The first is the notion that plans need to build in opportunities to achieve outcomes at short-, medium-, and long-term points of time. The initial ones can make or break continued commitment. The second lesson came from our dean at the time. We had initial successes, but we also had a changing culture that pushed people to stretch, and that defined excellence in ways that could be perceived as threatening to previous definitions of productivity and impact. It is of no surprise, then, that the beginning of our efforts had some challenge as well—and some very real potential for fracturing. The dean became a calm voice of reason to the department at a very critical time—supporting the vision, acknowledging the changing culture, and putting our efforts in the context of growth and reward. She also kept the provost informed. While these efforts helped the faculty, there was also the extremely important effect of having the department head's back, which was critical to keeping leadership momentum. Change rarely occurs in a vacuum, and this very obvious college and university support was critical to keeping us on track.

Overall, the essential take-home message for me about timing that emerged from this process is the importance of being proactive and being primed for change. We had the luck of timing that allowed us to develop a plan and start working on our goals during resource-rich times, and this reinforced and facilitated our aspirational thinking. Had we started the planning process a few years later, in the midst of budget cuts, I believe we would likely have had a minimalist and more survival-oriented strategic plan. We did face those hard questions that came from shrinking resources, but we had the ability to think about them in a different way. No one has a crystal ball of course, but my point is that I believe the most effective plans and processes are done proactively, when one is not forced to react to a specific set of circumstances. In turn, an articulated plan and vision provide an important scaffold when one is forced to respond to changing and challenging circumstances. Further, it makes it easier to then uphold strategic priorities, even under constrained conditions. Indeed, one could argue that the value of strategic planning becomes clearest under tough conditions because those conditions can be seen as having a "purifying effect" that cuts to the essence of what the unit is and is trying to achieve.

A related lesson learned about time has to do with patience. One of the challenges of setting ambitious goals is managing expectations about outcomes. Sometimes, maybe often, plans take time to come to tangible fruition. This is especially challenging when certain strategic aims are met that benefit one part of the unit, but maybe others are still in earlier stages of process where outcomes are not yet manifested. Frustration and resentment can occur and of course that can create challenges for further growth and commitment to the vision and strategic plan. This was true for us as well, and it instigated some very critical conversation about *collective* vision, and our *collective* efforts. So, for example, a key goal for us was to grow our grant dollars. Like with most units, at any point in its history, not all faculty members are equally funded or have equal opportunity or success in attracting dollars.

When grants started significantly growing, money became more available to investigators for course buyouts, summer salary, graduate assistants, travel, and other amenities. This was a great outcome, and surely provided incentive to keep working on that part of the strategic plan.

At the same time, however, our student population was exploding, and teaching demands were becoming more challenging. Not only were large classes and extra course sections threats, but the more someone taught, the less time they could possibly have to write grants and get funded to buy them out of this situation. Unfunded faculty members also did not have as ready access to money for travel or professional development, nor for funding graduate assistants to help them on their scholarship. One alternative would have been to back off the research goals and distribute teaching responsibilities equally. We chose a different path and chose to manage it through open conversation about these issues and affirmation about how mutually interdependent we are. Thus, salary savings and indirect cost returns *from research* (both of which stay at the department level at our institution) were used to invest *in teaching* through the hiring and support of well-qualified special-appointment teaching faculty. Indirect cost returns also helped us weather the economic downturn by buffering the budget cuts—a benefit that faculty members who had been critical of the greater emphasis on research and grant productivity had not anticipated. From all of this, we maintained significant momentum in our research aims, while bolstering our teaching goals (smaller classes, mores sections). However, time was a significant hurdle here, in terms of managing the varying paces of the two different areas of the strategic plan. Moreover, we all needed to take a long view of the situation, as it took several years to achieve an equilibrium where all felt they were equitably contributing and being rewarded equivalently.

(4) *Buy-in and continued commitment.* Commitment from stakeholders is critical. I have worked in units where the strategic plan was written by the unit leader or a small committee. Although arguably efficient, I would also say that commitment to the plan (my own and my colleagues) was not very strong. To be very honest, I simply did not know enough about it, or have enough personal investment in it, to take it as seriously as one would hope. We approached our plan with a more inclusive model by involving all of our faculty, who self-selected into areas of the plan they were most interested in (and in a few cases, were open to changing groups based on balance). Subgroups developed a part of the plan, but all faculty were involved in the final discussions and agreed by consensus (not majority rule) on the plan. Staff and administrative professionals were included in areas related to their job descriptions, and student input was gathered through significant surveys and focus groups. At the end of the day, there was a lot of skin in this game and a lot of commitment to success. I believe this to be largely due to the fact that everyone felt valued, everyone felt needed, and everyone had a voice.

(5) *Business plan as a complement.* Often the concepts of business and strategic planning are used interchangeably, especially in fields like mine where we are not trained in business principles, and these concepts develop through on-the-job learning that involves trial and (t)error. I personally do not see them as interchangeable, but I do consider their purposes to be essentially intertwined and overlapping. Earlier, I discussed the format of the strategic plan and what our department considers its purpose to be. Here, I want to highlight how we have utilized business plan principles as a complement to our strategic plan.

Whereas a strategic plan may be considered a plan to get everyone on the same course so that actions are coordinated to achieve specified goals and objectives, in large part it is an internal document used routinely as a roadmap for employees to achieve success in a timely manner. A business plan, on the other hand, provides a format used to evaluate the business one is in and what one chooses to do with the business in the future. We do not typically think about academic departments as businesses, but the analogy is important from the perspective of capital and support. In the corporate world, no one will risk their capital without evaluating an entity's business plan. I believe this to be equally true in academia when we consider investments by donors, deans, provosts, and vice presidents of research in a department. This tenet, then, invites a key conclusion: Although effective strategic plans are marked by successful achievement of outcomes, a business plan puts in sharp focus the concept of return on investment (ROI).

We have used ROI language repeatedly in the past several years as an argument for additional resources to meet strategic goals and as a factor in deciding what our goals are. We are not alone in seeing this metric's utility, as this language has ramped up significantly across our college and university in the past two years. I think it is important to distinguish between ROI related to evaluation and outcomes (i.e., we did "X" at a cost of "Y") and ROI related to planning (i.e., "What is the ROI of plan A and of plan B and how does that help us in deciding whether to choose between plan A and plan B"?). Our planning efforts utilize ROI in both of these ways.

A focus on ROI also serves a bigger purpose if it is communicated well. All departments want to be seen as a valuable asset to their campus. One way we are valuable is that we maximize resources as creatively and cost effectively as possible and then proceed to tell that story. Telling the story is critical, and that leads me to the last facet of the process I will address: don't keep it a secret.

(6) *Market the plan.* A strategic plan does not work well if no one knows what the plan is. I talked earlier about stakeholder commitment to developing and implementing the plan. Commitment, in my opinion, is directly correlated to investment in the plan, and investment results directly from input into the plan and perceived relevance of outcomes from the plan. To maintain

commitment, there needs to be communication and the opportunity to see the plan in action. The plan cannot sit on a shelf, but needs to be active. Beyond inclusion of relevant stakeholder groups, however, I believe the plan needs to be visible to those more distantly removed and with less direct stakeholder ties to the unit. For example, our unit's strategic plan is closely aligned with college and university aims. However, if the dean and provost and other relevant decision makers don't know what we are doing, and what our unit level aims are, how likely are they to invest? Part of our business plan is marketing, and we make it a point to talk about our strategic aims outside immediate circles whenever the opportunity presents itself.

I started with the analogy of a map, but I think at the end of the day that this analogy is only partially accurate. As an active document, a well-crafted and actionable strategic plan not only points us through time and space toward the destination—serving as a map—but also actively places us on the very real journey to get there. Any experienced journeyer knows that the best adventures are those that are not entirely comfortable, but are those that stretch us to move beyond our comfort zone, to try new things, and reach for goals that are slightly beyond our grasp. Our strategic planning process has been sometimes scary, has challenged our notions of who we are and what we want to be, and has dared us to be bold. We have thought about issues of context and timing, creativity and efficiency, and individual versus communal good. We have defined metrics that not only help us evaluate whether we are meeting our goals but also provide a story for demonstrating our value and the impact of our work. The process is exciting, fulfilling, and thank goodness, it is never ending—and that is the mark of a truly great adventure.

VI

Concluding Thoughts

Chapter Thirty-Three

Practical Ways of Increasing and Sustaining Morale

Jeffrey L. Buller

If there is a truism in higher education, it is that morale is always lower than it has ever been. Part of what lies behind this commonly expressed sentiment is the kind of nostalgia we all share that idealizes the past but sees every wart and wrinkle of the present day. Part, too, must be attributed to the type of pessimism many faculty members bring to their jobs; trained in graduate programs to identify problems and their causes in a specific discipline, they naturally apply these critical skills to their daily work and find challenges nearly everywhere they look. Nevertheless, perhaps the biggest reason why there is so often low morale at colleges and universities is that many academic leaders simply are not very good at understanding how to increase and sustain morale within their programs. They may know a great deal about budgeting, strategic planning, curriculum development, and all the other tasks commonly assigned to administrators, but in terms of genuine people skills—that expertise is all too frequently lacking.

This situation is unfortunate since there are a number of practical ways to improve morale in higher education. What is required is balance, that "middle way" that Aristotle described in the *Nicomachean Ethics* as the essence of most virtues. In other words, just as courage falls midway on a spectrum between cowardice and recklessness, so do the keys to promoting morale tend to fall between two morale-sapping extremes. Let's explore how that approach functions in a practical way in three important areas.

RECOGNITION

It is no secret that having their achievements recognized motivates people to even greater achievements in the future. Indeed, members of the faculty and staff often regard it as nearly as important to them as salary, and every now and then, when they are truly being honest, it rises to the top of the list of what people want most from their supervisors. But when it comes to recognition, it is easy to provide either too much or too little as an academic leader. When I became vice president for academic affairs at a small liberal arts college, it had been the school's custom for the provost to read a list of recent faculty accomplishments at the beginning of each meeting of the faculty assembly. Over time that custom had grown to the point where time would be spent praising people for every op-ed piece in the local paper, every Little League victory of the faculty members' children, and every thank you note a student had ever written a former advisor. By the time the minutes of the previous meeting were approved and we made our way through this long list of "achievements," there was often very little time for the meeting itself. You could often see people rolling their eyes, checking their email, or simply not paying attention. So, one day, I just stopped doing it.

Big mistake.

The impression I left was that I no longer cared what the faculty did. No one really wanted to go back to the old, boring, forced march through extremely minor accomplishments, but no one liked being ignored either. The solution was to come up with some guidelines about what really merited public recognition during faculty assembly. For instance, we would recognize books and articles if they were peer-reviewed or released by a university press. We would recognize grants if they were funded externally. We would recognize art openings and musical performances if they were invited or off-campus; merely mounting works in our own gallery or performing in our own theater might be mentioned in a weekly email update, but not recognized at a faculty meeting. It took a bit of negotiation and creativity to develop guidelines that we thought covered most eventualities, but the result was a vast improvement over what we had been doing before. Because standards and thresholds were set, public recognition really started to mean something. People began paying attention again during that part of the program, and morale improved as the genuine achievements of the faculty were consistently recognized.

CONSULTATION

That same middle path is important when it comes to giving members of the faculty and staff a voice in administrative decisions. Here again, it can be very easy to go to either extreme. If academic leaders do everything the faculty and staff suggest, there is no longer any reason for them to show up for work: reading the latest opinion poll will suffice. On the other hand, if they ask others for their opinion, but always do whatever they want anyway, they are sowing the seeds of cynicism. People know when they are being manipulated by being given the mere illusion of having a voice. In order to increase and sustain morale through effective consultation, it is important to discuss matters, when there actually is something to discuss, with a truly open mind. If you have already decided what you will do, and nothing at all is likely to dissuade you from that opinion, then you may as well admit it. People would rather know honestly that your mind is already made up than go through the motions of making arguments you are not going to listen to anyway. If you consult with others genuinely, there should always be the possibility that you will change your mind in the face of a persuasive enough argument.

This type of sincere consultation can be a wonderful way of increasing and sustaining morale. No one (or at least no rational person) expects his or her opinion to carry the day all the time. But if people understand that you truly are listening to their perspectives, giving the matter your best professional consideration, and then making your decision on the basis of reason you can explain, then they will know that their ideas have been properly valued. Recognize that not everyone will agree with your decision. But, there is value in expressing gratitude that everyone felt comfortable voicing his or her opinion, not merely agreeing with you because they were afraid to do otherwise.

VISION

A third area in which a moderate approach can have a positive impact on morale arises when the institution or unit is setting its vision for the future. Having no vision at all except perhaps a desire to "keep doing the great things we are already doing" will soon make the faculty and staff members feel like the university is adrift. They will start coming to work each day merely to put in their time and to receive their salaries, without any sense that they are part of an enterprise that is making a difference in anyone's life. But if you set a vision that is too lofty, the result can be just as destructive. People will feel that you do not value the work they are already doing and want the institution or program to become something it is not. Even worse, a failure to establish the *right* kind of visionary goals swiftly devolves into mission drift: the desire of every community college to be a state college, every state college to be a state university, every state university to be a research university, every research university to be a "Research I" university, and every

Research I" university to be among the top ten "Research I" universities in the world. That type of never-ending envy for the next level of success obscures an institution's identity, diverts resources from its most important activities, and destroys morale by causing people to feel that whatever they have done in the past was not good enough.

At schools that are always trying to "reach the next level of excellence," faculty members come to believe that the standards by which they are evaluated provide a constantly moving target. The staff feels that their work has been dismissed as unworthy of the type of institution you want the school to be. And students, who chose that college or university for what it currently is, may be puzzled as to why a school they selected because of what it is right now is somehow regarded by its academic leaders as not yet good enough for them. The key, in other words, is for administrators to inspire others through desirable but attainable goals and to develop plans that focus on making the institution even better at what it already does well than on transforming it into something that it is not—and possibly can never be.

CONCLUSION

The Russian psychologist Lev Vygotsky discovered that people learn best and are their happiest when they work in their "zone of proximal development": that Goldilocks region where the work is not so hard that it frustrates them and not so easy that it bores them. The practical way to increase and sustain morale is to keep the people we work with challenged in their own zones of proximal development. Recognize them for meaningful achievement, without providing recognition merely as a shallow management technique or because you think it is what you are supposed to do as an academic leader. Listen to their opinions genuinely and adopt their advice when it seems compelling. And challenge them to reach just a bit further than they normally do. It does not take advanced degrees in higher education leadership to make this kind of difference; it merely takes academic leaders who care as much about the people in their programs as they care about the programs themselves.

Chapter Thirty-Four

Conclusion

Distilling Advice about Academic Leadership

Robert J. Sternberg

As I read and edited the chapters of this book, I asked myself whether there are top pieces of advice mentioned by multiple contributors that would apply to virtually any academic leader at any level. I did not do any kind of statistical frequency analysis but, rather, kept in mind the pieces of advice from contributors that I thought were particularly valuable. Here are the top ten pieces of advice I came up with. Of course, other readers might come up with other lists!

1. *Don't compromise on ethical principles.* There will be lots of opportunities in virtually any administrative job to compromise on ethical principles. In many cases, one will be encouraged to make such compromises by people who have an agenda that is not your own. Some of these people will be powerful, perhaps more powerful than you are in the context of the position you occupy. If, however, one looks at what may be the number one cause of failed leadership, it is ethical lapses. Ethical lapses often occur on a slippery slope. As in John Grisham's book and the subsequent movie, *The Firm,* one starts off with just a small ethical lapse and graduates to larger ones until one is inured to them. In any administrative job, things can and will go wrong. About the only kind of thing that will make it virtually impossible for you to get another administrative job is an ethical lapse. Once it makes the media, it's yours forever and you will need to think about doing something else with your life. In contrast, acting ethically at all times will

not guarantee that you will continue living with your job, but it will guarantee that you can continue living with yourself and others, and with other opportunities within the academy.

2. *Suspend judgment.* You will hear a lot of people tell you many stories. Typically, they will believe, or at least half believe, the stories they tell you. The problem is that if you talk to someone else who is involved in the relevant situation, his or her story may be completely different. As part of my work as a psychologist, I have studied intimate relationships. If you ask couples to characterize a relationship, the stories they each tell are surprisingly different—and that's for couples who are intimately involved. So imagine how different the stories can be for unrelated individuals who have no particular stake in what others think. The phenomenon is sometimes called the "Rashomon effect," after the Akira Kurosawa movie in which four different observers give four different accounts of the same event. The accounts have little in common. Suspend judgment until you ensure you have heard a story from all relevant stakeholders.

3. *Adopt a mindset of servant leadership.* Academics are not used to power over peers. Rather, they are used to power over students, a wholly different phenomenon. When placed in positions of power over faculty as well as students, academics react in very different ways. Some seek to ascertain the needs of their constituents and serve them as best they can. Others let the power go to their heads and seem more to seek to meet their own needs than those of their constituents. The best leaders, of course, are the ones who serve their constituents. But it also can happen that a leader seeks to move constituents and the university well beyond where they are—to move them to the next level. This would sound like a strategy that would be universally welcomed but usually it is not. People, academics included, often become comfortable with the way things are. In many instances, the last thing they want is to move to the next level. So it often is not entirely clear what constitutes serving the people, as they may have different ideas of what is good for them than the leader does. You may have to move more slowly than you ideally would like. But in some cases, your constituents just won't see your vision as serving them. When that occurs, and it is widespread over constituencies, the leader might do well to move on and find a setting where his or her goals are more compatible with those of his or her constituents.

4. *Know who your stakeholders are.* In positions of leadership, one almost inevitably becomes somewhat isolated from the people one leads. The higher up one goes in leadership, the more removed one becomes. So it is important to remember who one's stakeholders are and to arrange ways to stay in touch with them. One may choose to

exercise "leadership by walking around," simply visiting different constituents both on and off campus. In every leadership position I have had, I continued to teach in order to stay in touch with students because I believed that they were the ultimate stakeholders in any university—they were the ones who were paying for an education. But no matter what position one is in, it is essential to stay in touch with the full range of stakeholders. It always seems to be the ones with whom one loses touch that prove to be problematical down the road.

5. *People hear what they want to hear.* In my various roles as an administrator—center director, acting chair, dean, provost, president—I always made a serious effort to make sure that I was clear in my communication. But there were two forces I was never entirely able to conquer—the megaphone effect and the egocentric-listening effect. The *megaphone effect* refers to the fact that people will hear what you say more loudly and more powerfully than you intend. They also will read into what you say all kinds of meanings you don't intend. The egocentric-listening effect means that people read into what you say what they want to hear or what they fear hearing. In other words, how they hear what you say is colored by their own personal and professional agendas. They may hear things entirely different from what you intended. Moreover, what they hear may depend on whether they wish you to succeed or fail. You are fortunate if your constituents want you to succeed and want to be part of your team. But if they do not want you to succeed or if they do not want to be part of your team, you will have to deal with the repercussions. In any university, there are negative leaders who make a career out of trying to sabotage administrators. In many cases, they have few or no ideas of their own—usually including scholarly ideas—and make a career out of opposing administrators, no matter what the administrators happen to say. Beware of negative leaders and prepare to deal with them. They will hear things that are different from what you say and will be prepared to broadcast those messages widely.

6. *You can't make everyone happy.* Different stakeholders want different things. At any given time, you probably can get one or two sets of stakeholders angry with you. You can't afford to lose them all! What makes things especially difficult is that different constituencies inevitably will want different things. So it is hard to be well liked by everyone with whom you deal. If you need to be well liked, you may want to consider a career other than academic administration. If you are too well liked, then you probably aren't getting much done. But if you are not well enough liked, you probably don't have long in your job.

7. *Learn the culture before moving too fast or far.* One would like to think that there is a single academic culture, or at worst, a small number of them, say, those found at large research universities, small teaching colleges, community colleges, and so forth. But there are innumerable academic cultures. And you can't effectively lead in any of those cultures if you don't understand well the culture in which you are operating. When you start in a new position, therefore, it is essential that you understand the culture in which you are operating. Most environments are what might be called "murky"—it is not clear exactly what they are all about. Many things are obscure. Your success in leadership will depend in large part upon being able to peer through the murk and see what is on the other side of it. Therefore, don't rush in. Even things that seem straightforward when you start in a new leadership position may turn out to be anything but. You may try to change the culture, but remember that changing an institutional culture is a bit like moving a graveyard. It is hard, messy, takes a long time, and has to be done one individual at a time!

8. *Your personal life and your privacy are up for grabs.* When I was a dean, the provost commissioned a 360-degree evaluation of my performance. There were many comments of many different kinds, but the ones I remember best are about the way I dressed, such as the ties I wore. Wow: I didn't realize anyone really noticed my ties. When I was a president, I received feedback that some constituents were upset that my wife was speaking to our children in German—in public, mind you! Well, you get the idea. Whatever your idea may be of personal, and even of acceptable private behavior, others will have different ideas. And once you are in an administrative position, many people won't hesitate to judge you in terms of their own standards. What is especially tricky is that you will know who many people are, but no matter how many people you recognize, more people will recognize you than you recognize. You need to be prepared to deal with the fallout of whatever you do, no matter how personal or private you feel it is. Once you are a public figure, like it or not, your private life is up for public grabs.

9. *Learn whom to trust.* When you start a new position, there will be a horde of people eager for you to trust them. And some of them even will be trustworthy. But no matter how astute you think you are at spotting trustworthy people, hang back. It will be a while before you find out whom you can trust. I must admit that despite my being a psychologist, and one who has studied nonverbal behavior, I've guessed wrong any number of times. And the cost can be critically high when you discover that someone whom you thought you can trust is working against your agenda or even stabbing you in the back. You

can fire them, but often, by then, the damage is done. You will need a team you can trust, but it will be a while before you find out who that team will be. Some administrators bring their old team from their previous position, which gives the administrator an immediately trust-worthy group. But if you do this, realize that the people you bring will not have the trust of your new constituents—and probably, neither will you—so you will need to work hard to earn that trust.

10. *The visions people most care about usually are their own.* On the one hand, universities need more educational leaders with a vision. Too many people go into administration because they have run out of ideas in whatever else they were doing, and administration seems like a safe and well-paying course. On the other hand, as a servant leader, you will need to learn other people's visions for where they want the university or the unit within the university to go, and it will behoove you to take the time to learn about their dreams and visions for the university because their visions are the ones they care about and hope you eventually will come to call your own. Administrative jobs can't be about your vision alone. To be successful, you need to develop a shared vision that well represents where the institution is and where it needs to go.

Index

About the Editors

Robert J. Sternberg is professor of Human Development at Cornell University. Previously he has been president of the University of Wyoming, provost and senior vice president of Oklahoma State University, and dean of Arts and Sciences at Tufts University. Before that, he was IBM Professor of Psychology and Education and professor of Management at Yale University. Sternberg is a former president of the American Psychological Association, Eastern Psychological Association, and Federation of Associations in Behavioral and Brain Sciences. He also was treasurer for the Association of American Colleges and Universities.

Elizabeth Davis has served as president of Furman University since July 1, 2014. She previously served as executive vice president and provost at Baylor University where she also served as interim provost, vice provost for academic and administrative affairs, associate dean for undergraduate business programs and acting chair of the Department of Accounting and Business Law. She holds the PhD from Duke University, and her research interests focus on judgment and decision making within business and accounting contexts.

April C. Mason, PhD, is provost and senior vice president of Kansas State University. Dr. Mason also holds the position of full professor in the Department of Human Nutrition at Kansas State University. Dr. Mason has previously held the position of dean, College of Applied Human Sciences at Colorado State University, and associate dean of Engagement and Discovery for the College of Consumer and Family Sciences at Purdue University. Her research involves determination of trace mineral availability from plant foods important as staple food products throughout the world. Dr. Mason has been involved in raising awareness of food insecurity in the United States and the world through research, public education, and student activities throughout her career.

Robert V. Smith is vice president of Collaborative Brain Trust University Consulting (CBT UC). Before joining CBT, he held academic administrative posts at Texas Tech University, the universities of Arkansas and Connecticut, and Washington State University. Smith is the author or coauthor of more than 330 articles and eight books, including *Where You Stand is Where You Sit: An Academic Administrator's Handbook* and *The Way of Oz: A Guide to Wisdom, Heart & Courage.* He holds master's and PhD degrees (pharmaceutical chemistry) from the University of Michigan, and a BS (pharmaceutical sciences), *cum laude,* from St. John's University (New York).

Jeffrey Scott Vitter is provost and executive vice chancellor and Roy A. Roberts Distinguished Professor at the University of Kansas. He co-led KU's strategic planning and has overseen the first-ever university-wide KU Core curriculum, expansion in engineering and business, multidisciplinary research initiatives, major growth of technology commercialization and corporate partnerships, and administrative efficiency. He received a BS with highest honors in mathematics in 1977 from the University of Notre Dame; a PhD in computer science in 1980 from Stanford University; and an MBA in 2002 from Duke University. He has over three hundred publications, primarily dealing with algorithmic aspects of big data, and is a fellow of the Guggenheim Society, AAAS, ACM, and IEEE.

Michele Wheatly received her BSc (hons) and PhD from Birmingham University in the UK and undertook postdoctoral training at the University of Calgary, Canada. She ascended the faculty ranks at the University of Florida (1984–1994). She served as chair of Biological Sciences (1994–2002) and then as dean of science and mathematics (2002–2009) at Wright State University. Recently she served as provost and vice president for academic affairs at West Virginia University (2009–2014). Dr. Wheatly is an internationally recognized STEM scholar/educator (more than one hundred refereed articles, two hundred conference proceedings, $25 million in career federal funding), working on temporal and spatial regulation of genes coding for calcium-transporting proteins. Recently, her scholarship has focused on opening the STEM pipeline at all levels (P–20) and more broadly on leadership in higher education.

About the Contributors

Anne L. Balazs (PhD University of Massachusetts, Amherst) is special assistant to the dean at the College of Business, Eastern Michigan University in Ypsilanti, Michigan. She served as the department head of marketing (2008–2014) and is vice president of EMU's Women in Philanthropy group. Balazs is a HERS graduate and spent the 2013–2014 academic year as an ACE Fellow at Bowling Green State University and the University of Toledo. Her research interests include elderly consumer behavior, healthcare marketing, and sales management.

Heidi Bostic is a professor of French and the chair of the Department of Modern Languages and Cultures at Baylor University. She previously served as interim chair of the Department of Humanities and as Director of Modern Languages at Michigan Technological University. In addition, she has taught at Minnesota State University, Moorhead, Concordia College (Minnesota), and the Universidad de Talca (Chile) as a Fulbright Scholar. Her research interests include eighteenth-century French literature, feminist theory, and narrative identity.

Jennifer Bott is the associate provost for learning initiatives and an associate professor of management at Ball State University, overseeing student success for online and blended education. Bott leads the Division of Online and Distance Education and the Integrated Learning Institute. These units bring together student support, instructional design, instructional technology, and faculty and administrative services for online and blended education. Bott earned her master's and doctoral degrees from the University of Akron. Since joining Ball State, she served in a variety of roles, including executive director of the MBA and graduate certificate programs in the Miller College of Business.

C. J. Brainerd is a professor and chair of the Department of Human Development and director of the PhD/JD Program in Law, Psychology, and Human Development at Cornell. He is a fellow of the Association for Psychological Science and of five divisions of the American Psychological Association. He has published over 250 research articles and chapters and over twenty books. His publications cover areas such as human memory and decision making, statistics and mathematical modeling, psychological assessment, learning, intelligence, cognitive development, and psychology and law. He is editor of *Developmental Review*, the leading journal of theory and literature review in developmental psychology.

Ann M. Brill is the dean of the William Allen White School of Journalism and Mass Communications at the University of Kansas. She previously taught at the Missouri School of Journalism, the University of Minnesota, and Marquette University in Milwaukee. She earned a doctoral degree from the University of Minnesota, a master's degree from Marquette, and a bachelor's degree from the University of Wisconsin, Eau Claire. Her areas of expertise include online journalism, online advertising, change and leadership, and effects of implementation of new technology. She is the president of the Association of Schools of Journalism and Mass Communication.

Jeffrey L. Buller has served in administrative positions ranging from department chair to vice president for academic affairs at a broad range of institutions: Loras College, Georgia Southern University, Mary Baldwin College, and Florida Atlantic University. He is the author of nine books on academic leadership. Since 2009, he has worked a consultant to the Ministry of Higher Education in Saudi Arabia, where he is assisting with the creation of the kingdom-wide Academic Leadership Center. Dr. Buller is also a senior partner in ATLAS: Academic Training, Leadership, and Assessment Services, which provides workshops on academic leadership all over the world.

Ana Mari Cauce is presently provost and executive vice president at the University of Washington, which includes serving as chief academic and budget officer. Previous administrative positions include dean of Arts and Sciences, executive vice provost, chair of Psychology, director of the honors program, chair of American Ethic Studies, and director of Clinical Training in psychology, all at the University of Washington. Her primary research focus is on risk and resilience in adolescence, and she has held numerous grants in support of this work. She has been recognized for her research and teaching with the James M. Jones Lifetime Achievement Award and Dalmas

Taylor Distinguished Contribution Award from the American Psychological Association and the UW Distinguished Teaching Award.

John D. Floros received his PhD from the University of Georgia in food science and technology, progressed through the faculty ranks at Purdue University, was head of the Department of Food Science at the Pennsylvania State University, and he is now the dean of Agriculture and director of K-State Research and Extension at Kansas State University. He has published more than 220 articles, book chapters, abstracts, and other publications, and has presented more than 150 papers and 200 invited lectures. He is a fellow and past president of the Institute of Food Technologists (IFT), and a fellow of the Food Systems Leadership Institute.

Don Foss was educated at the University of Minnesota, and followed with a post-doc at Harvard University. He has served on the faculties of the University of Texas at Austin, where he also was chair of the psychology department; Florida State University, where he was dean of the College of Arts and Sciences; and the University of Houston, where he served as senior vice president and provost. Foss's research interests have been in cognitive psychology, specializing in language comprehension, and in the factors that determine college success. He is the author of the recent book, *Your Complete Guide to College Success*, published by the American Psychological Association. The author thanks colleagues Randy Diehl, Janet Kistner, Judith Langlois, and especially Alan Witt, for reading and providing feedback on his chapter.

Pamela Martin Fry has served as associate provost and associate vice president of undergraduate education at Oklahoma State University since January 2011. Fry previously served six years as dean of the College of Education and three years as the school head of Teaching and Curriculum Leadership at OSU. Fry previously served twelve years as a faculty member and as an administrator at the University of Oklahoma with appointments at the associate dean, department chair, and program chair levels. Fry's research agenda continues to focus on the cultural and axiological analysis of teaching, learning, and curriculum at both the P–12 and collegiate levels.

Conrado "Bobby" Gempesaw became the seventeenth president of St. John's University on July 1, 2014. Previously, he served as provost and executive vice president for academic affairs at Miami University. At the University of Delaware, he served as dean of the Lerner College of Business and Economics, interim dean of the College of Arts and Sciences, vice-provost for academic and international programs, and chair of the Department of Food and Resource Economics. He obtained his BA in economics from Ateneo de Davao University, MS in agricultural economics from West Virginia University, and PhD in agricultural economics from Pennsylvania State University.

Thomas F. George is chancellor and professor of chemistry and physics at the University of Missouri, St. Louis. He holds a BA, *Phi Beta Kappa,* from Gettysburg College (chemistry and mathematics) and MS and PhD degrees from Yale University (chemistry), with postdoctoral appointments at MIT and UC, Berkeley. His research specialty is in laser/materials/chemical/nano-physics, including nanomedicine. He remains an active researcher with 750 papers, five authored and eighteen edited books. His awards include the Marlow Medal (UK Royal Society of Chemistry), Medal of Honor (Gulf University for Science and Technology, Kuwait), and Diploma of Honour (Seinäjoki University of Applied Sciences, Finland).

Diane Goddard is vice provost for administration and finance for the Lawrence Campus of the University of Kansas. Her principal responsibility is maintaining institutional fiscal integrity and accountability. She has served as associate vice provost/comptroller, acting budget director, director of purchasing, associate comptroller, and associate director of the Kansas Geological Survey at the University of Kansas. She previously served as chief accountant/controller at Yale University Health Services and as business manager for the Yale University art gallery. Goddard received her bachelor's degree in economics from Southern Connecticut State University, and her MBA from the University of Kansas.

Jane S. Halonen, a psychologist, has served as a dean (University of West Florida, a school director (James Madison University), and a division head and chair (Alverno College). Part-time administration opportunities included managing an outpatient mental health clinic as a co-owner and running the Psychology Advanced Placement Reading program for five years. Her research agenda has focused on critical thinking, assessment, and faculty and program development, including helping good departments become great ones. She was named the 2013 winner of the American Psychological Foundation's Award for Distinguished Applications in Education and Training. In 2000, she won the Foundation's Distinguished Teaching Award.

Diane F. Halpern is dean of the College of Social Sciences at the Minerva School at the Keck Graduate Institute and emeritus professor of psychology at Claremont McKenna College. Diane is a past president of the American Psychological Association, Western Psychological Association, Society for the Teaching of Psychology, and other academic societies. Other administrative positions include dean of undergraduate education at California State

University, San Bernardino, and department chair. Her work in the field of psychology is considered groundbreaking and pivotal, especially with respect to critical thinking, gender differences in cognition, and balancing work and family. She is a prolific author and editor with more than twenty books and hundreds of scholarly articles and other publications.

David Hodge has been president of Miami University since 2006. Previously, he served on the geography faculty of the University of Washington for thirty-one years, the last nine as the dean of the College of Arts and Sciences. He also served as a program director at the NSF, edited *The Professional Geographer*, and served two terms on the Board of Directors of AAC&U. His research has focused on urban and transportation geography including advisory work with the Puget Sound region and the state of Washington.

Elizabeth (Betsy) Hoffman is currently professor of economics at Iowa State, where she was executive vice president and provost from 2007 to 2012. Previously, she was president of the University of Colorado system. She also served as provost and vice chancellor for academic affairs at the University of Illinois at Chicago (UIC) and dean of the College of Liberal Arts and Sciences at Iowa State University. She is a well-known scholar in experimental/behavioral economics. She is a graduate of Smith College and holds doctoral degrees from the California Institute of Technology and the University of Pennsylvania.

Marc Johnson is president of the University of Nevada, Reno. Johnson previously served as interim president and executive vice president and provost at the university. Previously, Johnson was dean of the College of Agricultural Sciences at Colorado State University. He joined Colorado State in 2003 as vice provost for agriculture and outreach and dean of the College of Agricultural Sciences. Earlier, Johnson was dean of the Kansas State University College of Agriculture and director of the Kansas Agricultural Experiment Station and Cooperative Extension Service. Prior to that, he was a member of the faculty at Oklahoma State University and served in faculty and administrative roles at North Carolina State University. Johnson received his bachelor's degree in biology from Emporia State University and his doctorate in agricultural economics from Michigan State.

Frank Keil is the Charles C. and Dorathea S. Dilley Professor of Psychology, Linguistics, and Cognitive Science at Yale. He received a BS in biology from M.I.T. in 1973, a MA in psychology from Stanford University in 1975, and a PhD in psychology from the University of Pennsylvania in 1977. He was a faculty member in the Psychology Department at Cornell University from 1977 to 1998, and then joined Yale's faculty in 1998. For eleven years he served as master of Morse College, stepping down from that role in 2012. He currently serves as chair of the Department of Psychology.

Larry Lyon is director of the Center for Community Research and Development, vice provost, dean of the graduate school, and professor of sociology at Baylor University. His research has been in the field of local politics and community development. Since becoming dean of the graduate school in 1998, he has also published several articles based on his research concerning the challenges and opportunities associated with faith-based higher education.

Alan Mathios is the Rebecca Q. and James C. Morgan Dean of Cornell University's College of Human Ecology. He co-edits the *Journal of Consumer Policy*, serves on the boards of the *Journal of Consumer Affairs* and the *Journal of Public Policy and Marketing,* and has received the SUNY Chancellor's Award for Excellence in Teaching and the Cornell University Kendal S. Carpenter Advising Award. He worked at the Federal Trade Commission, where he received the Outstanding Scholarship Award, the Excellence in Economics Award, and the Award for Superior Service. He is currently serving as a commissioner on the Middle States Commission on Higher Education.

Mary Ellen Mazey (PhD, Cincinnati) was named the eleventh president of Bowling Green State University (Ohio) in 2011. She served as a faculty member at the University of Cincinnati, and as chair of the Department of Urban Affairs and Geography, director of the Center for Urban and Public Affairs, and dean of the College of Liberal Arts at Wright State University. In addition, she has served as dean of the Eberly College of Arts and Sciences at West Virginia University and as provost and vice president of academic affairs at Auburn University. Her expertise is in strategic planning and implementation with a facilitative leadership approach.

Richard McCarty received his PhD in pathobiology from Johns Hopkins University in 1976. Following a two-year postdoctoral fellowship at the National Institute of Mental Health, he accepted a faculty position at the University of Virginia, where he served as department chair from 1990–1998. He then moved to the American Psychological Association to be executive director for science. In 2001, he was recruited to Vanderbilt University as dean of the College of Arts and Science, and after seven years was named provost and executive vice chancellor for academic affairs. After serving as provost for six years, he returned to the faculty as professor of psychology in July 2014.

David D. Perlmutter is a professor at and dean of the College of Media and Communication at Texas Tech University. He is the author or editor of ten books on political communication and persuasion, several dozen research articles for academic journals, as well as more than 250 essays for U.S. and international newspapers and magazines. Perlmutter writes the "Career Confidential" advice column for the *Chronicle of Higher Education*. His book *Promotion and Tenure Confidential* was published by Harvard University Press in 2010.

Edward John Ray has served as president of Oregon State University since July 2003. He received the CASE District VIII Leadership Award and the Liberty Award from the Oregon League of Minority Voters in 2013 and an honorary doctorate from the University of Portland in 2014. Dr. Ray was on the economics faculty at Ohio State University from 1970 to 2003 and department chair from 1976 to 1992. He later served as provost, receiving the Distinguished Service Award in 2006; Dr. Ray holds a BA in mathematics from Queens College and master's and doctorate degrees in economics from Stanford University.

Sally M. Reis is the vice provost for academic affairs and a Board of Trustees Distinguished Professor at the University of Connecticut. She holds the Letitia N. Morgan Chair and is well known for her work on academically talented students. She was principal investigator for the National Research Center on the Gifted and Talented for twenty years and has authored or coauthored over 250 articles, books, book chapters, and technical reports. Her administrative responsibilities include all academic programs as well as Honors and Enrichment, Student Success, Career Development, Institutional Research and Analysis, Excellence in Teaching and Learning, and summer programs.

Henry L. Roediger III is the James S. McDonnell Distinguished University Professor and dean of academic planning at Washington University in St. Louis. He graduated with a BA in psychology from Washington and Lee University (1969) and received his PhD from Yale University (1973). He has served on the faculty of Purdue University, the University of Toronto, and Rice University. Roediger's research is focused on human learning and memory, and he has published about three hundred articles and chapters on various aspects of remembering. Roediger served as president of the Association for Psychological Science as well as several other organizations of psychologists.

Kenneth P. Ruscio is the twenty-sixth president of Washington and Lee University. Prior to assuming the presidency of his alma mater in 2006, he was the dean of the Jepson School of Leadership Studies at the University of Richmond. He served as a member of the Washington and Lee faculty from 1987 to 2002 in its politics department. He has written and taught in the areas of public policy, leadership, and democratic theory and is the author of the 2004 book *The Leadership Dilemma in Modern Democracy*. He is on the boards of directors of the Association of American Colleges and Universities and the Council of Independent Colleges.

Dr. Jean Sander is the dean of the Center for Veterinary Health Sciences at Oklahoma State University. She received her Doctor of Veterinary Medicine degree from the School of Veterinary Medicine, University of Wisconsin. Her graduate degree, a masters of avian medicine, was received from the University of Georgia, College of Veterinary Medicine, and she is a Diplomate of the American College of Poultry Veterinarians. While on faculty at UGA she oversaw the MAM program. She became associate dean for academic and student affairs, College of Veterinary Medicine, Ohio State University. Dr. Sander is a trustee of Elmhurst College, Elmhurst, Illinois.

Lise Youngblade, PhD, is a professor and the head of the Department of Human Development and Family Studies and associate dean for research and graduate programs in the College of Health and Human Sciences at Colorado State University. Dr. Youngblade is an applied developmental scientist whose areas of specialization include child and adolescent socio-emotional development; access to healthcare for vulnerable youth and families; program evaluation; and analysis of developmental processes in educational and community contexts, such as those related to child care, maternal employment, and risky behavior in adolescents. Her work has been funded by multiple federal and state agencies and has been published in more than fifty peer-reviewed articles.